To Larry
With Best Wishes
Lucy Thomlinson

Introduction to Shipboard Weapons

Titles in the
Fundamentals of Naval Science Series

Introduction
to
Shipboard Weapons

Carl D. Corse, Jr.
Lieutenant Commander
U.S. Navy

Naval Institute Press
Annapolis, Maryland

Fundamentals of Naval Science Series

But, in case Signals can neither be seen or perfectly understood, no Captain can do very wrong if he places his Ship alongside that of an Enemy.

Lord Nelson
(before Trafalgar)

Library of Congress Catalog Card Number: 74-25032
ISBN: 0-87021-750-X

Printed in the United States of America

Preface

This book was written to teach prospective naval officers about naval weapons. Too, the book will be a valuable reference for the junior officer at sea.

Surface ship weapons systems are described because they are representative of all the types used at sea, and are typical of the weapon systems most junior line officers are likely to encounter in their first duty assignment. Furthermore, to describe all submarine, surface, and airborne weapons systems is clearly beyond the scope of one book.

The newest weapons, either in service or being considered for service, are described within the limits imposed by classification.

The text has been organized so that it can be studied from beginning to end, or read in scattered assignments as desired by the instructor. The first chapters of each part are general, while the later chapters describe specific weapon elements; they serve as supporting examples for the general discussions. A beneficial consequence of this arrangement is that the reader has considerable freedom in exploiting the text to his best advantage. He may wish to study general descriptions without delving into particular weapons systems, or he may wish to become familiar with one weapon type by reading all the chapters that relate to it. If he wishes to read further about a subject beyond the scope of this text, the bibliography in the back will refer him to the pertinent publications.

Finally, the author is proud to note that this is the first unofficial textbook on U.S. Navy weapons to appear since the highly respected *Naval Ordnance* was discontinued in 1937.

Carl D. Corse, Jr.
Lieutenant Commander, U.S. Navy

Acknowledgments

The Naval Institute Press gratefully acknowledges the extensive assistance provided by the following U.S. naval officers and departments in the preparation of this textbook: Lieutenant Commanders Frederick D. Dyches, Griffith J. Winthrop, and Luke H. Miller; Commanders Ronald E. Adler and J. E. Reisinger; and Captains Maurice O. Muncie and R. S. Crenshaw, Jr.; the Department of Weapons Systems Engineering, U.S. Naval Academy; the U.S. Naval Ordnance Systems Command; the Chief of Naval Material; and the Chief of Naval Education and Training.

This book was produced under the editorial direction of Jan Snouck-Hurgronje. Mr. William J. Clipson executed the line drawings.

Photographs, with the exception of the following, are official U.S. Navy or U.S. Coast Guard. Figure 2–1: Robert de Gast; Figure 19–9: W. D. O'Neil, III; Figures 19–10, 19–12, 19–13, 19–14, 19–15: OTO Melara; Figure 19–16: General Electric Co.; Figure 22–6: Vitro Laboratories; Figure 22–10: McDonnell Douglas Corporation; Figure 22–11: FMC Corporation.

Contents

Part 5: Antisubmarine Weapons   338

Chapter

Introduction to Shipboard Weapons

Introduction

Naval weapons are employed in the air, across the surface of the earth, and under the sea. Both guns and missiles are used against air and surface targets, while torpedoes are directed at targets under the surface of the sea. The student of shipboard weapons must first of all gain a knowledge of the ways in which weapons are normally described and evaluated; that is, he must become conversant with the language and the characteristics of guns, missiles, and torpedoes.

The Selection of Weapons

The central considerations which govern the selection of weapon systems are the combat missions of a ship. A nuclear-powered guided missile cruiser, employed in escorting and protecting aircraft carriers, will carry a balanced armament of antiair warfare (AAW), antisurface warfare (SSW), and antisubmarine warfare (ASW) weapons. A tank landing ship (LST) will carry such last-resort self-defense weapons as three-inch, rapid-fire guns because the ship is not designed to be a weapon platform but a carrier of Marines and vehicles. A hydrofoil patrol boat (PHM) will carry surface-to-surface missiles with which to attack surface ships. She may also carry antiaircraft guns to protect herself against her greatest threat, airplanes.

Area Defense and Point Defense

In addition to the influence of mission considerations in weapon design, two tactical concepts are central to the design and employment of guns and missiles.

If the objective is to guard ships against attack by providing defense as far distant from a formation of ships as possible, then the sensors and weapons will be designed to function inside a large envelope which extends some distance from the launching ship. Ships of this kind provide protection for the entire formation with their weapons, and the weapons are called *area defense* weapons. Examples of ships designed to provide area defense are CGs. These cruisers provide area coverage to the full extent of their search and fire control radars. The weapons on board are able to attack any target that enters this envelope (figure 1–2).

Figure 1-1. The interdependence of modern naval ordnance tactically and technically is illustrated by this picture of a naval gun, under a missile, which is lofting a torpedo. Fire control and search radars hover over their brood on the superstructure and mainmast.

The concept of *point defense* involves providing self-protection for the single unit, regardless of the ship type. A ship armed for point defense will attempt to shoot down any target that enters a ring drawn closely around the ship. The guns and missiles should be effective at very close ranges to prevent the attacker from damaging the ship. The ships designed to carry out special tasks—aircraft carriers, fleet aux-

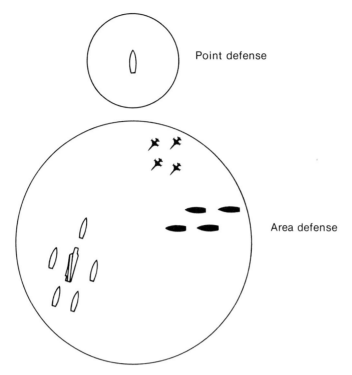

Figure 1–2. Area defense and point defense.

iliaries, amphibious ships, and destroyer escorts—are armed with short-range, point-defense weapons.

Weapon Characteristics

Turning from the general mission concepts of weapons to the terms with which they are described, the specific attributes of guns are shown below in the order in which they will be introduced.* The list is not necessarily complete, but most weapons personnel will be concerned with these aspects of gunnery.

Gun Characteristics

        Name/designation

        Year of introduction

        Arc of elevation

        Arc of train

* The terms introduced in this chapter will be defined and explained in later chapters. Special terms are defined in the glossary.

Range
Type of projectile
Firing rate
Muzzle velocity
Loading system
Weight and size
Speed of train and elevation
Degree of automation
Commonality and cost of materials
Maintainability

Name/designation

A gun is usually assigned a name by the manufacturer until it enters service with the Navy, when it acquires a *designation* for type and model. Sometimes it is still identified by the manufacturer's name alone. In any case, these names and designations are followed by terms which describe the gun's bore width and length of barrel, as well as its basic purpose. Examples might be: the "General Electric, Vulcan-Phalanx, 20mm, antiaircraft gun"; or the "Mark 42 Mod 10, 5-inch 54 caliber, dual-purpose gun."

Year of Introduction

This information is more useful than it may appear. Obviously it is important for the date of invention to be known, but many good gun systems are available long before they become operational in the Fleet; first, because of the need to test and improve them, and secondly, because political and financial factors affect the timing of their introduction. Thus, the year of introduction into the Fleet gives the knowledgeable observer a good idea of the value of a particular ship's gun armament and how it compares with the competition in other navies. For example, the 5-inch 38 caliber, dual-purpose gun was invented in the early part of this century, was used in the Navy with many successive improvements from the late 1930s, and is just now going out of service. A glance at a description of a ship's gun armament and at a table showing year of introduction can therefore provide a picture of the state of technology the ship's guns represent.

Arc of Elevation

The total vertical arc through which a gun barrel can be elevated and depressed determines whether a gun can be used against aircraft. Most marks of guns in service are dual purpose and can elevate to

85 degrees above and depress 15 degrees below the horizontal. The 5-inch 54 caliber, Mark 45, lightweight gun, on the other hand, can only elevate to 65 degrees, because it is limited by its loading system: it is designed to shoot at surface targets and low-flying aircraft.

Arc of Train

The total horizontal arc through which a gun may be trained and still fire without hitting part of the ship is a second significant characteristic of a gun's value. For example, if a gun were mounted well forward on the bow, it could have an uninterrupted field of fire of more than 320 degrees. A gun mounted aft could only have an arc of 180 degrees (beam to beam). If a gun has been poorly placed, because the placement was subordinated to other ship design considerations, then it may only be effective in a 90-degree arc. The *Leahy* class CGs have two three-inch gun mounts installed amidships, one on the port and one on the starboard side.

Range

The range at which a gun is effective against surface and air targets is an obvious consideration of a gun system, and it is determined among other things by the velocity imparted by the propellant, the weight of the projectile, the caliber of the gun, and the ability of sensors and fire control to observe the movements of the target.

Type of Projectile

The kind of target the gun will take under fire determines the type of projectile to be employed to achieve the most effective gunfire. U.S. naval guns can fire a standard round, a sub-caliber round, and a rocket-assisted projectile, all of which are described in Chapter 16.

Firing Rate

The rate at which a gun will fire, both in sustained firing and at the highest attainable rate, is an extremely important factor, especially when the gun is used to fire at approaching hostile aircraft and cruise missiles. A gun's rate of fire is greatly affected by the ability of the metal in the barrel to sustain the heat and the rapid cooling that takes place during a firing mission, and gun barrels are designed to withstand the stress of rapid fire according to their type. In smaller guns, such as the 20mm close-in weapon system (CIWS), this problem was addressed because of the very high rate of fire of this gun system by re-introducing the Gatling principle of revolving barrels. The firing rate of a manually loaded gun will depend upon the rate at which the crew can load it.

Muzzle Velocity

The velocity at which a projectile leaves the muzzle largely determines the range of a gun, and provides an indication of the time the round will take to reach a target at a given range.

Loading System

The way in which ammunition is stowed and fed to the gun is another governing factor in the usefulness and employment of a gun system. A large supply of ready-to-fire ammunition should be available to assure prolonged firing without the necessity for breaking out and passing more ammunition. Most current design efforts in gun systems are devoted to this consideration, as a slow or manual loading system could cripple an otherwise effective gun.

Weight and Size

The size and weight of a gun are determining factors in gun design, and they also affect the design of ships that will have to carry such guns. The lighter the weight of guns and gun directors, the more flexibility there is in the placement of guns on a ship to maintain its stability. This enables the Navy to use the same gun on many different sizes of ships, thus standardizing requirements for supply, repair and maintenance, and ammunition.

Speed of Train and Elevation

Medium and small caliber naval guns, such as the three-inch, should possess the ability to train and elevate quickly to keep pace with aircraft and missiles close at hand. It should be remembered that increases in train and elevation rates are only obtained by increasing the size of their motors, and thereby affecting the size of the gun.

Degree of Automation

The objective of automation is to increase the efficiency and speed of the gun, not necessarily to reduce the number of men in the system. Generally speaking, however, an increase in automation causing a reduction of men in the system decreases reaction time.

Commonality and Cost of Materials

The designer and user are further influenced by considerations of economy. They seek maximum commonality with other weapons when supplying a gun with spare parts. They also estimate the degree of maintenance that will have to be performed on board ship. The gun's components should be easy to obtain, they must be easy to repair, they need to be as simple as is allowed by the state of the technology, and they must be rugged and reliable. In gun systems, as with all other electronic equipment on board ship, there is a trend toward modular design. If a component in the system fails, the module is identified automatically by test equipment which monitors the system and is installed as part of the basic equipment. The module is replaced with another from the supply department, with the faulty module being repaired if possible or a replacement ordered.

Maintainability

If it becomes evident that it is difficult to keep a certain gun in operating condition while under way, the gun system would be a serious handicap to the Navy, both because of a loss in operational readiness, and cost. Unless the problem could be corrected, it is unlikely that the Navy would purchase the gun in question. Modern weapon manufacturers therefore insure as a matter of design that their product is relatively easy to maintain. As mentioned above, test equipment is included in the system to identify trouble and prevent failure.

Missiles

Like the naval gun, the ship-launched missile is used in several offensive and defensive roles. Missiles may be used to shoot at other ships, missiles, aircraft, or even submarines. They are characterized by their mission, by their propulsion systems, and by their guidance systems. Salient features are shown below, and they are discussed if they differ from those given for guns.

Naval Missile Characteristics

Name/designation

Year of introduction

Purpose – antisubmarine
surface-to-surface
surface-to-air

Warhead – continuous-rod
fragmentation
armor-piercing
nuclear

Airframe – length, weight

Propulsion – engine type
fuel
speed

Range

Launcher – single/double (1 or 2)

Guidance system

Magazine capacity and loading system

Number of targets system can
handle at one time

Cost

Maintainability

Warhead

The missile warhead is an important characteristic of a missile; it indicates the purpose of the missile. For example, a ship would fire a missile with a fragmentation warhead at a cruise missile, a continuous-rod warhead at an aircraft, or a high-explosive warhead at another surface ship. The warhead to be used will affect the design requirements of the guidance and propulsion systems to get the missile to the target. As an illustration, it is clear that if the warhead was only lethal within a small area, it could only be effective if placed on a missile that could be guided very close to the target.

Airframe

A missile must have a body structure strong enough to support and protect the internal missile parts in flight and light enough to keep fuel requirements low. Structural strength enables the missile components to withstand rapid acceleration at launch, and possible rapid changes in flight paths when chasing down a target. The size and weight of a missile are dependent upon such major considerations as stowage, transfer from magazine to launcher, propulsion, and guidance. Small missiles have several advantages over large missiles. First, they can be stowed in smaller magazines, freeing space on board ship for other requirements. Second, a larger number of missiles can be carried in a ship, cutting down the need for replenishment and making the ship more self-sufficient, with increased endurance in combat. Third, they are easier to transfer to their launchers and to load on the launcher arms, requiring less, and lighter, handling equipment. Finally, propelling a small missile through the air requires either less fuel over the same distance as a large missile, or it allows a longer flight to take place with the same fuel load as a large missile.

Propulsion

In the combat environment of aircraft and cruise missiles, fast-burning, hence, quick reaction time achieved with solid propellants recommend this type of propellant to the Navy. It is also safer to handle than liquid propellants. An example of the need for extremely fast reaction is the local self-defense missile, a missile designed to cope with incoming air targets in the last resort. In this combat situation, the incoming target has already penetrated to within a short distance of the ship. The *Sea Sparrow* missile is a missile of this type, and it uses a solid propellant (see Chapter 22). In contrast, some of the missiles that use liquid fuel in the sustained flight stage are the long-range missiles. The *Talos* missile is an example. Several engine types are in service and are often paired in one missile. For example, a rocket engine will carry the missile through the boost stage, while a ramjet engine may propel the missile during the rest of the flight. Many other missiles use two rocket motors: a booster motor and a sustaining rocket.

Guidance

As with propulsion, the guidance system is suited to the purpose of the missile. Missiles such as the *Poseidon* use inertial guidance suited for long flights. Other kinds of guidance are *preset, command-in-flight, radar and laser beam rider, homing,* and *composite* (see Chapter 23). The guidance system of the missile, moreover, depends on the fire control system available on the ship. For example, the long-range antiaircraft, surface-to-air missile requires extremely sophisticated electronic guidance from the ship in the form of computerized data processing equipment and big radar antennae. In contrast, the smallest short-range antiaircraft missile may have a relatively small, manual fire control system, using an optical sight with command guidance.

Number of Targets System Can Handle at One Time

The ideal missile system for combat at sea would be able to take all hostile targets under fire at the same time. The actual problems involved in detecting, classifying, tracking, and destroying a number of targets in a short time only allow a missile system a certain capacity for disposing of numerous attackers. Generally speaking, a ship's combat capability depends among other factors on the number of fire control radar directors available to track the targets after they are acquired by the search radars. Newer directors being introduced into the Navy can track several targets at one time, thus shifting the stress to the launcher, the magazine, and the loading system to keep up with firing orders. Most older gun and missile directors still in service cannot keep up with the capacity of the weapon-launching system on board, thus limiting a ship to firing at two to four targets simultaneously, depending on the number of directors on board.

Such characteristics as effective range, degree of automation, magazine and loading system, and cost and maintainability apply to missiles in the same way as they apply to guns.

Torpedoes

The antisubmarine weapon in service in the U.S. Navy is commonly the torpedo, although there are other means of destroying a submarine. Many navies carry varieties of rocket launchers and depth bombs as well as torpedoes.

Ship-launched torpedoes were originally designed for use against surface ships. However, once the submarine became the primary threat to our command of the sea, and reliable homing torpedoes were developed after World War II, most models of ship-launched torpedoes have been designed to attack submarines. The salient features of torpedoes depend on such factors as the method of their delivery to the target area, the length of their run in the water, the speed they achieve, their propulsive system, their guidance system, and their maximum operating depth.

Warheads generally consist of a sufficient amount of high explosive to crush the pressure hull of a submarine. Since submarines are already subjected to heavy pressure by the water, it takes less explosive to destroy a submarine than to sink a surface ship. As a result, torpedoes have generally become smaller than those that were used during World War II, when the targets were surface vessels. The antisubmarine warhead is normally detonated either by a contact fuze or by a fuze that senses the proximity of the submarine.

Some of the terms used to describe torpedoes are shown below and they are discussed where they differ from equivalent terms used to describe guns and missiles.

Torpedo Characteristics

> Designation
> Year of introduction
> Dimensions
> Delivery system
> Guidance
> Propulsion
> Magazines and loading systems
> Speed
> Endurance
> Depth Capacity
> Cost
> Maintainability

Designation

Torpedoes of the U.S. Navy are identified by a mark and model number, but they are rarely known by a name, as are missiles. An example is the surface-launched Mark 46 Mod 0 or Mod 1 torpedo. An exception is the submarine-launched Mark 45, ASTOR torpedo.

Dimensions

The diameter of a torpedo is an important descriptive statistic as will be shown in a later chapter, because it indicates the kind of target, the size of warhead, and the range of the torpedo. A 12.75-inch torpedo is currently the standard diameter in the surface fleet for antisubmarine work, while 21-inch torpedoes are also longer and heavier, indicating their greater range and sufficient destructive power for use against surface ships as well as submarines.

Delivery

The method of delivering the torpedo depends on the tactical situation, and the delivery systems all have definite capabilities and limitations. Torpedoes may be fired from tubes on deck, from a ship-launched helicopter, or from a rocket launcher (ASROC). Each launching system covers a different radius around the ship.

Guidance

Guiding a torpedo presents almost as difficult a technical problem as locating the target in the first place. Some torpedoes contain their own guidance system, which first takes the torpedo out to the target area, then develops a preset search pattern, and after acquisition finally steers to the target. Other torpedoes, especially the newest models, are guided during their run by wire, with corrective commands being transmitted through the wire to the torpedo.

Propulsion

Various systems for propelling torpedoes have been tested over the past 70 years (figure 1–3). The requirements for high speed through the water, silent running, and maximum range have caused the Navy to adopt several solutions. Steam-powered torpedoes used during World War II are still used for exercise and for training by submarines and torpedo boats. Others use hydrogen peroxide, electrical batteries, solid fuel and liquid oxidant, and liquid fuel. Each system has advantages and disadvantages. For example, electrically powered torpedoes may be fast and silent, but they may not have sufficient power to run as long as other systems. Liquid fuel is most useful when long range is an important consideration.

Figure 1–3. *The tactical use of torpedoes has evolved historically in much the same way as the surface-to-surface missile of today. They were first put on small vessels as a potent weapon against other surface ships, in restricted waters. Top, left: A torpedo is fired from a conventional tube on board a destroyer. Recently, efforts have been directed at launching torpedoes over the greatest possible distance within sonar range. Top, right: A torpedo in 1893. It soon went to sea in destroyer ship types to be used first against other surface ships and then against submarines. Bottom: An ASROC launching.*

Magazines and Loading

As with other weapons, problems of stowage, replenishment, and reloading are all fairly complicated with torpedoes, which are large, bulky, heavy, sophisticated, and delicate weapons. The most flexible stowage and loading system yet evolved for the rocket-propelled version in service may be found in the *Belknap*-class CG, which uses a dual-purpose launching ramp for either missiles or the rocket-boosted torpedoes (figure 1–4). Loading helicopters, deck-mounted tubes, and the older "box" antisubmarine rocket launchers (ASROC) is at best a slow, clumsy, manual process.

Figure 1–4. The USS Horne (CG-30) is equipped with a dual-purpose, automatically loaded launching ramp which may fire ASROC torpedoes or standard missiles as necessary. The Belknap *class is unique in the U.S. Navy in its combination of automatic loading and dual-purpose firing capabilities.*

Speed

The speed of the torpedo is of great importance tactically, because the modern submarine is extremely fast underwater and can run close to the same speed as an approaching torpedo. Thus, if a torpedo is launched behind a submarine that is going away from the launching platform, the speed advantage of the torpedo is small.

Endurance

The speed of modern submarines versus the speed of torpedoes points out the importance of the endurance of the torpedo in its run. If a torpedo is to capitalize on its somewhat superior speed to overtake an escaping submarine, the capacity for a long run is essential. If the run is too short in duration when the torpedo's engine stops, then the submarine may hope to outrun the pursuing torpedo.

Depth Capacity

Finally, it is evident that a torpedo must be able to search in deep water. A torpedo limited to 600 feet in its search is obviously not much use against a submarine lying at 800 feet. Thus both endurance and depth capacity are of importance.

PART 1

Introduction to Fire Control

The fundamental exercise in weaponry is getting the gun projectile, missile, or torpedo from its launcher to its target. This is called the fire control problem. The problem is stated by identifying all the factors which influence the travel of a weapon from the moment of firing until it reaches its target. This Part sets forth and explains the elements of the fire control problem as they apply to guns. Later consideration of the control of missiles and torpedoes will depend in principle on the detailed statement of the gun fire control problem, but will vary where the means used by those weapons to hit the target have their own requirements because of the medium (water, air, space) or the weapon involved.

There are four sets of calculations made in the gun fire control problem before firing. They are (1) ballistics, (2) target motion, (3) gun platform motion, (4) other minor corrections for mount location on the ship, and the like. The first two chapters in this Part explain the ballistic factors in the calculation, the third chapter explains all the factors together in one statement of the problem, and the remaining chapters describe gyroscopes and the operation of some modern naval gun fire control systems.

2

Interior Ballistics

Robert de Gast

Figure 2–1. Interior ballistics is the study of what happens from the moment the breech closes the chamber on the propellant and the projectile to the moment the shell leaves the muzzle.

Introduction

The ballistics of gun projectiles is a major component in the solution of the fire control problem. Gun ballistics is the science of the motions of projectiles; it is divided into interior and exterior ballistics.

The elements of interior ballistics combine to influence the motion of the projectile while it is in the gun. This includes the study of (1) the combustion of the powder, (2) the pressure developed within the gun, (3) the variations in pressures and velocities caused by the "conditions of loading," * and (4) erosion of the bore.

Exterior ballistics is concerned with the motion of gun projectiles in flight. This covers only the forces affecting a projectile after it leaves the barrel, traveling in a known direction, at a known speed. Exterior ballistics will be described in Chapter 3.

Propellant Combustion

In interior ballistics, the first consideration is the combustion of the propellant. Ideal propelling charges burn in the chamber of the gun in such a way that they develop maximum projectile velocity without excessive heat, pressure, or erosion. The most efficient propellant that a gun could have would be so balanced that the propellant charge is entirely consumed immediately before the projectile leaves the muzzle. That is, the ideal propellant burning would be such that the propellant gases would expand their effect during the entire length of travel of the projectile through the bore.

The Configuration of Powder Grain

Gun propellant powders are manufactured in grains of various shapes and sizes. Grain size is one of the factors that determine at what point in the gun barrel maximum pressure on the projectile will be reached. Each individual grain of powder burns in layers parallel to the surface that is ignited. For this reason, the powder with the greatest exposed surface area will burn faster and therefore produces greater pressures faster.

Propellant powders are manufactured either in solid form or with perforations. The three major types of propellant powders are solid, single-perforated, and multi-perforated.

---

* The "condition of loading" refers to the net adjustments in the amount, form, kind of charge, and the projectile weight that are made to obtain the desired tactical result.

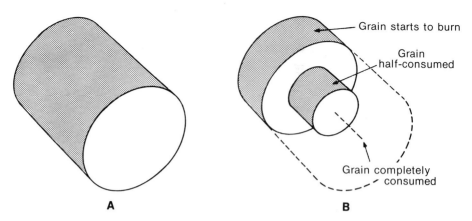

Figure 2–2. (a) *An unburned grain and* (b) *a burning grain of a degressive solid propellant.*

The solid propellant powder grain shown in figures 2–2a and 2–2b is termed a *degressive* powder because the area of the burning surface continually decreases during combustion.

The single-perforated propellant powder grain (figures 2–3a and 2–3b) is called a *neutral* powder, because the powder grain maintains an approximately constant burning surface during combustion.

The multi-perforated propellant powder grain (figures 2–4a and 2–4b) is called *progressive* because of the increasing burning surfaces during combustion.

The graph in figure 2–5 shows the relationship of the three types of grains when they are each burned in the same bore. Observe that

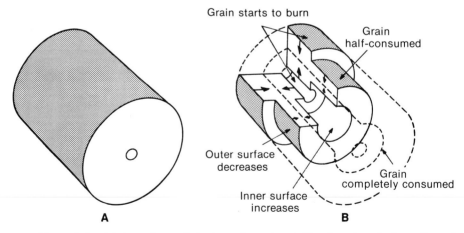

Figure 2–3. (a) *An unburned single-perforated and* (b) *a burning single-perforated* (*neutral*) *grain.*

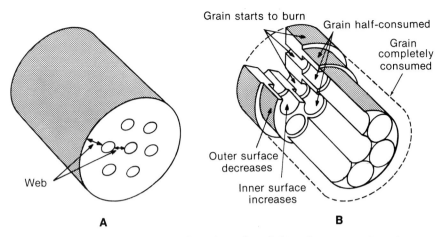

Figure 2–4. (a) An unburned multiperforated and (b) a burning multiperforated (progressive) grain.

the progressive powder reaches maximum pressure much later than a degressive powder and loses pressure much more gradually. It stands to reason that a degressive powder would provide more short-term pressure in a short barrel than a progressive powder.

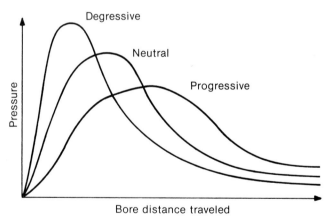

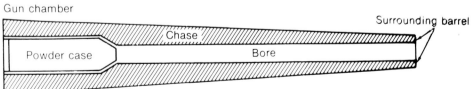

Figure 2–5. The pressure-travel curves of burning propellant powder grains.

Relationship of Gun Strength to Propellant Pressure

Figure 2–6 illustrates the basic principle of gun design and may be taken as typical of the strength-pressure relationship in gun barrels. As the graph indicates, the high breech strength is carried well forward of the point of maximum powder pressure. In five-inch guns this occurs before the chase.° The gun strength must exceed the powder pressure at every point by an amount that provides a suitable margin of safety so that the gun barrel will not burst.

The curve (figure 2–6) shows the pressure beginning at a value well above the zero axis. This shows that the pressure build-up occurs after the propelling charge begins to burn but before the projectile begins to move. The projectile begins to move only after the propellant gases reach the required force necessary to initiate projectile movement. The initial projectile movement is hampered by both the inertia and the engagement of the rotating band° in the rifling. It should be noted that the gun strength curve is a straight horizontal line above the area between the point of initial forcing pressure and the point of the powder's maximum pressure. The gun strength will run parallel to the pressure curve until this point, because the same pressure exerted by the expanding gases against the projectile base is also exerted in equal measure against all interior surfaces of the gun behind the

° See glossary.

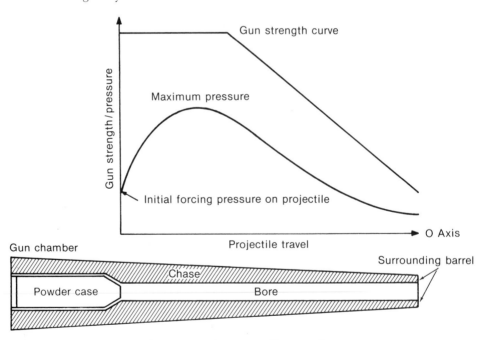

Figure 2–6. *Gun barrel strength vs. propellant powder pressures.*

projectile. Therefore, the breech end of the gun barrel is designed for the maximum pressure to be imposed on the gun.

After the projectile has passed the point of maximum propellant pressure, it will be accelerated by gas pressure until the projectile leaves the muzzle. The total area under the maximum pressure curve, up to the point where the projectile leaves the gun, is a rough measure of the projectile's initial velocity. The pressure remaining at the muzzle is an indication of muzzle loss.* A high muzzle pressure at this point increases the muzzle flash.

Charge Composition

There are several ways of manipulating the characteristics of the propellant to gain longer range, greater initial velocity, and steeper or more shallow trajectory in order to put the ship's guns to their best use in various tactical situations. The required objective may be attained by changing the weight, the density, the form, and the grain of the powder charge, as well as by altering the weight and shape of the projectile.

Powders

Powders are classified as "quick" or "slow" in relation to their rate of combustion. A small-grain powder is a quick powder since all the grains are consumed in a relatively short time. This powder is useful for mortar and small- through medium-caliber ammunition. Quick powders require a relatively high gun strength which makes their use impractical in large charges, because the large-caliber guns would have to be extremely thick. Larger grains of the same shape as the quick powder burn at a slower rate; thus they are slow powders. Slow powders have a lower maximum propellant pressure, and it is reached later in the travel of the projectile through the bore, as shown in figure 2–7. This figure compares slow powders and quick powders using the same weight of charge.

Weight of Powder Charge

Figure 2–8 shows typical gun pressure curves and the methods available to obtain an increased projectile velocity in a gun without increasing maximum pressure. The figure clearly shows that by increasing the amount (weight) of a slower powder (line 3) an increase in projectile velocity can be obtained over both the original powder charge (line 1) and a slower charge of the same weight (line 2).

* Any propellant gas pressure that is released to the atmosphere when the projectile leaves the bore.

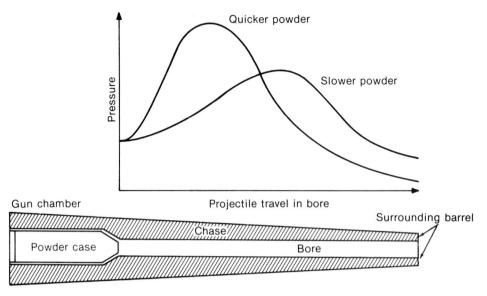

Figure 2-7. Comparison of slow and quick powder.

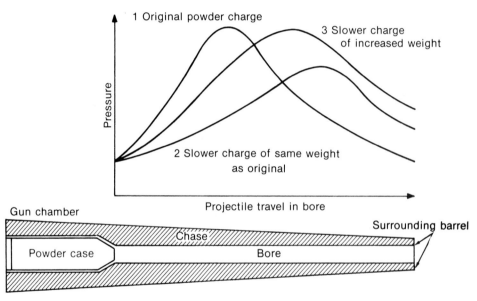

Figure 2-8. Powder weight vs. powder used, without increasing the maximum pressure attained in the original charge.

Density of Loading

Density of loading is the ratio of the powder charge weight to that of the volume of water which, at standard temperature, would fill the powder chamber. It is also a measure of the amount of space in which the combustion gases will expand before the projectile begins to move. A high density of loading leaves a very limited amount of space for

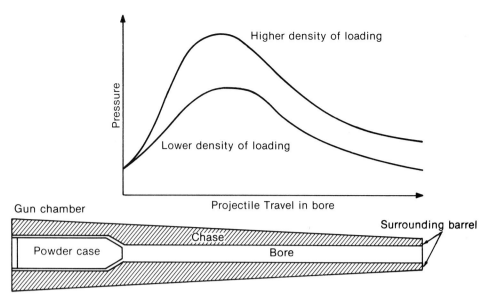

Figure 2–9. Comparative density-of-loading curves.

initial expansion, and gas pressure will build up rapidly (figure 2–9). With a lower density of loading, more gas expansion will take place before the projectile starts to move. With all other factors remaining equal, an increase in the density of loading will increase the maximum pressure, projectile velocity, and muzzle loss.

Volume and Form of Powder Chamber

After first establishing the desired projectile muzzle velocity, the gun designers determine from gun construction studies the limiting maximum pressure allowable in the gun and the weight of the propellant charge. The volume and form of the powder chamber is then established to meet the requirements of the above items. When the gun is built, the volume and form of the powder chamber will change only because of erosion at the origin of rifling and the related improper seating of the projectile.

Weight of Projectile

Different sorts of projectiles vary in weight. If a high-capacity projectile and an armor-piercing projectile, with no other factors considered, were fired from the same gun, the high-capacity projectile, being lighter, would have a slightly higher muzzle velocity.

Hypervelocity Guns

The less time a projectile spends in the air on its way to a target, the less time the target has to take defensive maneuvers. This is especially true as aircraft become faster and more maneuverable. Continued demands are being made for higher velocities in gun projectile muzzles. To increase muzzle velocities, the area under the projectile pressure-travel curve must be a maximum. This requires approaching a pressure-travel curve that is as flat as possible. Another approach to higher muzzle velocities is through the use of hyper-velocity gun projectiles described in Chapter 16.

For example, the muzzle velocity of a light-weight projectile can be increased to 4,000 feet per second from a typical muzzle velocity of 2,700 feet per second for a normal five-inch round.

Another approach to increasing muzzle velocity is the subcaliber projectile, which will also be described in Chapter 16.

High muzzle velocities and high rates of fire are commonly associated in the medium and small calibers with short-range and antiaircraft missions.

Exterior Ballistics

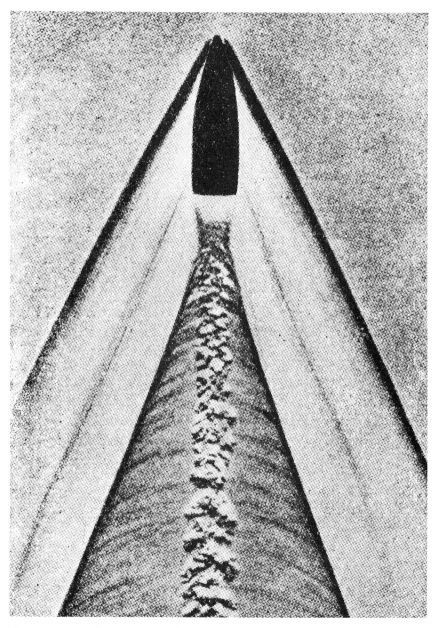

Figure 3–1. Shock waves set up by a projectile as it travels through the air.

Introduction

Exterior ballistics must be considered after the projectile leaves the gun bore, traveling at a known speed and in a known direction. It will be seen in Chapter 13, "Gun Barrels," that the known speed (initial velocity, IV°) is obtained through a computation of interior ballistic forces. The known direction is the direction of the center line or axis (line of fire) of the gun barrel. From the time that the projectile leaves the gun barrel until the warhead explodes, forces other than those generated in the gun affect the flight of the projectile. These forces will be grouped under the major headings of gravity, effects of the atmosphere, projectile weight, and projectile shape.

Gravity

Newton's first law of motion states that any moving body will continue to move in a straight line at the same speed until something interferes with it. This could be demonstrated if a projectile in outer space were shot from a muzzle; it would simply continue to travel indefinitely at the same speed along the line of fire until it hit something or came close to a body (such as the earth) that exerts an appreciable gravitational pull.

The Effect of Gravity in a Vacuum

If a projectile were picked up on the earth and let go, instead of remaining where it was, as it would in space, it would drop or fall, because on earth, bodies have weight owing to gravitational attraction.

Discounting air resistance, a falling object on earth will accelerate at a rate of 32.2 feet per second for every second of fall. This change in rate is the same for any body falling on the earth.

To show the effects of gravity, consider what would happen to a projectile that was fired in a vacuum from a gun bore sighted at zero degrees of elevation, compared with another projectile that was dropped over the side of a ship in the same hypothetical vacuum. Since all bodies fall in exactly the same way, the projectile that was dropped and the projectile that was fired will fall at the same speed and the same vertical distance in a given time interval, as shown in figure 3–2.

° The velocity at which the projectile is moving the instant it leaves the muzzle is called initial velocity (IV). It is generally measured in feet per second and it is a commonly used measurement in gunnery. For example, IV is needed to compute the fire control solution described in chapter 4.

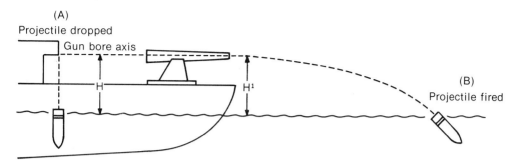

Figure 3–2. *A Projectile trajectory in a vacuum as it is affected by gravity. Projectile (B) fired from a* horizontally *aimed gun strikes the surface of the water at the same instant as projectile (A) dropped from same height. (Height H = height H¹.)*

The only difference is that the fired projectile is traveling forward and falling at the same time.

With the gun barrel elevated *above* the horizontal, the projectile will still have two motions. The first is an upward motion in the line of departure at a speed equal to the projectile's initial velocity (IV). The second is a falling motion straight down at a constantly accelerating speed after passing the maximum ordinate (the highest point of the trajectory). The projectile will be falling quite slowly away from the line of departure as it leaves the barrel, as most of its motion will be upward and forward in the line of departure. As it travels further, it will be retarded more and more in its upward motion until the force of gravity equals the force of upward motion. The point at which this occurs will be the maximum ordinate (point of travel). As the projectile continues on its path, gravity will be pulling it down faster than its momentum carries it upward, so its trajectory will continue to turn downward until it hits the ground.

Figure 3–3 illustrates in graph the two separate motions of a projectile in flight in a vacuum as it is affected by gravity. The three components of the projectile's movement are shown. The first vector is the vertical upward component of the projectile in the line of departure° from a barrel elevated 45 degrees. The second component is the equal horizontal distance traveled along the trajectory, which is not consid-

° The line of departure is the axis extending straight out in line with the bore axis along which a projectile would continue to travel in a vacuum without gravity.

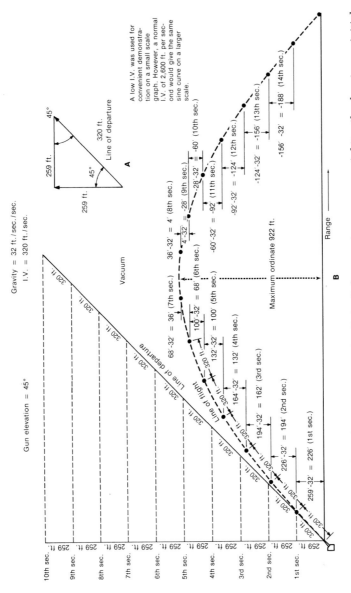

Figure 3-3. (a) The effect of gravity on a projectile in flight assuming a vacuum. Arbitrarily choosing an initial velocity of 320 feet per second with the gun barrel at the maximum ideal elevation of 45 degrees, the line of fire may be broken into a horizontal vector and a vertical vector of 259 feet each, for each second of travel. The vectors are equal because they are the sides of an equilateral right triangle, which has been constructed from knowing two angles (45° each) and a gun elevation side (320 feet). (b) Taking the vertical vector alone, it can be seen that it is acted upon by the opposite force of a vertical downward vector of the force of gravity (32 feet per second per second). Thus for every second of travel of the projectile, progressively subtract 32 feet. The result is shown by the dotted line representing the trajectory of a projectile affected by gravity alone. The solid line shows where the projectile would have gone (the line of departure) in a vacuum if the force of gravity were absent.

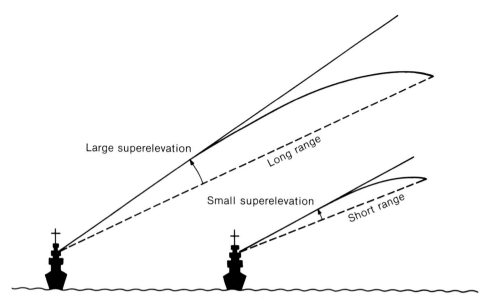

Figure 3–4. Angles of superelevation at long and short ranges.

ered here. The third vector is the vertical downward movement of the projectile's travel imparted by the force of gravity.

Even though the force of gravity is itself a constant value, it is a variable quantity in the fire control solution because the constant effect of gravity is measured in relation to the *time* that the projectile is in flight. This variable is then compensated for by a quantity called *superelevation*. Superelevation is defined as the angle that a gun must be elevated above the line of sight to compensate for the downward force of gravity (figure 3–4). Thus, a larger angle of superelevation is required for a long-range shot than for a short-range shot.

Gravitational Effect on Range in a Vacuum

The horizontal distance from the gun to the impact point where the projectile hits the ground is the range of the gun. The range will vary with any change in gun elevation. As the gun barrel is elevated, the projectile is given more upward movement. If the gun barrel is elevated above 45 degrees, the time the projectile is traveling will continue to increase, but the projectile's forward movement will be slower, resulting in a shorter range. Obviously, if the gun is shot straight up, the range will be zero. It can be noted that maximum range would be obtained in a vacuum affected only by gravity at a gun barrel elevation of approximately 45 degrees. These typical paths or trajectories for different gun barrel elevations in a vacuum are shown in figure 3–5.

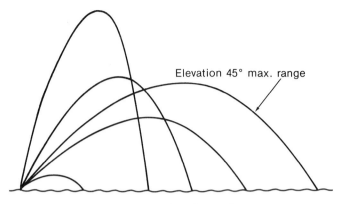

Figure 3–5. *Trajectories for different angles of gun elevation in a vacuum.*

Effects of the Atmosphere

When a projectile is moving through the air, the air becomes a force retarding the movement of the projectile.

In figure 3–6 it can be seen that the trajectory of a projectile fired in air differs significantly from that of a projectile fired at the same gun elevation in a vacuum. The range of the projectile in air is much less than the range in a vacuum. In order to give a projectile the same range in air that is obtained in a vacuum, it would first be necessary to increase the gun elevation. If the gun elevation were already set for maximum range (45 degrees), a range equal to that in a vacuum could not be achieved.

Air Density

Thin air will slow up the travel of a projectile as much as dense air. Air density decreases with altitude. Since the trajectory of a long-range shot rises high into the air, the projectile will be slowed less during each second that it is traveling in the upper reaches of the trajectory than when it is traversing the lower levels.

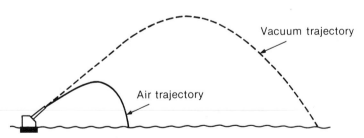

Figure 3–6. *A comparison of trajectories of projectile travel in air and in a vacuum for the same angle of gun elevation.*

Projectile Weight

The weight of a projectile also affects the trajectory of a shell that is in flight. A projectile that weighs more than another of the same dimensions but is fired at the same initial velocity is less affected by air resistance. The governing formula here is:

$$\text{Velocity} = \text{Mass} \times \text{Acceleration}$$

Projectile Shape

The projectile shape also makes a difference. The greater the diameter of the projectile, the larger a cross-section there is for the air to resist. A pointed nose on the projectile makes it easier for it to penetrate the air, thereby reducing air resistance. *Boattailing* or tapering the after end of the projectile reduces the drag resulting from the air turbulence directly behind the projectile.

Determining Range

The preceding discussion has shown that when a stationary gun is fired in the atmosphere, the projectile range depends on: the initial velocity of the projectile leaving the muzzle, elevation of the gun barrel above the horizontal plane, density of the air, weight of the projectile, and shape of the projectile.

It is possible to work out mathematically a range of a projectile, accounting for the factors summarized above. These items are considered together to obtain range, although there are more ballistic variables which affect the trajectory.

In considering a mathematical prediction of a trajectory, we can see for example that a 5-inch 54 projectile is designed to have an initial velocity of 2,650 feet per second. The gun elevation above the horizontal plane will be in increments from zero to 85 degrees. A standard atmosphere is used for the density of the air. This standard provides for a temperature of 59 degrees at sea level and a barometric pressure of 29.53 inches. The standard assumes that the air density decreases with an increase in altitude according to a standard formula. The weight of the 5-inch 54 round is 70 pounds. The shape is obtained from the applicable value of the coefficient of form. When these calculations have been made using increments of gun elevation, tables are created which provide the range, time of flight, and maximum ordinate of the projectile trajectory. These quantities are needed on board in most firing missions. Range is needed to set gun elevation, time of flight is used to determine when the projectile will hit the target, and maximum ordinate is used to ensure that the projectile will clear obstacles in indirect fire (i.e., shooting over a hill at a target on the other side).

These values are tabulated for easy reference by the gunnery officer in relation to a change in the range of the target. This is done because range is provided directly to the gunnery officer by the gun director. A range table is available aboard ship for each caliber gun carried and each type of projectile used.

Other Exterior Ballistic Factors

Drift

Every projectile fired by a naval gun drifts off to the right as it travels through the air, because of the clockwise rifling of the bore. This gyroscopic action causes the harmful characteristic, *motion of drift* (figure 3–7). A projectile's drift increases with range by a definite amount, which can be determined by experiments and can be tabulated. The amounts of drift to be expected from any trajectory of a naval gun are tabulated in the range tables. In order to make the correction, the drift in yards is converted into an angle in mils by the computer. A mil is an angle which will cause a deflection of one yard at a distance of 1,000 yards. Therefore, a 35-yard deflection at 1,000 yards would be equivalent to 35 mils.

Wind Effect

The effect that wind has on an object may be easily observed while watching a football game on a windy day. Depending on the wind direction and speed (velocity), the well-aimed "forward pass" may have curved to the right or left, or fallen short of or beyond the place where it was intended to land. Wind has exactly the same effect on a projectile that is in flight. The effects of wind must also be considered in the solution of the fire control problem.

Wind that is blowing at right angles (perpendicular) to the projec-

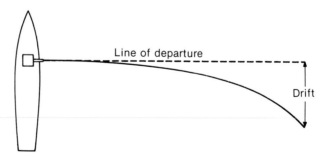

Figure 3-7. The effect of drift on the flight of a projectile.

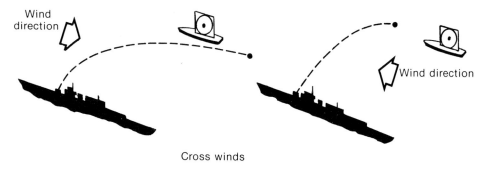

Cross winds

Figure 3–8. The effect of a cross wind on the line of fire of a projectile.

tile's line of fire (LOF) is defined as a *cross wind* (figure 3–8). If the wind is blowing along the line of fire, it is defined as a *range wind* (figure 3–9).

If the wind is blowing from the right at 90 degrees to the LOF, the projectile will land to the left of the target. To compensate for this the gun barrel must be trained to the right (figure 3–10). If the wind is blowing from the left at 90 degrees to the LOF, the projectile will land to the right of the target. To compensate for this the gun barrel must be trained to the left.

If the wind is blowing along the LOF against the projectile, the projectile will fall short of the target. To compensate for this the gun barrel must be elevated to increase the range of the projectile (figure 3–11). Under the same conditions, if the wind is blowing with the projectile, the projectile will tend to land beyond the target. To compensate for this the gun barrel must be depressed (lowered).

The examples shown above are very special cases. Winds do not usually blow directly at right angles to the line of fire or directly into the projectile's LOF. If the wind were to perform in this manner, it would be a relatively simple matter to compute the corrections re-

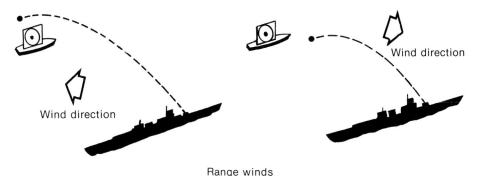

Range winds

Figure 3–9. The effect of a range wind on the line of fire of a projectile.

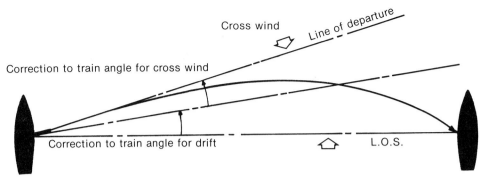

Figure 3–10. *Correcting for the effects of cross wind.*

quired for a known wind speed (velocity). In the majority of the cases, the wind will blow at some other angle in relation to the LOF. In order to correct for range and cross winds, it is necessary to resolve the true wind into two components which are in line with and perpendicular to the LOF. When this is done, each component can be treated individually and the proper gun LOF adjustments can be made.

The gun barrel corrections needed for cross and range winds increase with an increase in range. This is because when the projectile is first fired, it is traveling at such a high speed that the wind does not affect its flight very much. As the projectile slows down during its flight because of wind resistance, the wind affects its trajectory more and more.

Coriolis Effect

Coriolis force is the name for the deflection of a projectile to the right in the northern hemisphere and to the left in the southern hemisphere because of the rotation of the earth. This deflection is not normally considered in naval gunfire unless a shot is made over a long distance.

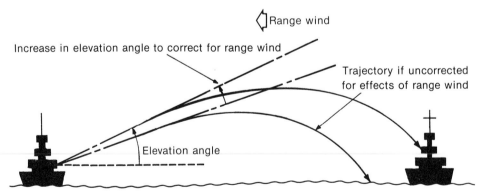

Figure 3–11. *Correcting for the effects of range wind.*

4

The Gun Fire Control Problem

Introduction

The ballistic factors which have been explained in the previous chapters combine to form part of the gun fire control problem and its solution.

The gun fire control problem is to consider and compute all the factors that govern the delivery of effective fire against a target. The type of target will determine the way in which the problem is solved. For example, the surface target position is measured in terms of bearing and range, but the position of an air target includes the third dimension of elevation. Other differences, such as target speed, also affect the solution. In addition to ballistics, the two other facets of the fire control problem are target motion, and own ship motion plus corrections for parallax and gun roller path tilt.

Command Decision

When a target has been detected by the combat information center and classified as an enemy target, all available information will be passed, with the evaluator's recommendations, as established in the ship's weapons doctrine. A decision will be made as to whether or not to engage the target. If the target is to be engaged, then the next question is which weapon should be used to accomplish the task. In this chapter it will be assumed that the decision has been made to use the ship's guns.

Aiming the gun bore so that the projectile will hit the target is not difficult if the target is stationary and within short range of the gun. However, when the range of the target increases, or the gun platform is moving as well as the target, many more factors are introduced. Some of the elements that must be considered have already been described in preceding chapters on interior and exterior ballistics. Since the gun bore cannot change the direction of the projectile after the projectile is in flight, the original aiming of the gun bore must be extremely accurate. As a result, the solution of the problem is the sum of all the individual corrections and events that take place between the detection and the destruction of the target.

All gun fire control problems are solved in the following five steps:

1. Locate the target.
2. Compute lead angles for gun elevation and bearing.
3. Correct for platform motion.
4. Actually position the gun.
5. Watch and, if necessary, correct the fall of shot (spotting).

Table 4–1 outlines all the variables that will be encountered in the solving of the fire control problem.

TABLE 4–1

Variables of the Entire Gun-laying Process to Achieve the Line of Fire

1. Bearing, range, and elevation of target
2. Own ship's course and speed
3. Interior ballistics
   a. muzzle velocity (IV) (sum of all internal forces)
4. Stable reference platform derives
   a. level
   b. cross-level
5. Factors of exterior ballistics
   a. wind speed and direction
   b. drift
   c. density
   d. gravity
   e. projectile weight
   f. projectile shape
   g. Coriolis effect (world's rotation)
6. Computer solves fire control problem in true vertical and horizontal planes for rates of bearing, range, and elevation. Reconverts to moving ship reference for gun elevation and train
7. Trunnion tilt
8. Parallax
   a. horizontal (train correction)
   b. vertical (elevation correction)
9. Roller path tilt (difference in horizontal plane of gun and director)
10. Spotting the fall of shot

The Theory of Linear and Relative Rate Systems

The two families of gun fire control systems currently in service in the Fleet are *linear rate* and *relative rate* systems. The most recent naval gun systems are often combinations of the two principles.

There are several ways to differentiate between the two; historically, distinctions can be seen by mission (expected character of the target), or by the approach employed by the computers to solve the problem.

The linear rate system was first used in the 1930s to control the then new 5-inch 38 dual-purpose gun. The relative rate systems appeared during World War II to meet the need to react quickly to close-in air attacks. Both systems are now in service and are employed in the newest guns.

The linear rate system is best suited for long ranges, especially when the target cannot be seen, and where the relative rate system cannot function as effectively because of the small angular changes in the target's movements. As a result, the linear rate system is usually associated with large and intermediate caliber guns; the relative rate system is used in intermediate and small caliber guns.

The Linear Rate Solution

The linear rate method of solving the problem of how the projectile is to intercept or hit the target is so named because it measures the *linear* distance a target travels between two points in relation to the *rate* (speed) at which the target is traversing that distance. The problem of where to aim the gun to destroy the target is submitted to the computer, which characteristically expresses the length of the line between any two points A and B as a linear value. The value is used to predict where the projectile (whose time of flight is known) can intercept the target, whose speed and range is being calculated (figure 4–1).

The Relative Rate Solution

The relative rate system is primarily designed for shooting at aerial targets. It depends on establishing the *rate* at which a close, fast-moving target traverses an angle whose second line is established relative to the first line of sight. The relative rate computer then generates a solution, which is a predicted collision point for target and projectile, using (1) the change in angular values, and (2) the time it takes for the change to occur. The relative rate computer solves the problem as described in figure 4–2. It can be seen from the different method of solving the problem that the relative rate system must be able to observe the target either visually or by radar to be able to establish the first line of reference.

Additionally, the relative rate system proves most effective when

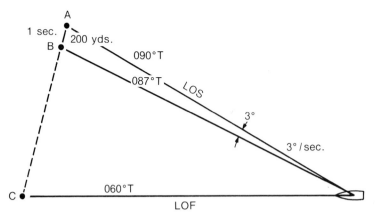

090° to 087° = 3° in 1 sec.   Time of projectile flight = 10 sec.

Lead angle will be 30° (090°T - 30° = 060°T)

Figure 4–1. Linear rate fire control systems measure the distance between one point of observation and the next over a period of time. The distance is measured between A and B along line AC, as well as the time taken to cover this distance. The range of the target from the ship is measured. The computer converts the linear value of the target's travel over distance and the time it takes into speed. Then it predicts the distance the target will travel during the time it will take the projectile to reach line AC. Assume the target was first sighted by the director at 090° true. One second later, the target has traveled 200 yards to 087°. Meanwhile, the computer calculates that the time of flight of the projectile will be 10 seconds to reach line AC. The gun is therefore trained to 060° true.

the target is moving fast enough to set up an appreciable angular change while the target is being tracked.

Shore Bombardment

The linear rate system lends itself to naval gun fire support missions, even though the computation is simplified for the linear rate system when aiming at a stationary target ashore. This is because there is no more change in range and bearing than is caused by the ship's own movement, and there is no elevation rate factor at all.

It is more precise than relative rate in this role because it uses the true coordinates as linear values for a reference. The relative rate system is not as well suited to naval gun fire support because it must see the target to obtain the first line of reference (line of sight) and because land targets are often stationary and so do not set up an angular rate of motion at all.

Rates of Target Motion

The most critical limitation inherent in any linear or relative rate system is the missile or aircraft which is approaching or going away from the ship directly along the line of sight. This critical movement

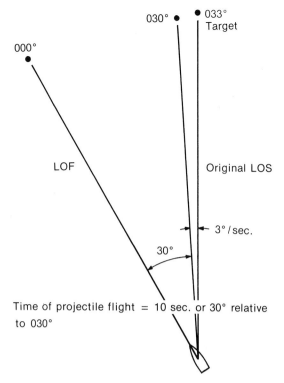

Figure 4–2. Relative rate fire control systems measure (by gyroscopic precession) the change in angle relative to the first line of sight over a period of time. The range of the target is also measured. Let us assume that a LOS is established at 033° relative to the ship's head. One second later, the target bears 033° relative. The computer calculates the time of flight the projectile requires to reach the target at that range. A time of flight of 10 seconds will be used in this example. Using the angular rate of 3° per second (determined above) times 10 seconds, the gun must point 30° to the left of the LOS at 030° to intercept the target. The line of fire shown will be 000° relative, or dead ahead.

along the line of sight is called *range rate*. Range rate is computed as a value expressed in knots of the closing or opening rate of target motion in the line of sight. Of less critical nature are rates of target motion in bearing and elevation as they do not immediately threaten the ship. *Bearing rate* is a measure of target motion perpendicular to and across the line of sight. *Elevation rate* is a measure of target motion perpendicular to the line of sight in a vertical plane. Newer computers are capable of handling very rapid changes in the range of closing high-speed targets.

The Fire Control Problem

Having described the theoretical difference between both ways of finding the point at which to aim the gun, we can now describe the actual steps taken to ensure that all corrections are made for all the variables in the problem, so that the calculated prediction will produce faultless gun positioning orders.

Establishing Present Target Positioning—Step One

As previously discussed, the target position is measured in terms of bearing, elevation, and range.

Bearings

Relative bearings are measured clockwise in degrees and minutes from the ship's bow to the vertical plane of the line of sight to the target. True bearings are expressed clockwise in degrees and minutes in reference to true north rather than to the centerline of one's own ship (figure 4–3).

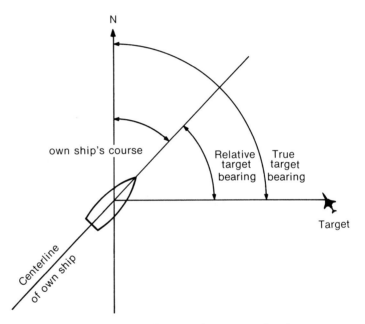

Figure 4–3. Distinctions between relative and true target bearings.

Elevation

To obtain target elevation, a vertical plane is imagined passing through the line of sight from the surface. It is measured in minutes from the surface to the target (figure 4–4). Degrees are not used in gun fire control systems.

Range

There are two types of target ranges—*horizontal* and *slant* (figure 4–5). The range that is measured along the line of sight from one's

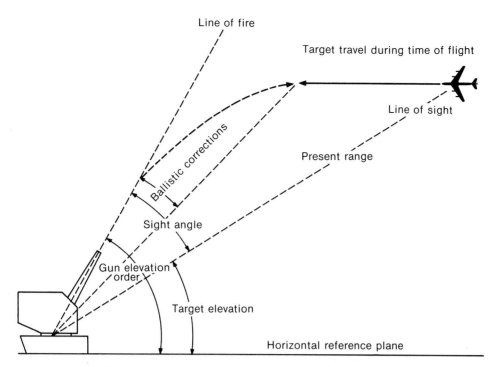

Figure 4–4. *The basic gun elevation order.*

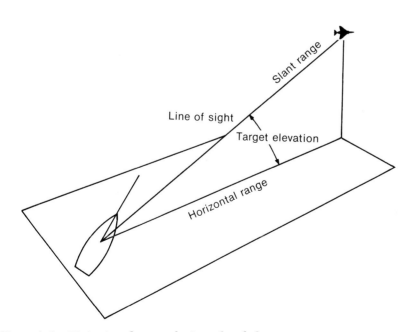

Figure 4–5. *Distinctions between horizontal and slant ranges.*

own ship to the target is called the *slant range* measured in yards.

Another value which has been mentioned is range rate (yds/sec).

Range rate, elevation rate (if any), and bearing rate are the actual values computed in the linear and relative systems as previously described. They provide present target motion.

Computing Gun Lead Angles—Step Two

There are two gun lead angles (elevation and train) to compute in order to hit a moving target, just as a hunter aims his shotgun at a point in front of a flying duck. The line of fire must be such that the projectile and the target will reach the same point in space at the same time.

Gun Elevation Order

After the computer has calculated where the projectile and target will meet, an elevation order must go to the guns. Since the computer solved the fire control problem using a horizontal plane, the original gun elevation order is in relation to this horizontal plane (figure 4-4). Notice that the gun elevation order goes from the horizontal reference plane up to the line of fire (gun bore axis); whereas the sight angle goes from the line of sight up to the line of fire.

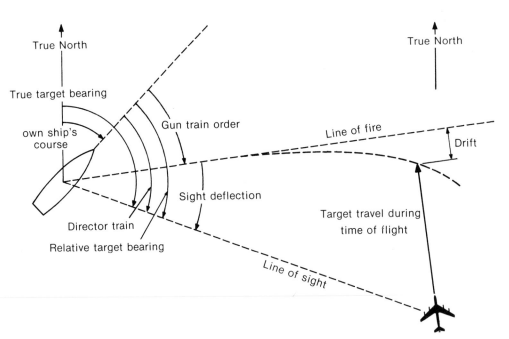

Figure 4-6. A plan view of the basic gun train order.

Gun Train Order

A gun train order goes to the guns after the computer has calculated where the target and projectile will collide, in the same way as the gun elevation order (figure 4–6).

There are more factors used in determining the gun train order. Notice that the angles for relative target bearing and director train are the same, because the director train is measured in the deck plane. However, this is only true when the ship is not rolling or pitching. Notice that the gun train order goes from the ship's head to the line of fire; whereas, the sight deflection goes from the line of sight to the line of fire. Sight deflection is the algebraic sum of the corrections for drift and the target's travel during the projectile's time of flight.

Correcting for Gun Platform Motion—Step Three

The gun mount moves as the ship rolls and pitches. As it is impractical to stabilize the ship, two alternatives have been tried. The first requires that the gun mount drive motors must continuously reposition the gun bore axis to maintain the correct line of fire regardless of the ship's movements. The second method, less frequently used, is to control the firing circuit so that the gun will only fire when the gun bore axis is in the correct position for the projectile to hit the target.

The terms used in the corrections required for the combined effect of ship's roll and pitch are called *level* and *cross level*. The level correction takes care of the ship's deck movements in the line of sight to the target. Cross level is the correction made for the ship's deck movements at right angles to the line of sight. Both these quantities are measured in their relationship to the true horizontal plane, as shown in figure 4–7.

Deck Plane (Trunnion) Tilt

The gun barrel rotates up and down on trunnions, which are fixed to the ship's deck. Therefore, the gun mount tilts with the ship's motion, and when the ship rolls and pitches, the gun is not always elevating in a plane perpendicular to the horizontal plane. Because of this, when the gun is elevated, the gun bore axis shifts in train (figure 4–8, point A). Both elevation and train corrections must be made to compensate for this deck tilt. Figure 4–8 shows the train correction necessary, from point A to point B, for the indicated deck tilt. Point B to point C shows the elevation correction.

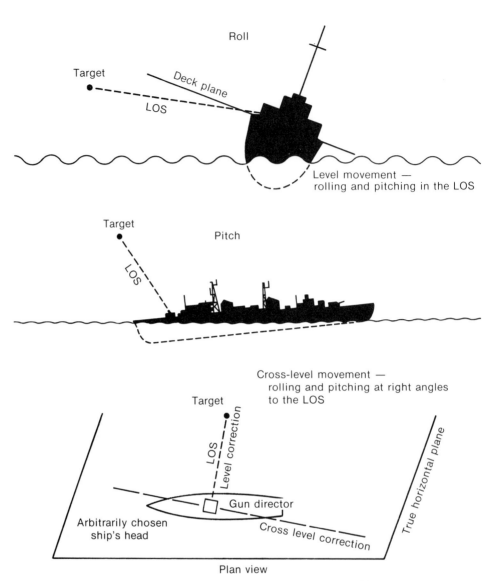

Figure 4-7. Profile and plan views of level and cross-level motion.

Establishing Gun Positioning Orders—Step Four

With the previous steps completed, a solution to the fire control problem (gun train and gun elevation orders) is available from the computer in relation to the unit (director) that established the line of sight. Since the gun mounts are not at the same location as the director, corrections must be made to the fire control solution to establish the gun positioning orders. With corrections for parallax and roller path tilt, the gun-laying process is concluded.

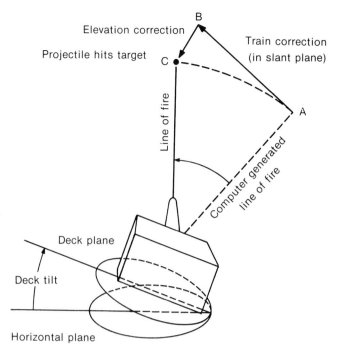

Figure 4–8. *Corrections in train and elevation for deck tilt.*

Parallax

In the fire control problem, *parallax* is the displacement in vertical and horizontal position of the gun mount as observed from the position of its director on the ship. Figure 4–9 illustrates the parallax correction for train and elevation required to bring the forward mount to bear on the same target that the director sees. An elevation parallax correction is necessary in certain ships where the director is much higher in the ship than the gun mount. The train parallax correction is computed from target range and relative target bearings from the director.

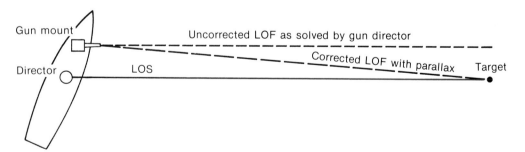

Figure 4–9. *Horizontal and vertical parallax requiring a correction in gun train and elevation.*

Roller Path Tilt

As the fire control problem is solved using the director's roller path as a reference plane, the gun mounts should have their roller paths in a plane parallel to the director's. Ideally, they are. However, because of changes in the way the ship's hull is supported while it is being built in a shipyard compared to when it is afloat, the gun mount's roller paths may differ from the director's roller path. As a result, individual corrections are necessary for each gun mount.

This correction is made in gun elevation orders at the gun mount with an amount depending on the bearing at which the mount is trained. Figure 4–10 shows a gun mount roller path tilt in a much exaggerated form.

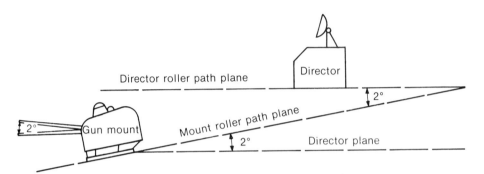

Figure 4–10. Roller path tilt.

Correcting for Fall of Shot—Step 5

Even with the major refinements in new fire control systems, there are still factors which affect the flight of a projectile that cannot be precisely evaluated in advance of firing the guns. In firing at surface targets, the first shot does not necessarily hit exactly at the desired point, even with the most efficient fire control personnel operating the best fire control equipment and with the most experienced gun crews operating the guns.

Corrections called "spots" are applied to the initial firing solution at the computer after the fall of shot has been observed.*

Three spots are available and used to correct for the errors in the fall of shot. They are deflection (bearing), elevation, and range. The deflection spot is normally made in mils, converted from degrees and

---

* A spot is a correction obtained from observing the fall of shot in relation to the target.

minutes of arc. The elevation spot is made in yards, meters, or mils. The range spot is made in yards. A typical command in spotting the fall of shot could be:

Left five mils
Up two mils
Add 100 yards.

The elevation spot is only used when concerned with target height in shore bombardment. Should the subsequent salvos not fall at the desired point, additional spotting may be required.

Spotting air targets is practically impossible for the guns in service although tracer rounds may be fired from guns, and pyrotechnic rockets can be fired on outgoing missiles to assist the observer in following the line of fire. Nevertheless, the Vulcan-Phalanx 20mm gun system employs an advanced integrated spotting system called closed loop spotting, which corrects the gun's aim after comparing the stream of projectiles with the line of sight.

Lethality of the Warhead and Vulnerability of the Target

Aerial Targets

From the preceding discussions of the interior ballistics of gun projectiles, exterior ballistics, and the solution of the fire control problem, it is evident that shooting down aerial targets presents certain peculiar problems in fire control. First of all, the effectiveness of a gun system depends on the way an air target moves. A missile can follow a maneuvering aircraft, but a gun projectile cannot. As a result fire control consists of setting up an accurate prediction of the point of collision between the projectile and air target. This prediction is dependent, as can be seen, on all the factors in the fire control solution just reviewed.

Because the gun system depends on target motion, a pilot will attempt to maneuver in such a way that his aircraft moves in the least predictable way. Target speed and maneuver are critical in achieving a kill. For example, an aircraft flying directly down the line of sight has a high range rate, and if it is low, it is hard to track with all the clutter of the *sea return.* * This movement places a particular kind of stress on the computer and sensor in providing range rate. A quick change of altitude or direction by an air target changes the collision point and requires the director to recompute the solution. Thus it can be seen that aerial targets will be flown to put unbearable stress on

* See glossary.

the weak points of the defending ship's gun system. Once the round reaches a point of interception, the kill becomes dependent on the effectiveness of fuze and warhead, which are pitted against the kind of protection the target is provided with.

If the burst pattern is highly directional because of the payload's location relative to the fuze, it may be particularly effective in certain kinds of engagements and ill-suited to others. For example, a fragmentation round behind a noze fuze would have a doughnutlike pattern well suited to cutting down an incoming missile at deck level, but it might be too planar or directional to destroy an airplane. Again, as far as the warhead is concerned, if the aircraft is protected in the critical parts with armor, perhaps armor-piercing projectiles would be required instead of a fragmentation warhead (figure 4–11).

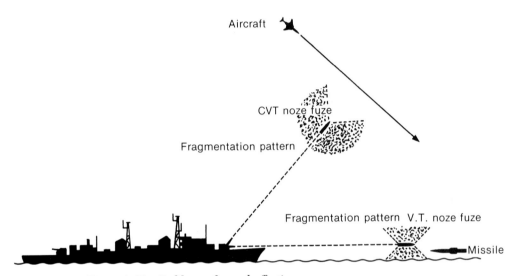

Figure 4–11. Problems of round effectiveness.

In addition to the considerations of gun-laying and round effectiveness in engaging aerial targets, gun effectiveness tends to increase on a statistical basis as the number of rounds fired at a target increases. The cumulative effect of a large number of "somewhat accurately" placed rounds may produce the desired kill effectiveness against the air target. This concept presents a contrast to the large-caliber gun and guided missile concept where a single round or missile is employed, each having a probability of kill higher than the rapid fire gun projectile.

In practice, both the concepts of maximizing the accuracy of each round and salvo firing are applied together, with one consideration dominating the other in a particular gun or missile system.

Surface Targets

Land targets also pose individual fire control and warhead selection problems. If the target is moving, such as a truck or tank, the projectile will require less penetrating force, but more effect over a cubic area.

On the other hand if the target is stationary and heavily fortified, the round will be armor-piercing and the trajectory will be steep for accuracy at the desired range. A steep trajectory will also help the projectile to penetrate the roof of the structure.

Computers

The three basic kinds of fire control computers are analogue, digital, and gyroscopic. They use electronic, electro-mechanical, or gyroscopic calculating equipment.

Analogue and Digital Concepts

The magnitude of a variable is normally determined by measurement or by counting. For example, the weight of an object can be found using either a spring scale or a balance (figure 4–12). In the spring scale, the deflection of the scale is proportional to the weight and, therefore, measures weight directly.

In the balance, unit weights are added to one side of the scale until the unknown is counterbalanced, then the unit weights are counted. The first method (measurement) is called *analogue*, and the second method (counting) is called *digital*. The difference is a fundamental one, corresponding to the mathematical distinction between the con-

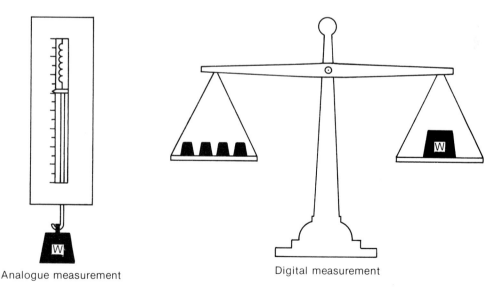

Analogue measurement

Digital measurement

Figure 4–12. Analogue and digital measurement.

tinuous (analogue) and the discrete (digital). The analogue device recognizes any increment of a variable as a whole quantity, as in the displacement of a point, rotation of a shaft, or voltage in a circuit. The digital device recognizes a quantity as a number of basic units, such as a number of weights on a balance, or days on a calendar.

One significant aspect of the analogue device is that it will continuously measure a changing variable. For example, if the object to be weighed were a leaking bucket of water, the spring scale would show the exact weight of the bucket and water at all times. The balance, however, will give a value which is correct only for one weight. If more weight is put on the balance then new counterweights must be put in the counter-balance before the scale is even once again.

Examples of each computer can be found in current naval weapon systems. The Mark 56 and Mark 68 fire control systems, which will be discussed in following chapters, use analogue computers, while the Mark 86 employs a digital computer. The digital computer can provide a faster solution to the problem than the analogue equivalent because it calculates the entire problem in one operation at one time. The analogue computer calculates different segments of the problem in different data banks, then feeds the increments to the director. Furthermore, the digital computers are compatible with other computers aboard ship, such as the NTDS computers described in Chapter 21.

Gyroscopic Computers

Gyroscopic Computers were devised to provide rapid and accurate solutions against close-in aerial targets. Some fire control systems use the principles of gyroscopic rigidity and precession in their computers. Basically, various gyroscopes measure the required angles in target motion, platform motion, and the other minor anomalies needed for the fire control solution. They do this electrically by measuring changes in voltages and resistances. These directly measurable quantities are employed by the computer. The gyros function to generate bearing and elevation lead angles for the gun mount. More insight on how this is accomplished will be found in the next chapter on gyros and relative rate systems.

Electromechanical Computers

Before the gyroscopic computers came into service, the Navy had already developed electromechanical computers to serve the 5-inch 38 dual-purpose gun mount.

In this type of computer, electrical values of bearing, elevation, and range go to the computer from the director. These electrical signals are changed into mechanical motions inside the computer. Other variables, such as the ship's course and speed, are also entered into the computer electrically. The remaining ballistic factors, such as initial velocity, are entered into the computer by hand. The electromechanical computer takes all of these inputs and solves the fire control problem by performing a series of mechanical analogue operations. The computer solution is also a mechanical output, but it is translated into electrical signals for positioning the gun.

Electronic Computers

Electronic computers are rapidly replacing the older electromechanical computers in the Fleet, because they are faster in solving the fire control problem. Speed is an essential factor in weapon system effectiveness because there is less time for the target to change position. Electronic computers use specific circuits or electric elements to perform the mathematical functions that the electromechanical computer did mechanically. When alternating current voltages are used in an electronic computer, two voltages can be added or subtracted by changing their phase relationship, which yields a voltage representing the vectorial sum of the voltages. Electronic computers are smaller, lighter, and have a greater problem-solving capacity than electromechanical devices.

5

Principles and Applications
of Fire Control Gyroscopes

Introduction

It has become evident in the preceding discussion that gyroscopes are widely used in weapon systems; it is important, therefore, to understand their principles and their use in fire control. In order to understand the terminology of basic gyroscopes, certain definitions follow:

Gyroscope The Greek words *gyro,* meaning revolution, and *skopein,* meaning to view, were combined by Leon Foucault, a French scientist, to name his invention in 1852. It was a way, he said, to "view the revolution of the world."

Rotor A spinning mass (wheel) rotating about an axis (shaft) through the center of the mass (figure 5–1).

Gimbal A ring containing a spinning rotor, which is pivoted on an axis and is given the freedom to swing (figure 5–1).

Stand or *Case* The mounting to which the gimbal is attached (figure 5–1).

Degree of freedom The number of gimbals between the rotor and the stand. Figure 5–1 shows a gyro with two degrees of freedom. Figure 5–2 shows a gyro with one degree of freedom.

Rigidity The tendency of the rotor spin axis to remain in a fixed attitude (angle of inclination) if no external force is applied to it.

Precession The tendency of the rotor spin axis to turn right angles to the direction of an externally applied force.

Principles and Applications

Construction

A gyro is made up of a rotor, a gimbal or gimbals, and a base or support. The *universally* mounted gyro can rotate about three axes.°

° It is also called a universally mounted gyroscope because it can assume any axis orientation or direction in space without it being necessary to move the stand.

54

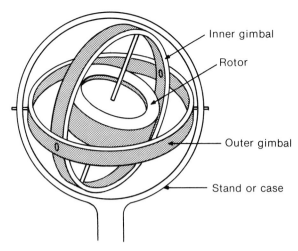

Figure 5–1. *The parts of a gyroscope.*

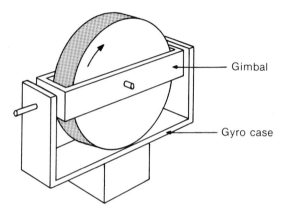

Figure 5–2. *A one-degree-of-freedom gyroscope.*

The first of the three axes is indicated by the *x* in figure 5–3 about which the gyro rotor spins. The inner gimbal, which holds the rotor, is free to rotate about the *y* axis. The outer gimbal rotates about the *z* axis.

Properties

The two gyro properties of *rigidity in space* and *gyroscopic precession* make the gyro useful in numerous fire control systems. Rigidity in space is used to maintain a reference axis in space, which is unaffected by the motion of its supporting platform (i.e., ship, aircraft, or missile). It is then possible to compensate for that motion, because there is a reference to measure movement against.

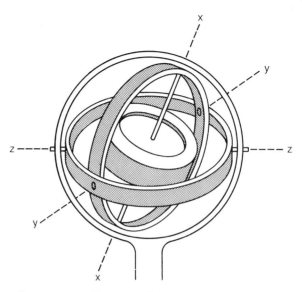

Figure 5–3. A basic universally mounted gyroscope.

Rigidity in Space

Rigidity in space is demonstrated in any number of objects we see every day. An example is a toy top which, when spinning rapidly, stays balanced on its point. Again, when riding a bicycle, it is easier to maintain balance at high speeds than it is at low speeds. The high speed of the bicycle wheels acting as a gyro tends to keep the bicycle wheel rigid in space (at right angles to the ground). The universally mounted gyro shown in figure 5–3 also demonstrates rigidity in space. If the rotor were spun rapidly, the x axis would remain pointed in the direction illustrated. If the rotor were stopped and the rotor axis moved in another direction, spinning the rotor again would cause the x axis to remain in its new direction. Taking this into account, observe what happens when the base is moved. If the base is moved in any direction, the spinning rotor axis remains pointed in the same direction because the only thing that actually moves is the gimbal system.

Application of Rigidity

To make the universally mounted gyro useful in the fire control problem, an erecting system is added. The erecting system keeps the gyro axis in a true vertical direction in relation to the surface of the earth. This is accomplished by the force of gravity. There are several erecting systems being used in fire control systems. Further information on erecting systems can be obtained from the Ordnance Publications for particular systems.

As described in the preceding chapter, the true vertical and horizontal planes are used for reference in solving a fire control problem (figure 5–4).

The y axis of the gyro is aligned through the centerline of a ship from the ship's bow to its stern, the z axis of the gyro is aligned to port and starboard. After the erecting system has pointed the gyro axis (x) in the true vertical, gyroscopic rigidity will tend to keep it there. Thus, rigidity is the principle employed to establish the true vertical plane against which is measured the degree of horizontal motion in level and cross level, because when the spin axis (x) is set on a true vertical, the plane of the spinning rotor indicates the true horizontal plane. With the gyro case bolted to the deck of the ship, the ship will pitch and roll about the rotor. The rotation about the y axis in figure 5–4 will provide a measurement of the ship's pitch, while the rotation about the x axis provides the amount of the ship's roll.

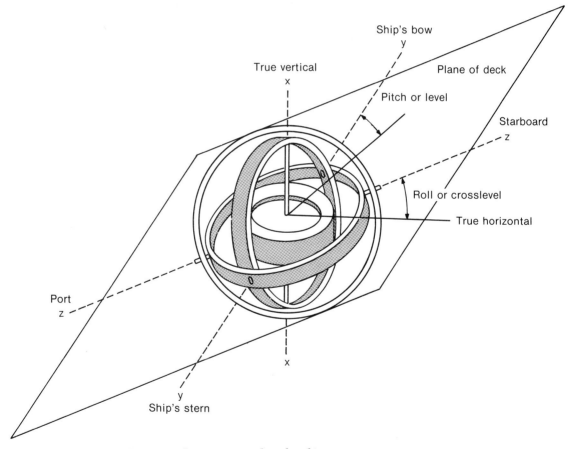

Figure 5–4. A universally mounted gyroscope on board a ship.

Rigidity is applied in both linear and relative rate systems for establishing the true horizontal and vertical planes.

Precession

While rigidity provides continuous measurement of the angle between the platform in motion and the reference planes in linear and relative rate systems, the second property of a gyro, precession, is used in relative rate systems alone to solve for target motion. Precession is used to measure the degree of change in angle when a fire control director is slewed to track a target, keeping the line of sight (LOS) on the target. The principle of precession may be stated as the tendency of the rotor (y) axis to realign itself to parallel the axis of any external force (a) applied to the rotor in figure 5–5. The angle between the original rotor axis and the new axis is used to measure the change in direction (degree) a target has moved from point A (original LOS) to point B (new LOS the director was slewed to) (figure 5–6). The speed (rate) at which the rotor axis moves from point A to point B provides the angular rate of motion of the target. This is derived from the rule that the speed of the gyro's precession is proportional to the magnitude of the applied force. One application of precession in relative rate gun fire control systems may be found in the one-degree-of-freedom gyro (figure 5–7).

Use of Precession

Should a force be applied to the case (figure 5–7), the force will tend to change the direction of the gyro rotor and precession will

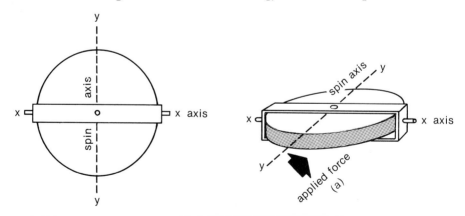

Figure 5–5. Precession. Force a *applied to the rotor causes the rotor to precess 90° to the direction of force* a. *Stated another way, the application of force* a *to the rotor causes the gimbal to align itself with force* a.

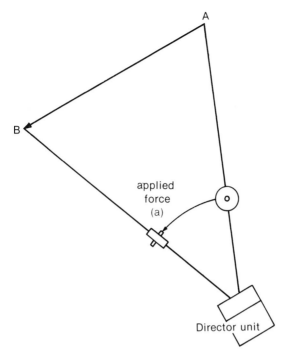

Figure 5–6.   *Measurement by gyroscope of director movement.*

result. If the force moving the case is stopped, the rotor axis will remain in the plane in which it was pointing when the precession stopped.

In relative rate fire control systems, this one-degree-of-freedom gyro motion principle will be applied in two ways: in *rate-of-turn* gyros and in *rate* gyros.

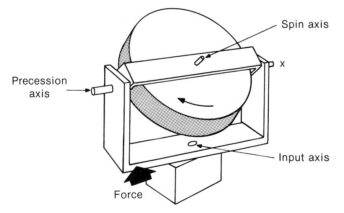

Figure 5–7.   *The precession of a one-degree-of-freedom gyroscope.*

Rate-of-Turn Gyros

Rate-of-turn gyros provide a measurement of the force applied to the gyro case. This is accomplished by adding a restraining mechanism, such as a spring, to the rotor's gimbal. The tension placed on the spring by the attempt of the rotor to precess to its new position measures the force applied to the case. This force is the speed of the director as it slews to follow the target. Thus the rate-of-turn gyro, as its name implies, provides the rate of the target's movement through a given angle (degrees per second). With the precessional torque being directly proportional to the rate of turn of the line of sight about its z axis, the proper gun orders are generated, with some modification.

Rate Gyros

As discussed above, rate-of-turn gyros are a means of calculating degrees-per-second using a particular method of engineering. Rate gyros can also provide degrees-per-second information to the relative rate fire control solution, but they work in a different way. A rate gyro receives an electrical order from the slewing controls, which are attempting to maintain the LOS to the target to precess the same

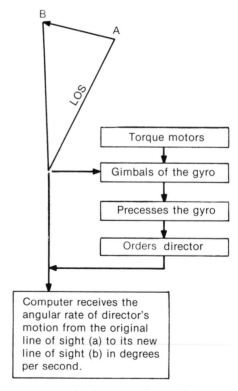

Figure 5–8. The transmission of information derived by gyroscope.

amount the control unit moved while tracking. The degrees per second the gyro rotor precesses is sent to the computer, while at the same time the gyro orders the director to slew to the new line of sight (figure 5–8).

Summary

Some of the essential ways in which gyroscopes are used to help generate the solution to the naval gun fire control problem have been described. The gyroscopic actions used in linear rate and relative rate gun fire control systems are based on *rigidity* and *precession.* Rigidity helps the system compensate for platform motion, while precession is used in relative rate systems to generate lead angle and lead sight solutions in the gun fire control problem. Precession applies in two methods of engineering fire control/gunfire control systems—in rate-of-turn gyros and in rate gyros. These kinds of gyros show up in all relative rate gun fire control systems.

6

The Mark 68 Linear Rate
Gun Fire Control System

*Figure 6–1. Mark 68 gun director with optical sights uncovered and radar antenna
is mounted high in the superstructure of the USS Bigelow (DD-942).*

Introduction

Having offered an explanation of the theoretical basis for solving the gun fire control problem, the application of that theory is presented in the following chapters. They describe the way in which some representative fire control systems in service and some of the newest systems available function on board ship.

The two most common gun fire control systems in the U.S. Navy today are the Mark 68 linear rate system and the Mark 56 relative rate system. The Mark 56 will be discussed in Chapter 7. Newer systems are described in Chapter 8.

A gun fire control system (GFCS) is a combination of elements: a *director* (establishes the line of sight from the ship to the target and measures the target's present position in bearing and elevation), a *computer* (solves the fire control problem), a *stable element* (establishes the horizontal reference plane that is used in the computer to solve for lead angles), and a tracking *radar* (measures the present range to the target and the rate at which the target is moving in range).

The Mark 68 GFCS is installed on most destroyer ship types (figure 6–2). It is a dual-purpose (for surface and air targets), linear rate system that is used to control the fire of 5-inch 54 caliber or 3-inch 50 caliber guns. The system can automatically track and engage surface targets and aircraft as well as missiles that travel at speeds of less than 2,000 knots. The Mark 68 GFCS can provide continuous orders (gun train, gun elevation, fuze order, sight angle, sight deflection and parallax) to the gun mounts.

The Mark 68 Gun Director

The gun director, figure 6–3, determines the present target's position in bearing and elevation along the line of sight. It is always located high in the ship to increase the visual detection range and reduce interference from the ship's superstructure. The director may track the target either optically or with the fire control radar. The fire control radar antenna is located on top of the director, figure 6–3, and the axis of the radar beam is parallel to the optical line of sight. Optical sights in the director consist of the director officer's binoculars, the director tracker's telescope, and a stereoscopic rangefinder. Slip rings, an assembly of brushes and circular rings, enable the director to have unlimited train.

To stabilize the line of sight in *cross-level* (motion across the line of sight), the major part of the director is stabilized and pivots on the cross-level gears attached to the director supporting member. The

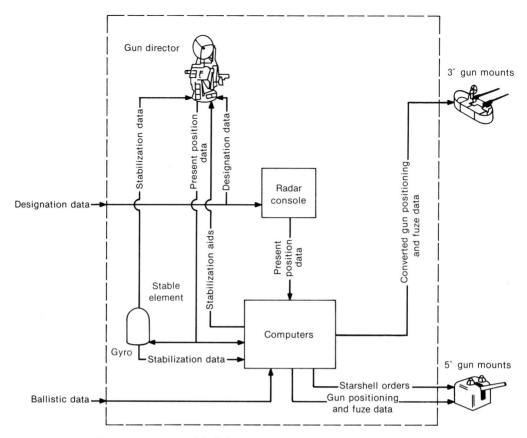

Figure 6–2. A simplified diagram of the flow of information in the Mark 68 system.

radar antenna and director optics are stabilized in *level,* up and down motion in the line of sight. Level and cross-level are sent to the director from the stable element. Movement of the director in cross-level and train is accomplished by small amplidyne power drives. The radar antenna and director optics in level and elevation are also driven by small amplidyne motors.

Director Officer's Station

From this station (figures 6–4 and 6–5), located on the left side of the director, the director officer supervises the operation of the gun fire control system. A slew sight, with a pair of 7 x 50 power binoculars, is mounted outside the director and is used for the initial acquisition of targets. The *one-man control unit* (OMC), figure 6–5, is used to control the train of the director and to control the elevation of the optical sights and radar antenna. To train the director, the entire

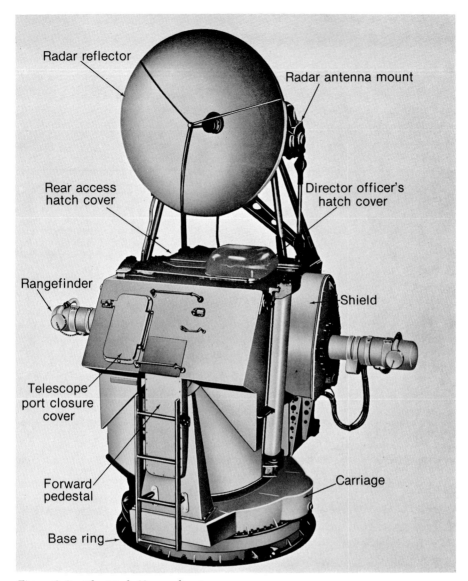

Figure 6–3. The Mark 68 gun director.

one-man control unit is rotated horizontally in the desired direction. To elevate the director optics and radar antenna, the one-man control unit is raised to the desired angle. A trigger switch on the right hand grip allows the director officer to take control over all modes of operation. In the manual operating mode, the hand wheel unit located at the top of the director officer's one-man control unit is used to move the director optics and radar antenna in elevation only.

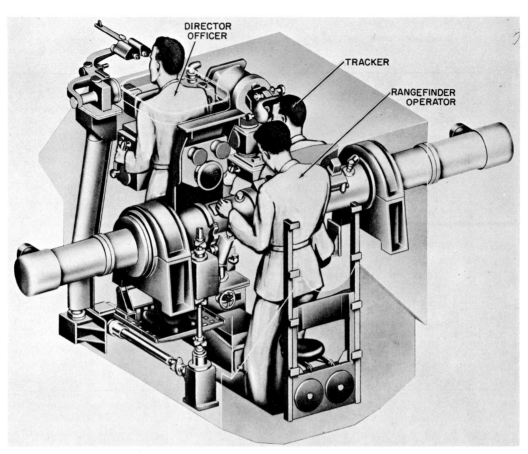

DIRECTOR OFFICER

TRACKER

RANGEFINDER OPERATOR

Figure 6–4. Crew stations inside the director.

The *director officer's control panel,* located above the director officer's one-man control unit, enables him to turn on the director power drives and select the director operating mode. The director officer has a firing key, but the tracker usually fires the gun.

Director Tracker's Station

The tracker's station (figure 6–4) is located on the right side of the director. A six or ten power telescope is used for visual target tracking. The *director tracker's one-man control unit* (OMC), figure 6–6, is similar to the director officer's unit, except that the right trigger switch is the tracker's firing key. When manually operated, the tracker's hand wheel is used to move the director in train only. Therefore, coordination between the director officer and tracker is important when tracking a target visually in this mode.

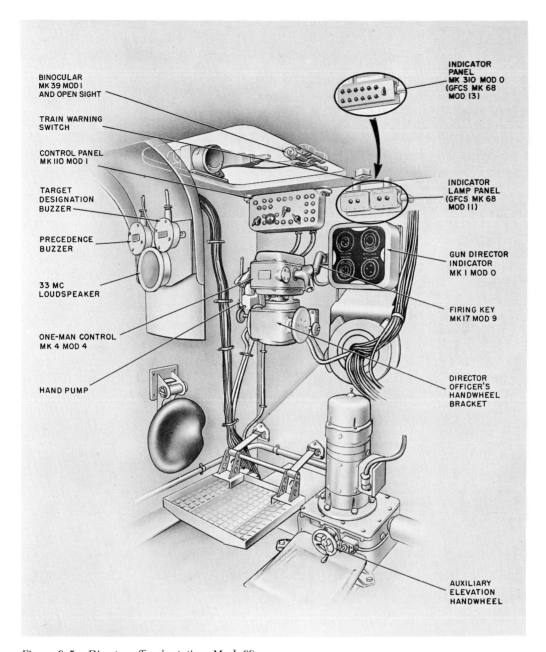

BINOCULAR
MK 39 MOD I
AND OPEN SIGHT

TRAIN WARNING
SWITCH

CONTROL PANEL
MK IIO MOD I

TARGET
DESIGNATION
BUZZER

PRECEDENCE
BUZZER

33 MC
LOUDSPEAKER

ONE-MAN CONTROL
MK 4 MOD 4

HAND PUMP

INDICATOR
PANEL
MK 310 MOD 0
(GFCS MK 68
MOD I3)

INDICATOR
LAMP PANEL
(GFCS MK 68
MOD I I)

GUN DIRECTOR
INDICATOR
MK I MOD 0

FIRING KEY
MK I7 MOD 9

DIRECTOR
OFFICER'S
HANDWHEEL
BRACKET

AUXILIARY
ELEVATION
HANDWHEEL

Figure 6–5. Director officer's station, Mark 68.

Rangefinder Operator's Station

This station (figure 6–4) is located at the rear in the center of the director. The rangefinder is a 16-power stereoscopic optical sight that is used to obtain ranges to surface or shore targets. To obtain range,

The Mark 68 Linear Rate Gun Fire Control System   **67**

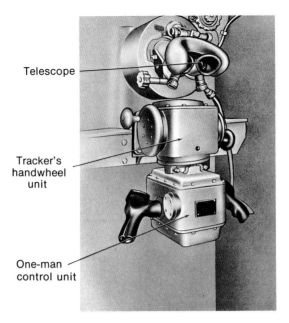

Telescope

Tracker's
handwheel
unit

One-man
control unit

Figure 6–6. The tracker's station.

a series of diamond shapes are placed, by rotating the rangefinder range knob, in front of and behind the target. When this has been accomplished, range is read from a dial.

Radar

The gun fire control radar (AN/SPG-53A)* is used to search for, acquire, and track air or surface targets automatically or manually. When used with Radar Signal Processing Equipment (RSPE), the radar will automatically acquire and track a target. In addition, the RSPE improves radar operation in an electronic jamming environment. The radar supplies target range and range rate (the rate at which a target's range is changing) to the computer. Electrical positioning signals are sent from the radar to the director train and elevation power drives to keep the director line of sight on target in the automatic target tracking mode of operation. The parabolic radar antenna is mounted on top of the director and the radar beam axis is parallel to the director tracker's telescope. Thus radar ranges can be obtained when the target is tracked visually. The radar beam has two scan patterns—*spiral* (12 degrees wide) for search and acquisition and *conical* (3 degrees wide) for tracking. A radar display console, located in the fire control room

---

* See appendix for an explanation and breakdown of the AN/ equipment nomenclature system.

below the main deck, contains all the necessary operating controls and radar scope displays.

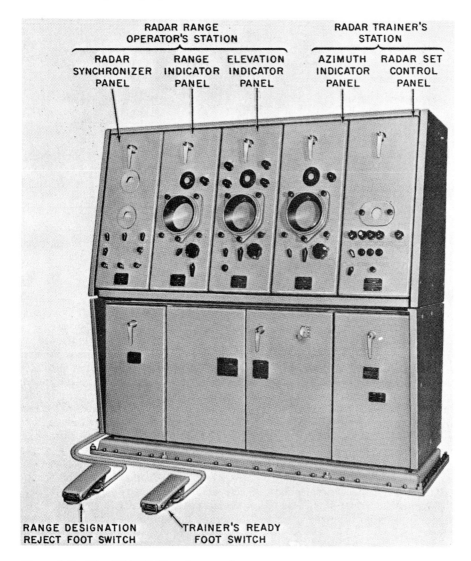

RADAR RANGE OPERATOR'S STATION

RADAR TRAINER'S STATION

RADAR SYNCHRONIZER PANEL | RANGE INDICATOR PANEL | ELEVATION INDICATOR PANEL | AZIMUTH INDICATOR PANEL | RADAR SET CONTROL PANEL

RANGE DESIGNATION REJECT FOOT SWITCH

TRAINER'S READY FOOT SWITCH

Figure 6–7. The AN/SPG-53 radar console.

The Fire Control Room

The *radar range operator's station* (figure 6–7) is located on the left side of the radar console and includes the radar synchronizer panel, the range indicator panel (R scope),* the elevation indicator panel

---

* Chapter 10 contains an explanation of various fire control radar indicator scope displays.

(E scope), the range designation reject foot switch, and the RSPE operating control panel.

The *radar synchronizer panel* contains controls for tuning the radar transmitter and receiver, varying the transmission frequency, and varying the pulse repetition rate.

The *range indicator panel (R scope)* contains controls and a radar display of range. Range and target data are shown on two horizontal sweeps (figure 6–8), a main sweep (bottom) and a precision sweep (top), the main sweep showing 120,000 yards of range. The transmitted (outgoing) pulse appears as an upward deflection at zero range. Target echoes appear as upward deflections from the horizontal line (sweep). A downward step called the range step can be moved over to a target and corresponds to the range notch on the precision sweep. The position of the range step is an indication of radar range and will be displayed on a range dial.

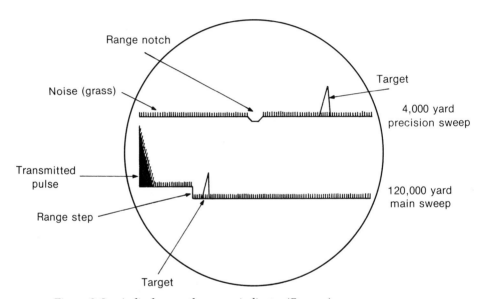

Figure 6–8. A display on the range indicator (R scope).

The precision sweep (upper horizontal line) shows 4,000 yards of range, 2,000 yards on either side of the range notch, which always remains fixed at the center of the precision sweep. The range notch corresponds to the range step on the main sweep. The radar is ranged correctly when the selected echo is centered in the range notch of the precision sweep.

The *elevation indicator panel* (E scope), figure 6–9, provides for a display of target elevation sent to the computer. The elevation scope

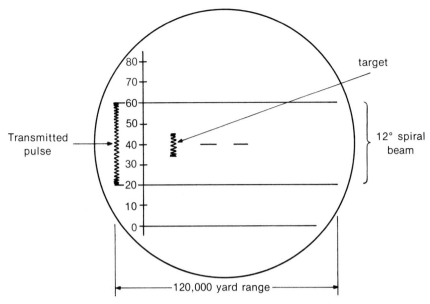

Figure 6–9. The main sweep of the elevation indicator (E scope) in spiral scan.

shows range horizontally and elevation vertically. A sweep control switch allows the radar range operator to select a main, or precision, radar presentation.

The *RSPE operating control* panel, figure 6–10, is used to turn RSPE on and off, to tune it, and test it. When the RSPE is used, the radar will be placed on target in spiral scan by the director or the ship's weapon designation equipment (WDE). Weapon designation equipment is used to transfer fire control data of target bearing, elevation, and range from one fire control element to another. When the target appears in the radar beam, the RSPE will cause the radar to automatically acquire the target in conical scan and lock on to track it. This RSPE eliminates the need to manually acquire the target using the range, elevation, and bearing radar displays.

The *radar trainer's station*, figure 6–7, is located on the right side of the radar console and includes the azimuth indicator panel (bearing scope) and radar trainer's ready foot switch.

The *azimuth (bearing) indicator panel*, figure 6–11, provides for control of target bearing input into the computer. The azimuth indicator displays range vertically and bearing horizontally. A sweep control switch provides a choice of a main (120,000 yard) or precision (4,000 yard) video presentation.

The *radar trainer's ready foot switch* when depressed shifts the radar scan from spiral (12 degrees) to conical (3 degrees), causing the radar

The Mark 68 Linear Rate Gun Fire Control System **71**

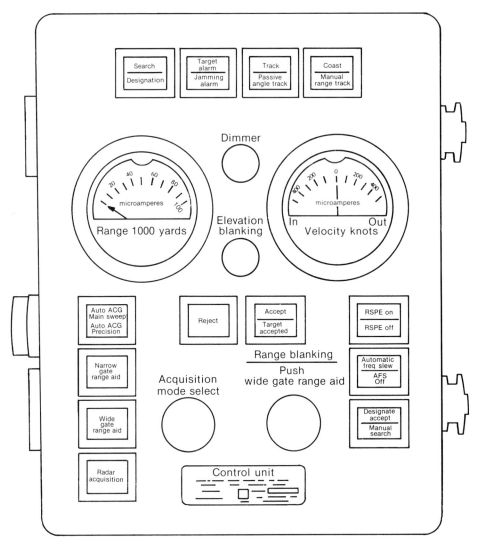

Figure 6–10. The radar signal processing equipment control unit.

to track the target automatically. To cease tracking and return the radar to spiral scan, the ready foot switch is depressed again.

Computers

The *Mark 47 computer* is a dual-purpose computer designed to solve the antiaircraft and surface-shore fire control problems and calculates gun and fuze setting orders for 5-inch 54 caliber guns. This analogue computer is fully transistorized and has operating controls on the front cover along with dials that show computer outputs and inputs.

Automatic and continuous inputs to the computer include the ship's speed from the pit log, the ship's course from the gyrocompass, target range and range rate from the fire control radar, target bearing and elevation from the director, and level and cross-level from the stable element.

Manual inputs to the computer include initial velocity (IV), wind direction and speed, and spotting data.

The fire control radar and director measure present target position continuously. When the computer's *generated present target position* equals the *actual present target position* established by the director, the computer can predict a *future target position*. It is at this future target position that the projectile will intercept the target. When the ballistic variables (superelevation, drift, wind and IV) have been added to or subtracted from future target position, the aiming point for the gun mount has been calculated. This aiming point will be sent to the gun mount as a gun train order and gun elevation order that will change continuously as the range, bearing and elevation to the target's present position changes. When the computer solves the fire control problem, it uses true horizontal and true vertical reference planes to develop gun orders. These references are provided by the gyroscopes of the stable element. Nevertheless, since the gun is located on the moving deck, these gun orders must be converted to account for gun platform motion in level, cross-level, and deck plane (trunnion) tilt

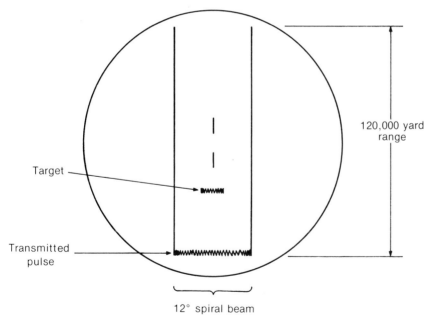

Figure 6–11. The main sweep of the azimuth indicator (B scope) in spiral scan.

The Mark 68 Linear Rate Gun Fire Control System   **73**

before being sent to the gun. Further corrections compensate for horizontal and vertical parallax, as well as roller path tilt to complete the positioning of the gun.

The *Mark 47 computer* calculates gun orders for the 5-inch 54 caliber gun mount. If the ship is equipped with 3-inch 50 caliber guns, then the 5-inch 54 gun orders are sent directly to a Mark 116 computer which converts these gun orders to 3-inch 50 caliber gun orders by compensating for the differences in the ballistic characteristics between the two guns. The Mark 116 computer can also modify the 5-inch 54 gun orders to position the gun mount for firing illumination projectiles (star shells). The gun will be positioned to cause an illumination round to burst above and beyond the surface target rather than to collide with it. This will make the target visible to the firing ship.

Stable Element

The stable element (Mark 16) is located in the gun fire control room next to the Mark 47 computer. In general, its primary function is to measure the angles of level and cross-level. The stable element does this by using a gyroscope to establish true vertical and true horizontal. When the ship pitches and rolls, she will cause the director line of sight to move off target when tracking optically, or induce deceptive errors when in full automatic radar track. To keep the director line of sight on target, the stable element continuously sends orders compensating for cross-level motion to the director. It also sends level and cross-level to the computer.

Operation of the System

The mode (table 6–1) of fire control that is chosen to operate the guns is dependent upon the type of target—a missile, an aircraft, a ship, or a shore target—and the tactical situations. Two primary modes are the *normal* and the *manual* mode. For example, the manual mode is used for bombarding relatively slow moving shore targets in a minimum air and submarine threat environment. It would also be used when battle damage has caused a loss of power and when maintenance to the equipment is required. The normal mode is used, as the name indicates, in every other situation.

In the normal mode of operation, the director officer determines a subordinate mode; that is, whether director movement is governed by controls within the director (optical search mode); by controls at the radar console (console search mode); by the target designation system (target designation mode); or by radar automatic tracking circuits (automatic radar tracking mode). Alternately, with handwheel

TABLE 6–1
Mark 68 Gun Fire Control System Operating Modes

Mode	Sub-mode	Angle Tracking By	Ranging By	Used For
	Auto-track	Auto-radar tracker	Radar circuitry, performed automatically	AA, Surface
N	Console	Handcranks and scopes at radar console	Handcranks and scopes at radar console	AA, Surface
O	Director officer's control unit	One-man control unit and binoculars	Radar (at console) or rangefinder	AA, Surface
R				
M	Director tracker's control unit	One-man control unit and tracking telescope	Radar (at console) or rangefinder	AA, Surface
A				
L	CIC target designation	Target designation source	Target designation source	AA, Surface
HANDWHEEL		Director officer's and tracker's handwheel unit and optics	Radar (at console) or rangefinder	AA, Surface

mode operation, director movement is controlled only by the director officer's and tracker's handwheel units. The director determines the mode of operation, and can cancel one mode in favor of another.

Optical Search Mode

In this mode, the director crew searches for the target with optical sights. Director movement can be controlled either from the director officer's station, using the one-man control unit and open sight and binoculars, or from the tracker's station, using the one-man control unit and tracking telescope. Target acquisition by the tracker sighting through his telescope is restricted to slow-moving and surface targets. Target range is obtained either optically with the rangefinder or by radar.

Console Search Mode

This mode is used primarily for searching; however, it can also be used to track both surface and low-speed air targets. Under this mode of operation, controls at the radar console are employed to position the director in train and elevation.

Target Designation Mode

This mode supplies target range, bearing, and elevation information to a gun director from another sensing element—from search sensors in CIC, another director, or from another ship by computer data link. Signals from the target designation system slew the director to a position in train and elevation, and also cause the radar range step to move to a designated range position at the radar range indicator. When the director and radar range have been positioned, they are not necessarily placed directly on target. The radar operator and radar trainer use controls at their stations to perform this function. To control radar range manually, the radar operator must press the range designation reject foot switch for the entire period that manual control of range is desired.

Radar Automatic Tracking Mode

This radar mode is employed for tracking air targets, and also other types of targets in which the tactical situation requires a rapid solution of the fire control problem. In this mode, angle tracking of the target in bearing, elevation, and target ranging is performed automatically by radar circuitry.

Radar automatic tracking is activated automatically from either the console search or target designation modes if the following conditions have been met:

1. The director has been placed on target in train and elevation.

2. The target has been gated in range (placed in the range notch on the precision range sweep).

3. The ready foot switch at the radar trainer's station has been depressed.

Handwheel mode

This mode is independent of all normal operating modes and is usually employed for slow-moving surface targets and shore targets.

In this mode, the handwheels at the director officer's and tracker's stations are turned to elevate the director optical sights and radar antenna, and to train the director, respectively. Each 360-degree rotation of the handwheels at the director officer's station either elevates or depresses the director optical sights and radar antenna one degree, depending upon the direction of rotation. The same degree of rotation of the handwheels at the tracker's station trains the director by one degree. Range can be obtained either optically with the range-finder or by radar, as determined by the director officer.

Summary

The Mark 68 Gun Fire Control System has been modernized to make it more reliable and effective and to make it compatible with today's shipboard antimissile systems. Newer gun fire control systems, such as the Mark 86 and 92, have been developed and may eventually replace the Mark 68 system, but at present the Mark 68 system controls many of the Fleet's guns.

7

The Mark 56 Relative Rate
Gun Fire Control System

Introduction

When it became necessary during World War II to develop fire control systems which could greatly reduce the time required for the solution to the antiaircraft fire control problem, it was decided that an individual system, such as the Mark 56, would be provided to control each mount. It was also decided that since the greatest danger to the ship was from incoming targets at close range, many of the ballistics computed by the existing linear rate fire control system could be safely ignored.

Purpose of the Mark 56

As the Mark 56 is installed on many U.S. Navy ships to direct 3-inch 50 caliber guns, it will be discussed as an example of the relative rate systems currently in service. The Mark 56 is most frequently associated

Figure 7–1. A Mark 56 fire control director, visible above the five-inch gun mount on the deck of a cruiser.

with 3-inch guns, but it may also control 5-inch guns. The Mark 56 is primarily designed to fire upon subsonic aircraft at intermediate ranges with an additional limited ability to fire upon ships and shore targets. These targets would have to be within a maximum radar acquisition range of 30,000 yards. It can track and compute gun orders for a target having a range rate of 420 (opening) and 640 (closing) knots. The time lag required from the "lock on" in conical scan of automatic radar tracking to a fire control solution is from two to three seconds. The Mark 56 system is a hybrid, or composite, fire control system. It uses angular rates to establish target motion, and then converts the angular rates to linear rates in order to solve the problem. This combination is designed to emphasize the strong points of each method.

Control Stations

The Mark 56 system is operated by four men: a *director officer* (control officer), a *director operator* (pointer), a *radar operator* (senior man), and a *radar tracker*. The director officer and director operator are located in the director for optical target acquisition and tracking of visible targets. The other two men are located at the Mark 4 console in the fire control room below decks.

System Components

The Mark 56 gun fire control system is made up of the subassemblies shown in figure 7–2. They are the gun director (Mark 56), the radar (AN/SPG–35)*, the console, a gun order converter, a wind speed transmitter, and a horizontal parallax (train) corrector unit.

The Gun Director

The Mark 56 gun director is installed aboard ship in a position that provides maximum visibility. As shown in figure 7–3, the director crew is stationed in the left section (cockpit) with the director officer behind the director operator. The director's right section is made up of four watertight compartments that house the gyro unit and above-deck Mark 35 radar equipment units. Mounted on the exterior of the director are the director power drives and a radar antenna.

Director Officer's Station

The director officer uses a slew control unit and a cockpit data unit to control the system. The slew control unit (figure 7–4) sits on a

---

* See appendix.

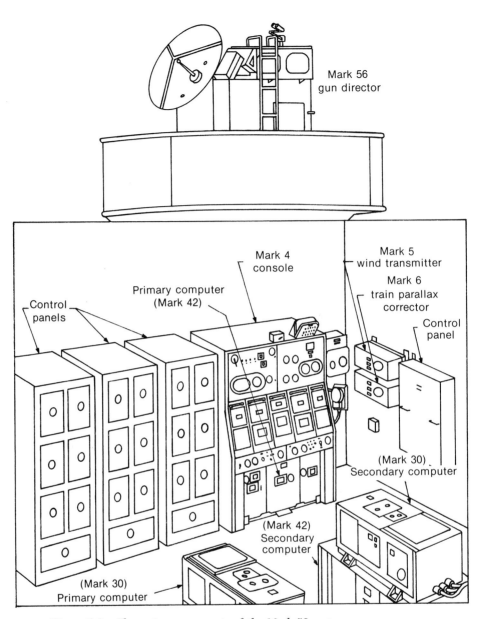

Figure 7–2. *The major components of the Mark 56 system.*

pedestal in front of the director officer. Connected to the slew control unit is an elevating cross arm on which the director officer's binoculars are mounted, providing a ready means of optically tracking a target. A slew switch on the unit permits the director officer to slew the director in bearing and elevation, and it also gives him positive control of the director at any time he wishes.

The director officer's cockpit data unit contains dials, switches, and lights which show the officer what his system is doing. The "radar-optical" switch provides for the type of target tracking to be accomplished. For example, if the director officer turns to *radar*, the radar console located below decks will control the director power drives. In the *optical* position, the tracking control unit director operator controls the director power drives. The sequence of events for changing from director officer's slew control to optical or radar tracking follows:

1. The director officer closes his slew switch to bring the director onto the line of sight as fast as possible.

2. Once the director officer has his binoculars' crosshairs on the target, he determines which station (radar or optical) will track the target.

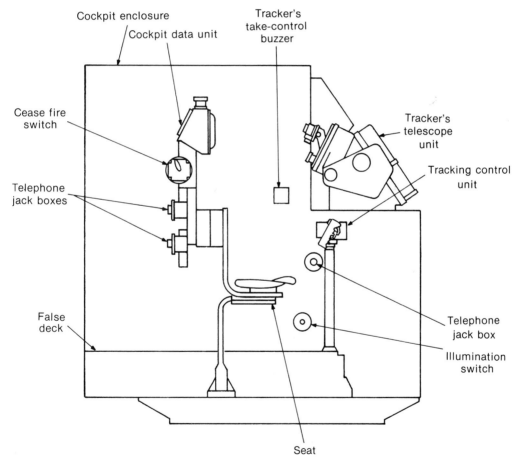

Figure 7–3. The Mark 56 director cockpit.

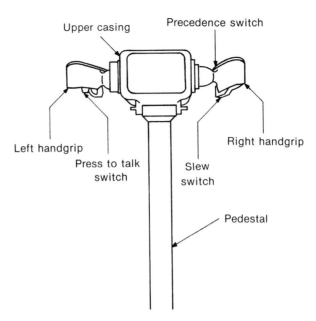

Upper casing

Precedence switch

Left handgrip

Right handgrip

Press to talk
switch

Slew
switch

Pedestal

Figure 7–4. The director officer's slew control unit.

3. He then places the radar-optical switch in the desired position, depending on weather conditions and combat situation.

4. While still maintaining the director line of sight on the target with his slew control, he closes a "precedence switch" on his handgrip (figure 7–4). This causes a take-over buzzer to sound at the designated station. If optical has been designated, the director operator closes an "optical precedence" switch on his tracking control unit (figure 7–5) and continues to track the target. If *radar* has been designated, the radar tracker pushes his radar "scan control" foot switch and the radar goes into full automatic radar tracking. This permits the director officer to relinquish tracking control of the director while still slewing by releasing his slew switch.

5. To regain control of the director, the director officer again presses his slew switch.

Director Operator's Controls

The director operator also uses two major units in performing his duties—a tracking control unit and a telescope.

The tracking control unit (figure 7–5) sits on a pedestal between the legs of the director operator. Rotation of the head and/or handgrips generates electrical signals which indirectly control the director's train and elevation drive motors.

The telescope (a Mark 79) located directly in front of the director operator, has an eight-power magnification and a seven-degree field of vision. While tracking a target optically, the director operator moves his tracking control unit to maintain the target in the center of the crosshairs in his telescope.

Director Power Drives

Direct-current (DC) drive motors controlled by below-deck amplidyne generators drive the director in train and drive the radar antenna and optics in elevation. Manual handwheels are provided at the base of the director for securing purposes only.

The Radar

The radar antenna is made up of a parabolic reflector (a concave dish), a nutating antenna feed horn, and a scanning mechanism. The entire assembly elevates to coincide with the elevation of the line of sight. The antenna feed horn forms a narrow PP beam a few degrees in diameter (conical scan [see Chapter 10 for a full description]). When *searching* for the target, the scanning mechanism nutates the radar feed horn in a spiral scan that provides a total coverage of 12 degrees,

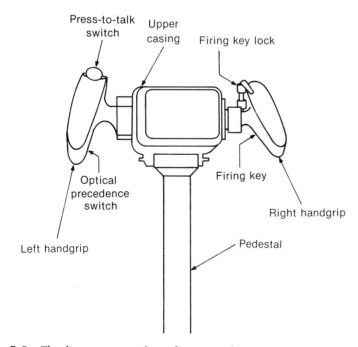

Figure 7–5. The director operator's tracking control unit.

The Mark 56 Relative Rate Gun Fire Control System   **83**

with the line of sight at the center (figure 7–6). When *tracking* the target, the scanning mechanism nutates the radar feed horn in a conical scan that provides a total coverage of three degrees about the line of sight.

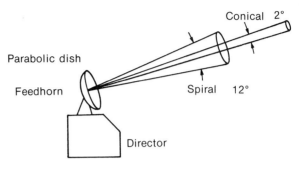

Figure 7–6. *Spiral scan and conical scan.*

The AN/SPG–35 radar supplies the Mark 56 GFCS with continuous values of target ranges for both optical and radar target tracking. The Mark 56 GFCS has no optical/manual ranging capability. When the radar is "locked" on a target in full automatic radar tracking, it supplies train and elevation signals to the director, as well as range, to maintain the director's line of sight on the target. Automatic tracking is only possible when the radar is in the conical scan mode of operation. The antenna, transmitter, and receiver are located on the director, while the radar indicators, range controls, and automatic tracking circuits are located below decks in the Mark 4 console.

The Console

The Mark 4 console (figure 7–2) consists of four main sections: a dial section, a radar section, an operational section, and the Mark 42 computer. The dial section allows the operator to manually insert data into the system, and it has dials indicating target range, bearing, and elevation. The radar section, consisting of five panels, contains the A/R indicator scope, E indicator scope, B indicator scope, and switches for controlling the radar operation. The indicator scopes and their displays are described in Chapter 10. The left-hand (radar operator's) and right-hand (radar tracker's) operational sections contain the controlling devices for director train and elevation and for radar range and antenna scan from the console.

The Computer

The Mark 42 analogue computer provides the Mark 56 system with the ballistic computations needed to solve the fire control problem.

In a dual ballistic system (where two different gun calibers are controlled), the primary Mark 42 computer is located under the Mark 4 console with a second Mark 42 computer, located elsewhere in the radar control room, furnishing the secondary battery ballistic computations.

Establishing Present Target Position

The first step in solving the fire control problem by the Mark 56 GFCS is resolved at the Mark 56 director, which measures the three coordinates of director train, director elevation, and present range. The Mark 56 director's line of sight may be initially placed on the target either optically or by target designation from acquisition by radar.

Optically

To initially acquire a target, the director officer must see the target or be told where to look to see the target.

Target Designation

The target designation sequence of events is the same as discussed for the Mark 68 GFCS in Chapter 6, up to the point where the target information positions the director in train and elevation. Should the target not be seen optically or on the radar scopes, the radar operator, controlling the director's drive motors, starts a search pattern. Once the target is acquired, the radar is switched to its automatic tracking mode of operation.

Target Position Transmission

In the full radar mode of operation, the director line of sight is kept on the target by the automatic tracking radar circuits. In the optical mode of operation, the director line of sight is kept on the target by the director operator moving his OMC to keep the target in the center of his telescope. The values of director train and direction elevation are sent by a synchro transmission system to the Mark 4 console in the fire control radar room. The values of present target range are obtained directly from the radar indicator scopes located at the Mark 4 console.

Computing Gun Lead Angles

The target lead angles are supplied by the gyro unit, located in the Mark 56 director, and the radar range rate servo motor. The Mark 42 computer receives these target lead angles and adds the ballistic corrections to form the gun lead angles.

The system uses the angular motion of the target in two mutually perpendicular planes—elevation and traverse. These angular motions are called the *elevation* rate and the *traverse* rate. Using these rates plus the range rate, the Mark 56 GFCS resolves the fire control problem into three linear rates of target motion—linear elevation rate, linear bearing rate, and range rate.

The Measurement of Angular Motion

The measuring of the angular motion of the target is accomplished by two gyros located in the gyro unit of the Mark 56 director—a rate gyro whose precession during tracking develops lead angles with respect to the line of sight and a vertical gyro which maintains the true horizontal and vertical reference planes (figure 7–7).

The rate gyro uses the principles of rigidity in space and precession. With the gyro rotor spinning, the rate gyro remains stationary in space until acted upon by some force. The force that moves the gimbals of the rate gyro is introduced by means of elevation and traverse torque motors. As the director officer and director operator move the director by turning their one-man control (OMC) unit, the OMC sends an

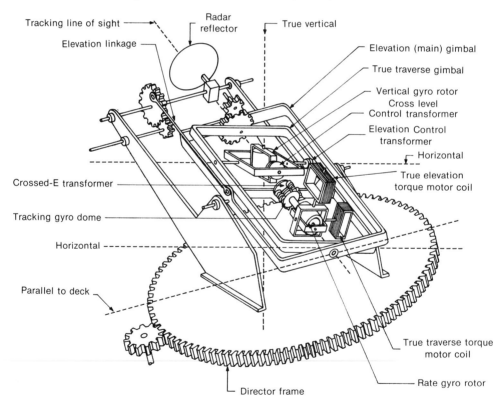

Figure 7–7. The Mark 56 director gyro unit.

electrical voltage to the correct torque motor. This in turn precesses the rate gyro. A second gyroscope maintains a true horizontal and vertical reference plane.

Range Rate

The third factor required in computing target lead angles is range rate. Range rate is obtained from a tachometer which is attached to the shaft of the range servo motor. This tachometer is a small generator whose output voltage will vary with the speed (change in range) of rotation.

Computation to Linear Rates

The computer (Mark 42) converts the angular rates of target motion to linear rates, then calculates superelevation and drift. It corrects for the effects of wind by receiving electrical values of own ship's course and manual inputs of true wind speed and direction, initial velocity, and own ship's speed. An additional manual input of "dead time" may be used to compensate for the delay of the gun crew loading time upon fuze time orders.

Correcting for Gun Platform Motion

The Mark 30 computer (gun order converter) is the component of the Mark 56 GFCS that corrects for gun platform motion.

Establishing Gun Positioning Orders

The quantities necessary for establishing gun positioning orders, roller path tilt and parallax are the same as discussed in Chapter 4.

Correcting for the Fall of Shot

"Spotting" can only be accomplished at the Mark 4 console. It is done after the radar operator has estimated the corrections. He inserts them at the console using "spot elevation," "spot deflection," or "fuze spot" inputs.

Summary

In the Mark 56 GFCS, the director and radar antenna are installed as high as possible in the ship's superstructure, while the console, computer, gun order converter computer and radar are placed in protected radar rooms below deck. All of the system elements are connected by a synchro transmission system.

The director, manned by two crew members, contains the optical devices and radar antenna which establish the line of sight and range to the target, and sends values of angular target motion through the

Mark 4 console to the Mark 42 computer. Two crew members operate the console and establish target range rates which are also sent to the Mark 42 computer.

With the establishment of target motion and ballistic inputs, the computer generates a solution to the fire control problem in true coordinates, which are then sent to the Mark 30 computer.

The Mark 30 computer takes the above inputs and compares them against the actual deck plane to provide continuous gun positioning orders containing corrections for all significant factors that affect medium-range antiaircraft and surface firings.

8

Recent Digital Gun Fire Control Systems
(Mark 86, 87, 92 and Vulcan-Phalanx)

The Mark 86

The Mark 86 gun fire control system (GFCS) was designed and developed as part of the Navy's lightweight gun program for control of the 5-inch 54 Mark 45 lightweight gun mount. It is the primary fire control system for the DD–963 *Spruance*-class destroyers and the LHA amphibious assault ships. It is basically a linear rate system. The Mark 86 includes a surface search, track-while-scan radar (AN/SPQ–9), and air tracking radar (AN/SPG–60). The surface search, two-dimensional radar with a slow data rate of one sweep per second is adequate for the surface track-while-scan function against ships or boats. A separate fire control system includes the three-dimensional AN/SPG–60 air search radar to provide continuous linear rates for air targets. The track-while-scan surface radar permits the tracking of several targets simultaneously. A remote optical sighting system (television cameras) eliminates the requirement for topside operating personnel. In Condition III watches, a single operator can fire the first several rounds in a gunnery engagement. Figure 8–2 is a simplified block diagram of the main elements in the system.

Digital Computer Mark 152

The computer (figure 8–3) is a general purpose, stored-program digital computer. The program that is stored within the computer memory section contains all the instructions and fixed constants required to perform the data processing functions in solving the surface, shore, or air fire control problems. The computer is programmed to track surface targets automatically while the surface radar, the AN/SPQ–9, scans. It also simultaneously performs the computations required by the AN/SPG–60 air fire control director radar during the acquisition and tracking of air targets.

The fire control problem is solved in the same manner as in the previously described Mark 68 analogue computer, but in digital language representing linear values. Present target position data is used

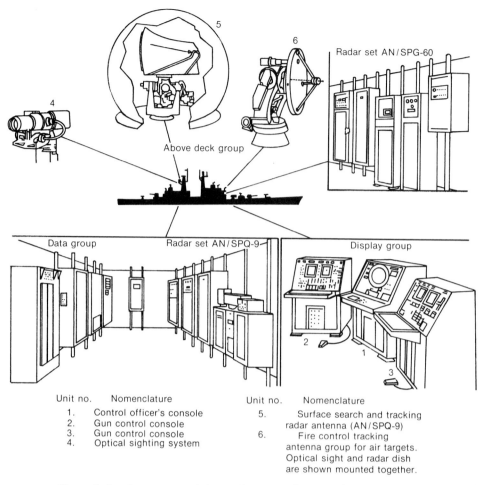

Unit no.	Nomenclature	Unit no.	Nomenclature
1.	Control officer's console	5.	Surface search and tracking radar antenna (AN/SPQ-9)
2.	Gun control console		
3.	Gun control console	6.	Fire control tracking antenna group for air targets. Optical sight and radar dish are shown mounted together.
4.	Optical sighting system		

Figure 8–1. Components of the Mark 86 gun fire control system.

to develop linear rates of target motion that are used to predict a future target position. Interior and exterior ballistic quantities are added to the future target position to obtain gun train and elevation orders, the fuze order, parallax, sight angle, and sight deflection orders to the gun mount. The computer displays target and ballistic data on the operating consoles located at the gun control station, below decks, in CIC.

The Signal Data Translator (Mark 1)

The signal data translator acts as an interface between the digital Mark 152 computer and the other units of the fire control system and gun mounts that use angular information instead of digital information (figure 8–2). Outgoing digital symbols from the computer are translated into synchro information and incoming synchro information is translated into digital words representing the angular position (setting in mils) of each synchro dial.

The Optical Sight System (Mark 1)

The optical sight system (Mark 1) is a closed circuit television camera that has replaced the optically sighted gun director, and thus removed the requirement for topside personnel (figure 8–4). Two or three, depending upon the Mod of the system, closed circuit television cameras with light filters and zoom lenses provide visual tracking and area surveillance for the gun control consoles. One television camera is mounted on, and aligned with, the AN/SPG–60 air fire control radar antenna axis (figure 8–1) and provides a visual display of the air target being tracked by that antenna. One or two television cameras, depending upon the Mod, are mounted on a single roll and pitch stabilized pedestal. This unit is called the Remote Operated Sight, and is located high above the ship's superstructure to provide maximum visibility (figure 8–1). The remotely operated sight is used during engagements with other ships and also for firing upon targets ashore. All television cameras can be controlled from the gun control consoles.

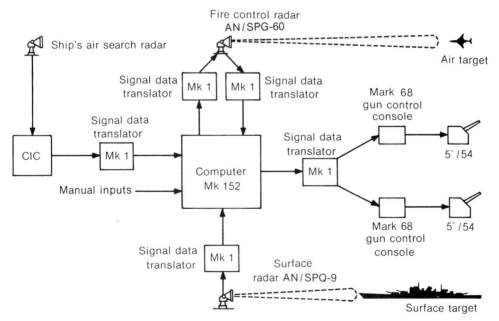

Figure 8–2. A block diagram of the Mark 86 gun fire control system. Note that only one signal data translator is used.

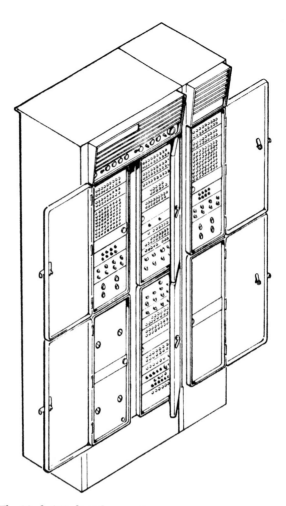

Figure 8–3. The Mark 152 digital computer.

The Surface Radar (AN/SPQ–9)

The radar is the primary sensor that provides range and bearing data on surface and low altitude air targets for the Mark 86 GFCS (figure 8–1). It provides a 360-degree surface search and it can track several surface ship targets. It rotates at a rate of one radar scan per second. Target bearing and range information is sent automatically to the GFCS computer for targets that have been assigned to tracking channels. The radar is a conventional surface search radar except for its somewhat higher scanning rate and the employment of a new technique, called *optical pulse compression*, which permits the radar to operate at lower power levels, thereby improving its ECCM flexi-

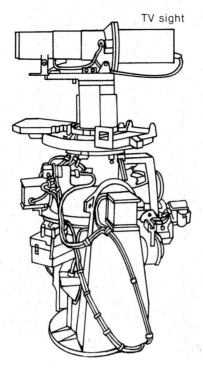

TV sight

Figure 8–4. The remote optical sight.

bility in electronic warfare. The control officer's console provides for control of the radar and its employment in electronic warfare.

The Air Fire Control Radar (AN/SPG–60)

The air fire control radar (AN/SPG–60) is used to track air targets acquired by the ship's air search radar. A television camera, part of the optical sighting system, is boresighted with the line of sight and provides a visual display of the target being tracked on the gun control consoles (figure 8–1).

Operator Control Consoles

The Control Officer's Console (Mark 67)

The Mark 67 console controls and monitors the system. The console provides a PPI display of returns from the AN/SPQ–9 surface track-while-scan radar antenna (figure 8–5). A surface or low-altitude air target is assigned for tracking to the computer by positioning a symbol over the selected target on the PPI display, and assigning the target to a selected tracking channel in the computer. The coordinates of

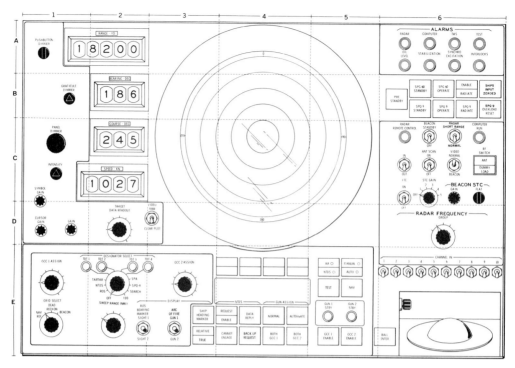

Figure 8–5. PPI display of contacts detected by the AN/SPQ-9 radar antenna on the control officer's console.

the selected target are applied to the computer to initiate track-while-scan. Target data, such as target course and speed, may be displayed as an output from the computer. Additional functions of the console are to feed electrical power to system components, operate the AN/SPQ–9 track-while-scan radar, perform radar surveillance, and monitor the operation of the entire GFCS.

Gun Control Console (Mark 68)

There is a gun control console for each 5-inch 54 gun mount on board (figure 8–6). Each operator controls the fire of a single gun, or all guns, against a surface or air target assigned to his console. The gun control console performs the following functions: it provides ballistic data to the computer; selects the type of ammunition to be fired; monitors targets visually that are tracked by the AN/SPG–60 air fire control radar; tracks surface and low level air targets visually using the remote optical sight; monitors the 5-inch 54 Mark 45 gun-loading operation; controls the 5-inch 54 Mark 45 gun-laying system; controls the firing of the gun and enters spots when required by observing television displays on the console.

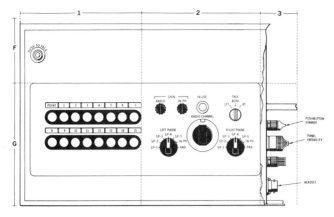

Figure 8–6.   TV monitor and radar (PPI or B scope) panels of the gun control console.

Integrated Digital Fire Control Systems under Development (Mark 87 and 92)

The principle of modern integrated fire control systems such as the Mark 87 or Mark 92, which can provide fire control for the 76mm 62 caliber compact, for example, will be applied in new units, especially in antiair warfare. The most important characteristic of these new systems is the combination in one system of all of the weapon functions from target detection, acquisition, identification, and threat evaluation, to ballistic computation, launch order calculations, and damage assessment. The combination of the search and track functions into a single antenna system for surface-to-surface engagements is also an improvement. It is only through such integration, with no electrical or mechanical "language barrier" between the search and track functions, that very accurate systems with very short reaction times will eventually be achieved. In these modern integrated systems, a weapon can be launched against a surface target within range in six seconds from the time that the target is discovered.

Because surface search and track functions are integrated into a single unit, duplicate transmitters, receivers, control consoles, and interface equipment normally found in separated systems are eliminated. The number of elements in the weapon system is reduced to the essential and coordinated by a digital computer at the center. It is this coordinating function, as much as performing actual computations, that makes the advent of the digital computer so important. Once the digital computer has been instructed by introducing the control program, it can be depended upon to carry out the sequence of command and operational functions required to bring a weapon system into action in the shortest possible time and in the most effective way.

Typical of the decision automation which is possible with a digital computer is the video processing capability of such a system. The length and character of the return signal, the speed of the target, and the number of echoes received per sweep are all entered into the digital logic section for evaluation to decide whether a given return is a target, a bit of weather, or other clutter. Once identified as a target, the return is interrogated by the integral IFF system and, if not identified as a friend, is immediately designated and acquired by the tracking radar, so that in a few seconds the ship can open fire. Because of integration, the entire operation can be controlled by a single man who observes the engagement on a central PPI and commands the necessary actions by pushing control buttons in front of him. At General Quarters, he can be assisted by a second man who manipulates the weapon control console, permitting the weapon control officer to concentrate on the tactical and operational picture.

As the engagement progresses, the digital computer does a great deal more than compute ballistics. Capable of absorbing a great mass of information and storing it for future use, the computer controls the search sequences, analyzes the radar returns, assists in the target acquisition, computes for stabilization, computes present target position and rates, calculates the external ballistics, and monitors the overall engagement of one target while simultaneously tracking and analyzing one or more other targets, depending upon the capacity of the installation.

Almost as important as the capacity to calculate are the digital computer's technical characteristics which aid in its maintenance and repair. Modern digital computers are low-voltage, solid state units which are inherently so reliable that despite the enormous number of components included in their design, they have design specification goals for Mean Time Between Failure (MTBF) of approximately 5,000 hours. When they do fail, the trouble can usually be identified quickly by using the computer's diagnostic routines (integral test equipment) and repairs can be made easily by substituting spare circuit cards for the faulty ones.

Digital Computation

A solid state digital computer can handle a relatively large number of different calculations in a fraction of a second—in "real time" for all practical purposes. With an analogue computer, on the other hand, even after the input is sufficiently accurate, a solution time of at least two or three seconds is required for the accuracy of the output to be appropriate to the input.

Digital Transmission

The advantages of the digital computer will be appreciated when digital transmission of control signals becomes available to replace analogue transmission by synchro systems. Digital transmission can reduce time lags, particularly where transmissions are made serially over a single pair of conductors. This invention would reduce the control wiring throughout the ship.

The Phalanx Close-In Weapon System

The Phalanx system has been developed for shipboard use employing a naval version of the Vulcan 20mm aircraft gun described in Chapter 19. It was developed to provide completely automatic defense against low-flying, antiship cruise missiles at very short ranges (figure 8–7).

Design Considerations

As the missile attack may come without warning from any direction, and the gun has a short range, the system must be continuously alert to detect and engage targets in a minimum amount of time. Detection and acquisition of the target and the firing of the gun must be entirely automatic, eliminating men from the functional sequence of events in the gun system. It continually searches for low elevation air contacts, and it has a fast reaction time and a high probability of destroying its target.

Description

The Phalanx CIWS (figure 8–8) is a single unit including search and fire control radars and the gun itself. It can be installed on board any ship type. Housed in the upper dome is a tracking radar antenna and a 360-degree radar search antenna, which shares a common pulse Doppler radar transmitter with the tracking radar. Beneath the antenna dome is the six-barrel 20mm Vulcan gun. The entire unit is $15\frac{1}{2}$ feet high, weighs 10,000 pounds, and requires 54 square feet of deck space.

A projectile that is employed against missiles must have a high-muzzle velocity to effectively destroy the surface-to-surface missile. To accomplish this, a very dense, subcaliber, spin-stabilized, projectile was developed. It has a discarding sabot and pusher (figure 8–9) to make it compatible with a 20mm gun barrel which imparts the spin to the projectile. The projectile has a muzzle velocity of 3,650 feet per second. The extra-high velocity is achieved by using a subcaliber

Figure 8–7. The Vulcan-Phalanx naval gun mount.

projectile, explained in Chapter 16, which travels in a relatively flat trajectory for approximately one mile.

The gun mount can train at an approximate rate of 100 degrees per second and elevate at about 86 degrees per second. The self-contained electronics section has a computer and the necessary equipment to operate the radars, solve the fire control problem, and correct the line of fire.

Spotting is automatic using an electronic spotting system, which accurately measures the system error between the target and the stream of projectiles. Corrections are then made to bring the line of fire on target.

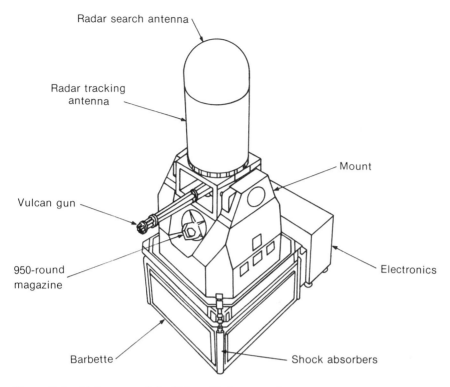

Figure 8–8. *Main parts of the Vulcan-Phalanx naval gun mount.*

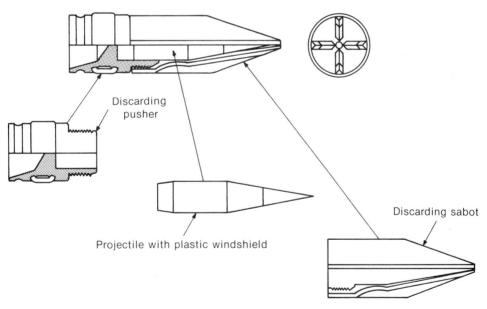

Figure 8–9. *The sub-20mm, spin-stabilized projectile with discarding pusher and sabot.*

99

Operation

The operation of the Phalanx system is completely automatic after the power to it is turned on, and operates continuously. Since the system is not manned, there is an extremely fast reaction time. The 950-round magazine (figure 8–10) is a single-ended, linkless ammunition feed system, which discards empty cases and misfired rounds. It is designed to be sufficient for three engagements and can be reloaded in a few minutes if necessary.

When a target enters the Phalanx search radar beam, the return is analyzed for Doppler. If the Doppler return is classified as target Doppler by the computer, the gun slews around to the target bearing. As soon as the tracking radar locks on the target, the gun opens fire at a rate of 3,000 rounds per minute. Firing will continue until the target is destroyed; then the gun will cease fire, and Phalanx will automatically search again for another target.

Figure 8–10. The 950-round magazine drum is a linkless ammunition feed system for the Vulcan gun. The single-ended design discards spent cases and misfires.

PART 2

Sensors and Detection Devices

Sensors and detectors are needed in every weapon system to detect, locate, and identify a target. Any device performing the first of these functions should be capable of detecting the target as far away as possible. It should also establish with rapidity and precision the target's location, orientation, and velocity with respect to one's ship. Moreover, this device should establish what the target is and whether it is hostile or friendly. The ideal device would be equally efficient regardless of the medium in which it is operating. It should be able to disregard any interference caused by the enemy, friendly forces, or nature.

No detecting device or system yet developed or in use can achieve all of these requirements. Nevertheless, these requirements can be applied as standards for measuring the effectiveness of detecting devices.

In the next few chapters the kinds of shipboard sensors and detectors currently employed in the Fleet will be discussed in the order in which they appear in the frequency spectrum. They are:

> Optical and electro-optical devices
> Radar
> Electronic Support Measures (ESM)
> Sonar
> Magnetic Anomaly Detectors (MAD).

9

Optics

Introduction

Figure 9–1 shows the range of energy employed by ship's sensor and fire control systems. *Visible light* is shown at the high end of the frequency spectrum of wavelengths and is employed by the optical and electro-optical systems. It is followed by *infrared* energy, which is used in chemical, photo, thermal, and luminescent detectors. *Radar* frequency wavelengths follow in order and are adapted to many shipboard detection and fire control functions. Next are *radio* waves, which are used in weapon systems to detect the presence of other forces by picking up their emissions. Radio receivers in missile or gun fire control systems provide tracking information on any targets which emit electronic energy. At the low end of the spectrum, *audio* frequencies are used to detect the presence of objects in the water with sound navigation and ranging (sonar) equipment. Sound waves may be generated by the ship, which will be reflected by an object in the water in active sonar, or alternatively, the ship's passive sonar (hydrophones) can be used to detect the sound energy radiated by an object in the water.

The two parts of the frequency spectrum discussed in this chapter are visible light and infrared. Optics have been used in naval weapons for a long time but infrared has only recently been put to use in shipboard sensors. As the applications are classified, the discussion of infrared will be limited to the principles used in infrared detectors.

Optical devices in weapon systems always establish target bearing and target elevation. Some optical devices can also measure the range to the target. Except for highly unusual atmospheric conditions where the light rays reflected from the target are perceptibly bent by refraction, the line of sight is, practically speaking, a straight line from the target to the observer. To extend the capabilities of the human eye in target detection and identification, some optical devices use lens systems designed to magnify the target image.

Target acquisition and tracking by television, used in some weapon systems, are an outgrowth of this need to enhance vision. Optical devices that depend on infrared light invisible to the unaided eye are

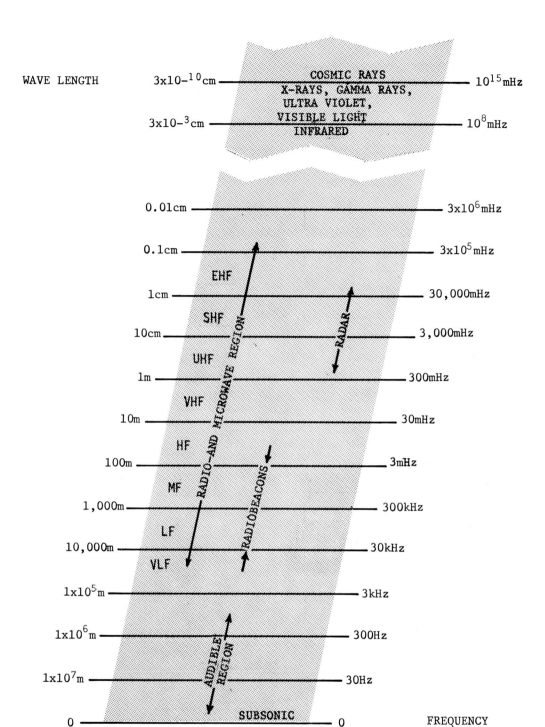

Figure 9-1. Frequency spectrum.

also available for observing targets at night. Most optical devices depend on visible light reflected from the target and therefore are handicapped by darkness, fog, and visible obstacles. However, optical devices have many strengths not shared by other detection, acquisition, and tracking devices. For example, optical sights do not require electrical power to operate. They are hard to jam and confuse. They are valuable in positively identifying a target as friend or foe, and much information about the target is available to the viewer that is hidden from operators of sound and electronic equipment. Optical sights are precise.

Fire Control Optical Instruments

The optical instruments used in fire control systems present an enlarged image of the target to the observer's eye. At the same time, the observer sees an image of a reference mark inside the instrument itself. By accurately lining up the reference mark on the target image, the observer can establish the true line of sight to the target. The optical rangefinder establishes two separate lines of sight and makes it possible to find the target range by a form of triangulation. Lenses, prisms, mirrors, or some combination of these elements control the path of the light that passes through an optical instrument. Lenses may consist of two or three separate lenses in a simple telescope arrangement. The interior parts and cementing compounds must be protected against mishandling, moisture, and other causes of deterioration, such as dirt. Navy optical equipment is hermetically sealed. Fixed optical equipment, such as sight telescopes and rangefinders, is charged with dry helium or nitrogen gas.

Sights

Three general optical systems are employed in fire control system sights—simple sights without lenses, telescopic sights with fixed optical components, and sights with movable optical components.

Simple Sights without Lenses The observer looks through the eyepiece (figure 9–2), and when he has aligned the target with the center of the front sight, the line of sight to the target is parallel with the gun bore axis. To provide for ballistic and target lead angle corrections, the observer must offset the line of sight so that the projectile will hit the target. The amount of offset is accomplished by using the cocentric rings and spokes of this simple sight instead of the sight's center. The value of the sight is restricted to targets within a short range when the gun is in local control and when other aiming methods are not available. Effective use of the sight to direct gunfire requires

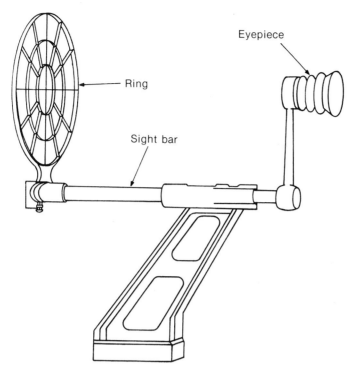

Figure 9–2. An open ring sight.

considerable practice. The simple sight without lenses is less accurate than other optical systems.

Telescopic Sights with Fixed Optical Components This kind of sight is used in some antiaircraft rapid-fire gun mounts and fire control directors for shooting at either air or surface targets from the director or just at surface targets from the gun mount. There are two typical systems—the direct system and the indirect system. In the direct system (figure 9–3) the magnifying lens (called the objective lens) will form an inverted image of the target. This image falls on the engraved surface of the crossline lens. Between the crossline lens and the erect-

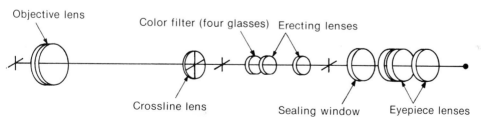

Figure 9–3. Direct telescopic sights with fixed optical components.

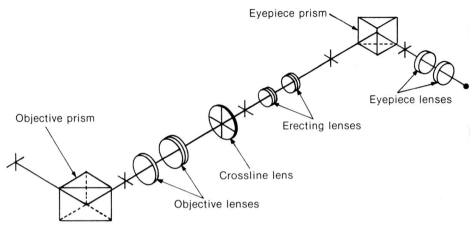

Figure 9–4. Indirect telescopic sights with fixed optical components.

ing lenses* are three color filters and a plain glass filter. The operator can bring any one of them into the line of sight. The color filters increase the contrast of the target image and decrease the glare from the sky and water. The erecting lenses erect the target image, and form the target image near the crossline eyepiece. The plain glass sealing window keeps out dirt and moisture. The eyepiece may be moved in and out for focusing the target image without affecting the seal of the rest of the telescope.

The indirect optical system (figure 9–4) is basically similar. The only major difference is that the line of sight is twice reflected by prisms.

* Erecting lenses reinvert the image to right side up; thus images made upside down by the objective lens are corrected by the erecting lens.

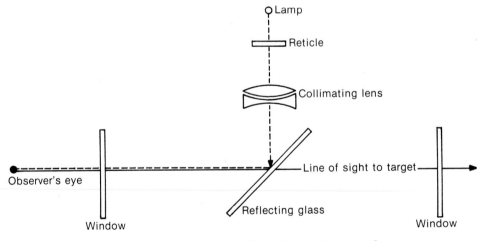

Figure 9–5. Direct sights with movable lead-computing optical components.

As a result, most of the telescope lies at right angles to the line of sight, giving greatest efficiency and compactness of design in the gun director.

Sights with Movable Optical Components Movable optical components are needed to enable the gun layer to offset his line of sight from the gun barrel or the line of fire. The sight is offset the amount needed for the projectile to reach the target, as a hunter leads a flying duck.

There are two main types of sights with movable optical components. The first resembles the open sight in figure 9–2. The only difference is that an additional prism and the objective prism are linked mechanically to a sight-setting system on the gun mount. This kind of sight is used in some antiaircraft gun mounts. The other type of sight (figure 9–5) includes a reflecting glass, a collimating lens, and a lamp, and it is used with gyroscopic lead-computing sights. The advantage of movable components is that the line of sight can be offset without moving the entire telescope.

Rangefinders

One important piece of information needed to solve the fire control problem is the range to the target, and one way of getting this information is by using an optical rangefinder with two eyepieces (stereoscopic). Mark 37 and 68 gun directors are equipped with rangefinders which are used to obtain a range when electronic emission conditions prevent the use of the radar, or when the radar is inoperable.

The rangefinder (figure 9–6) is composed of optical units assembled

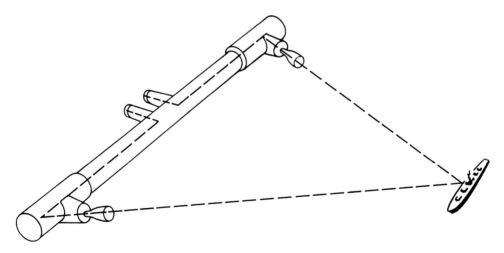

Figure 9–6. An optical rangefinder.

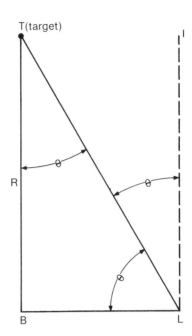

Figure 9–7. The optical rangefinder range triangle.

in a cylindrical tube, mounted in a director, with only the protruding ends of the telescope exposed. On its forward surface, the tube has a window at each end. Through the windows on the ends of the tube, the operator establishes two separate lines of sight to the target. The distance between the windows is called the base length.

The optical rangefinder determines range by solving a right triangle (figure 9–7) in which one side (the base length of the rangefinder windows) and two angles (one at each rangefinder window) are known. As shown in figure 9–7, BL is the rangefinder base length. BT is the range (R) to the target (T). With the left end window always at a right angle to the rangefinder tube axis, TBL is always a right angle. The two lines of sight (BT and TL) converge at the target forming the indicated angle theta (θ). LI is an imaginary line parallel to the range line BT. Angle TLI is thereby equal to the angle BTL. Angle TLB is measured at the rangefinder and subtracted from 90°. This gives the value of the angle θ. The problem is now solved by Euclidean theorem for the side TB (range) by saying TB = base length (BL) times the cosine of theta (θ).

Figure 9–8 shows in simplified schematic the arrangement of the optical system in a stereoscopic rangefinder. The erector lenses have been omitted for the sake of simplicity. The diamonds shown represent

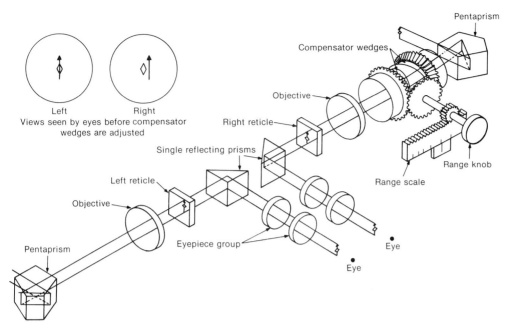

Figure 9–8. *A simplified diagram of a stereoscopic rangefinder.*

the reticle pattern and the arrows represent the two images of the target. As shown in the figure view insert, the diamond and the arrow do not match up in the right window. To match up the views, the knob (range) on the right side of the rangefinder tube is turned to rotate two compensator wedges (thin prisms with sides nearly parallel) through which the light from the target passes. Rotating the prisms

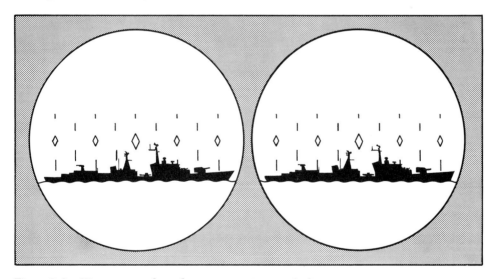

Figure 9–9. *View as seen through a stereoscopic rangefinder.*

will deflect the line of sight. This changes the angle theta (see figure 9–7) with range being read from the dial.

Figure 9–9 shows the right and left images as seen through a stereoscopic rangefinder eyepiece. With the large diamond placed at the same place on the target, the operator can read the actual range to the target on the range scale.

Radar and Electronic Warfare

Figure 10–1. The macks of the USS South Carolina (CGN-37) are equipped with a sophisticated array of radar and electronic warfare sensors. The air-search radar on the forward mack is the most prominent.

Introduction to Radar

Radar (originally an acronym made up of the words *Radio Detection And Ranging*) is one of the greatest scientific developments that emerged from World War II. It makes possible the detection and tracking of ships and aircraft over long distances and during reduced visibility.

Theory of Operation

The basic principles of radar are similar to the echo of a sound or wave reflection. If a person shouts in the direction of a cliff or some other sound-reflecting surface, he hears his shout return from the direction of the cliff. Sound waves, generated by the shout, travel through the air until they strike the cliff. Then they are reflected and some return to the spot where they originated. These reflected waves are the echoes that the person hears (figure 10–2). Radar emits waves of radio frequency (RF). These waves can be considered to travel in a straight line until all their energy is expended. If the waves strike an object, some of the RF energy is reflected and is called the target

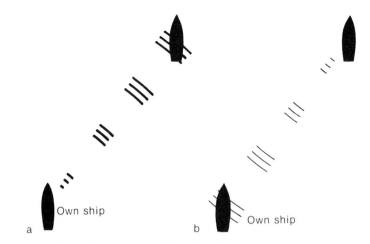

Figure 10-2. (a) Radar pulses and (b) reflected waves.

echo. This echo returns to the radar by a reciprocal path and indicates the presence of an object in the wave's path.

Limitations of Radar

Radar is unaffected by darkness, but it often is affected by various weather conditions; for example, heavy rain. Because radar waves travel in a straight line from the antenna in a line of sight—that is, radar waves cannot follow the curvature of the earth—the ability to detect objects on the surface of the sea is further limited to the horizon. The distance at which objects can be detected on the surface therefore depends on the height of the antenna above the surface, in the same way that visual range is limited by the height of eye. This line-of-sight characteristic is typical of the high frequencies found in the part of the electromagnetic energy spectrum used in radar equipment.

Radar Spectrum

Although the principles of radar detection have been applied over the whole radio frequency spectrum (from 10 kHz to 10^9 mHz), the highest frequency, or microwave, end of the region has been used primarily for military radar. To offer some specific examples of the use of the RF spectrum by shipboard radars, a typical air search radar radiates in the vicinity of 1200 mHz, a typical surface search radar employs approximately 5500 mHz, and a fire control radar transmits near 8200 mHz.

Types of Energy Transmission

Radar systems transmit energy either in pulses or continuous waves (CW). The principle of pulsed radar is that the transmitter sends out radio waves in series of short, powerful pulses and then rests during the remainder of its cycle. During the period in which the transmitter is at rest, echo signals may be received by the same antenna and timed to determine the range to the target.

In continuous wave radar, the transmitter sends out a more or less continuous signal. If a stationary target is in the path of the transmitted wave, the frequency of the reflected echo will be the same as that of the transmitted signal. If the target is moving, the frequency of the reflected echo will be higher or lower than the transmitted signal. The difference in frequency, or Doppler, between the transmitted signal and the echo is used to detect and track moving targets.

Range Determination

The employment of radar to determine the range (distance) to a target is made possible by knowledge of the velocity of the transmitted RF energy in space, and the measurement of the time required for the energy to reach a target and return.

Once radiated, RF energy travels at the speed of light. It travels approximately 186,000 miles per second, or 164,000 nautical miles per second. To make practical use of this velocity-distance relationship, it is necessary to consider distance in terms of yards and time in terms of microseconds. By simple computation, we find that RF energy travels 328 nautical yards in one microsecond. This means that approximately 6.18 microseconds are required for the energy to travel one nautical mile. Range measurement is simply accomplished by using the following formula:

Radar range (in nautical miles)
$$= \frac{\text{microseconds between transmission and echo return}}{12.4 \text{ microseconds}}$$

The figure 12.4 is the time it takes the RF energy to travel two nautical miles; remember that the reflected energy must make a round trip between the transmitting ship and the target. It would be impossible for a person to count off the microseconds, but it can be done easily with radar electronic circuits.

Bearing Determination

Bearing (also called azimuth) is the direction of an object from the observer, expressed in degrees clockwise through 360 degrees around the horizon. True bearing is measured from true north; relative bearing is measured from the heading of the ship. In radar, bearing (true or relative) of the target may be determined by concentrating the radiated energy in a narrow beam, and by knowing the beam's direction when a target has been picked up.

Altitude Determination

The remaining dimension necessary to precisely locate an object in space can be expressed either as an angle of elevation or as an altitude. If one is known, the other can be calculated from one of the basic trigonometric ratios. A method of determining the angle of elevation and the altitude is shown in figure 10–3. Slant range is obtained from the radar as the range to the target. The angle of elevation is the same as that of the radar antenna. Altitude is equal to the slant range, multiplied by the size of the angle of elevation. In radar equipment with antennae that can be elevated, altitude determination by slant range is computed automatically by electronic means.

Radar Functions and Characteristics

No single radar set has yet been developed to perform all the combined functions of air search, surface search, altitude determination, and fire control because of size, weight, power requirements, frequency band limitations, and so on. As a result, individual sets have been developed to perform each function separately.

Surface Search Radars

The principal function of surface search radars is the detection and determination of accurate range and bearing of surface targets and low-flying aircraft while conducting a 360-degree search for all surface targets within the horizon of the radar antenna. The system constants of this radar vary from those of the air search radar. Because the maximum range requirement of a surface search radar is limited mainly by the radar horizon, very high frequencies are used to give maximum reflection from such small target-reflecting areas as ship mast structures and submarine periscopes. Narrow pulse widths permit short minimum ranges, a high degree of range resolution, and greater range accuracy. Wide vertical beam widths are used to compensate for pitch and roll of own ship and to detect low-flying aircraft. Narrow horizontal beam widths permit accurate bearing determination and good bearing resolution.

Air Search Radars

The chief function of an air search radar is the detection and determination of ranges and bearings of aircraft targets at long ranges (greater than 50 miles), maintaining a complete 360-degree search from the surface to high altitude. Low frequencies are chosen to permit long-range transmissions with minimum loss of signal. Wide pulse widths (two to four microseconds) increase the transmitting power and are used to aid in detecting small targets at greater distances. Low pulse repetition rates are selected for greater maximum measurable range. Wide vertical beam width is used to ensure detection of targets from the surface to relatively high altitude and to compensate for the pitch and roll of the ship (figure 10–3).

Fire Control Radars

The principal function of fire control radars is to acquire (pick up) targets originally detected and designated (relayed) from search radars to determine accurate ranges, bearings, and elevation angles of targets. Antennas are "stabilized" by compensating in the computer calculation for pitch and roll of the ship. Very high frequencies are chosen to permit the formation of narrow beam widths with comparatively small antenna arrays, detection of targets with small reflecting areas, and good definition of all targets. Narrow vertical and horizontal beam widths (0.9 degrees to 3 degrees) provide accurate bearing and position angles and a high degree of bearing and elevation resolution.

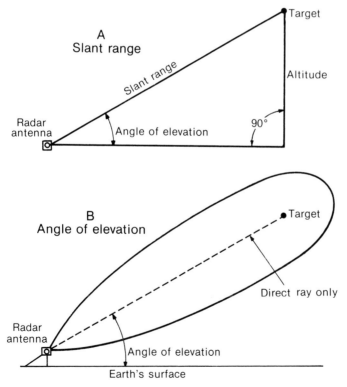

Figure 10–3. Determining the altitude (A) or the angle of elevation (B) of an object.

Missile Guidance Radars

In general, missile guidance radars operate on the same principles as fire control radars and will be described in a later chapter.

Basic Pulse Radar System

A block diagram of the basic units of a pulse-modulated radar system is shown in figure 10–4. Modulation is the process of varying the amplitude or the frequency of a radio frequency signal. The modulation produces the timing pulses that trigger the transmitter and indicator. These timing pulses are converted by the transmitter into high-power pulses of RF energy at the assigned frequency. The use of one antenna for both transmitting and receiving is made possible by the duplexer. It directs the transmitter's outgoing pulses to the antenna and the echo pulses to the receiver. The antenna system radiates the RF energy as a directional beam, and receives the echo pulses only from the direction in which the antenna reflector is pointing. The receiver amplifies the received echo pulses reflected from the target, and applies them to the indicator. There they are displayed on the face of a cathode-ray tube. A more detailed description of some of the individual elements follows.

Synchronizer

The synchronizer is the timing unit. It is the heart of the entire system. It produces trigger pulses which control and coordinate the circuits of the system so that each operates at the correct time. In pulse-modulated radars it governs the number of pulses the transmitter

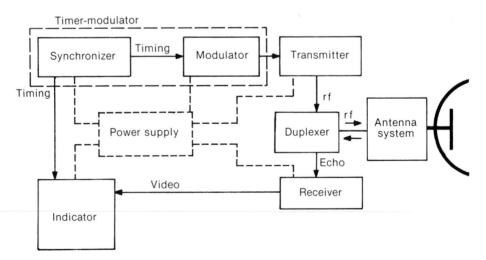

Figure 10–4. The elements of a radar system.

produces in each second (called the pulse repetition frequency (PRF) cathode ray tube indicator with the firing of the transmitter, and contains provision for delaying the beginning of the sweep to give special types of displays, such as the A, E, B, and PPI presentations described below.

Modulator

The modulator controls the transmit-receive periods by providing a high voltage pulse, which modulates the transmitter and forms the transmitted pulse.

Transmitter

An outgoing RF pulse of extremely short duration is generated by the transmitter each time a keying pulse is received from the modulator. A special microwave oscillator tube, called a *magnetron* (figure 10–5), frequently is used as the transmitting tube in radar systems. A pulse from the modulator, shaped and amplified to form a strong negative pulse, is applied to the magnetron cathode. The presence of this pulse causes the tube to oscillate for the duration of the pulse.

Duplexer

In a radar system using a magnetron, the magnetron output is fed to the radar antenna through a duplexer and a waveguide. The duplexer consists of anti-transmit-receive (ATR) and transmit-receive (TR) switches that prevent the high-powered RF output of the trans-

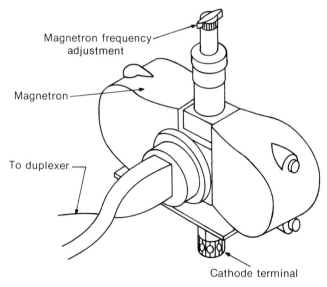

Figure 10–5. A magnetron.

mitter from entering the receiver, but permit the return signal to enter the receiver unimpeded. The duplexer and the waveguide physically connect the transmitter to the antenna.

Antenna

The antenna system has two general purposes. It radiates microwave energy developed by the transmitter, confining the waves in a narrow beam. In addition, it receives the echo signals from the target and sends them via the duplexer by means of the waveguide to the receiver.

Types of Antenna

The Bedspring Array

The bedspring array (figure 10–6), so called because of its resemblance to a bedspring, is used with air search radars. It consists of a stacked dipole array. One method of obtaining a directional effect is to arrange two or more dipoles so that radiation from the dipoles adds in some directions and cancels in other directions. (Dipoles are

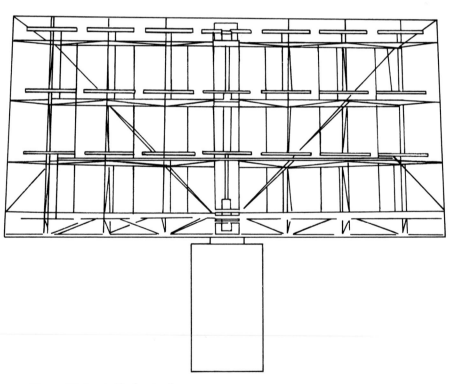

Figure 10–6. A "bedspring" array.

conductors that are one-half wavelength long at the carrier frequency of the radar.)

The Paraboloidal Antenna

The type of reflector generally employed in fire control radars is the parabolic disk. It is similar in appearance to the reflector used in automobile headlights, and is used in both the Mark 56 and 68 fire control systems. One of the important advantages of radar operation in the microwave region of the electromagnetic spectrum is that microwaves have properties and characteristics similar to those of light. This permits the use of well-known optical design techniques.

The action of the reflecting surface of the reflector is a result of its parabolic shape and the fact that the rays striking and reflecting from the metallic surface make equal angles with the surface at the point of reflection. This action is illustrated in figure 10–7. In A of the figure, consider that the focal point is a feedhorn radiator and is a point source of energy. Electromagnetic energy is emitted from a point source in spherical waves like ripples that fan out from a pebble thrown into a pond of still water. The primary purpose of the parabolic

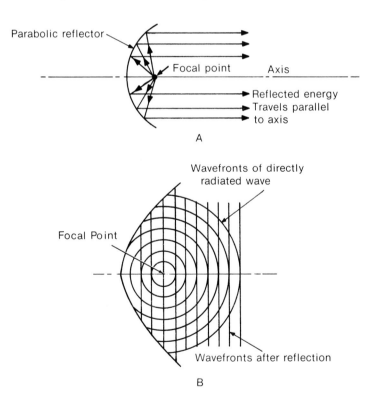

Figure 10–7. *The principle of the parabolic reflector antenna design.*

reflector is to change the spherical wavefronts of the radiated energy into flat (plane) waves and focus them into a circular beam. Part B of figure 10–7 shows spherical wavefronts coming from a radiating feedhorn at the focal point of a parabolic reflector. As the waves strike the reflector they are straightened and concentrated into a narrow circular beam of energy containing parallel flat wavefronts.

When the radar is receiving reflected energy, the incoming rays are concentrated and focused on the feedhorn when they enter the dish as parallel rays. The waves reflected from a distant target can be considered to be parallel if they were transmitted in this form. The action of the reflector during reception can be visualized by reversing the arrowheads in part A of the figure. Therefore, we can state that in any antenna system the transmitting and receiving patterns are essentially the same. For this reason one antenna can be used for transmission and reception. The parabolic reflector produces a "pencil beam" in which most of the energy is confined to a small cone of nearly circular cross section. The concentration of the energy into a beam increases the amount of radiation illuminating a target.

Receiver

The function of a radar receiver is to amplify the comparatively weak echo pulses received from the antenna system, and feed the video output of the receiver to the indicator so that it may produce a visual indication of the desired information. The power contained in the echo pulse that returns to the antenna from distant objects is microscopic when compared with the power of the transmitted pulse. The energy potential that the radar antenna can discern may be a few millionths of a millionth of a watt. The radar receiver must amplify the small, minute voltages several millionfold. The receiver must accomplish this amplification with the least possible introduction of noise or other disturbances which may be present. A high signal-to-noise ratio is required so that the receiver can detect a weak signal from a distant target and override the noise generated in the receiver.

Indicator (Repeater)

The purpose of the indicator is to present visually the information gathered by the radar set. In the early days of radar, the indicator was a part of the main radar console. With the increase in numbers and purposes of radar sets aboard ship, however, remote indicators (radar repeaters) became necessary.

When the modulator sends a keying pulse to the transmitter, it also sends a triggering pulse to the indicator. This trigger pulse, processed through the sweep generating section of the indicator, appears on the face of the scope coincidentally with the transmission of the RF pulse from the antenna. In other words, the trigger pulse initiates the trace or sweep across the face of the scope, and the beginning of the trace indicates the time the radar signal is transmitted.

The target echo pulse (video) from the receiver is increased in amplitude by video amplifiers. It then is applied to the scope via matching impedance circuits. Depending on the type of presentation employed, the echo appears on the trace (or sweep) as a pip or a bright spot. As stated earlier, the time of appearance of the echo pulse is the indicator of the target range. Information from the ship's gyro-compass and the radar antenna assembly is applied to the indicator through a sweep-positioning system. This system puts the sweep on to a true bearing. At the same time the sweep-positioning system synchronizes the rotation of the sweep with the rotation of the antenna. Without true bearing data from the gyro, the position of the sweep indicates a relative bearing. Range markers can be displayed on the screen to aid the operator in estimating the range of a target. In addition, most radar repeaters are equipped with a mechanical or electronic cursor that facilitates the accurate reading of bearing. Some radar repeaters are also equipped with a range strobe that permits accurate measurement of range.

The Cathode Ray Tube

All cathode-ray tubes have some common elements. There is an electron gun that produces a beam of electrons. The face of the tube is covered on the inside surface with a phosphor coating that emits light when excited by the electron beam. The walls of the tube are coated with a conducting material that is kept at a high potential with respect to the cathode. This conducting material acts as an anode and collects the electrons after they have excited the phosphor coating on the face of the scope. Most cathode-ray tubes have one or more grids, as well, to regulate the electron beam in direction and intensity. The basic difference between cathode-ray tubes lies in the method by which the electron beam is deflected, or moved, across the face of the tube. There are two widely used methods of deflecting the electron beam. One is known as *electrostatic* deflection and the other as *electromagnetic* deflection. The following discussion will be of the electrostatic deflection type since it is the simpler method. Four plates—two horizontal and two vertical—are in the tube. Each plate is an equal distance from the center path of the electron beam (figure 10–8). In an electrostatic tube using the type-A scan described below, the sweep is caused by applying a linear sawtooth voltage to the vertical deflection plates. As the electric field between these plates

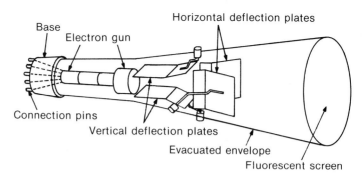

Figure 10–8. Components of a cathode ray tube.

is increased linearly, the electron beam is deflected across the face of the tube in a horizontal sweep. Incoming signals are applied to the horizontal deflection plates, where they cause the beam to deflect up or down on the face of the tube. The electrostatic cathode-ray tube is focused by changing the potential on the first anode in the neck of the tube. Most tubes of this type are used in type-A scopes and provide a range only indication. Some tubes of this type are used for B-scope presentations, although the sweeps are not generated quite like those just described for the A-scan. Electrostatic scopes are used extensively in oscilloscopes and small indicator scopes. However, the larger the face of the tube, the greater must be the deflecting voltage on the deflection plates; hence, electrostatic scopes that are more than 7 inches in diameter are rare.

Types of presentations

PPI Scope

The PPI (Plan Position Indicator) scope presents both range and bearing information. Usually this scope is employed in a radar system whose antenna is uniformly rotated around the vertical axis. The trace on the scope rotates in synchronization with the antenna (see figure 10–9). Large numbers of pulses are transmitted for each rotation of the antenna. As each pulse is transmitted, the scan spot starts at the center of the screen and moves toward the edge of the screen along a radial line.

Upon reaching the edge, the spot quickly returns to the center and begins another trace with the next transmitted pulse. The return trace of the spot is eliminated from the screen by a process called blanking. When an echo is received, the intensity of the scanning spot increases considerably, and a bright spot remains at that point on the screen.

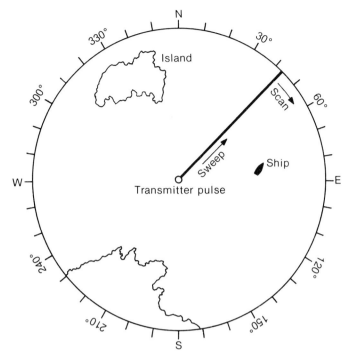

Figure 10–9. Radar scope traces.

The position of the radial line on which the echo appears indicates the target bearing. The distance of the target pip from the origin of the radial line indicates the target range. Because of the characteristic of persistence, it is possible to produce a map of the surrounding territory on the scope face, making the PPI presentation useful as an aid to navigation. The PPI scope presentation also provides the observer with instantaneous changes of target positions in all directions.

A/R Scope

The A/R scope (figure 10–10) has a double-trace presentation. The lower trace (A-sweep) has a notch called the range mark which is movable and can be set on the target pip by the radar operator. The upper trace (R-sweep) is an expansion of that portion of the A-sweep representing several hundred yards either side of the range mark. Thus by adjusting the position of the range mark, the operator can examine any desired portion of the A-sweep on the expanded R-sweep. By adjusting the position of the range mark the target pip can be brought exactly to the edge of the range step, which is simply a drop in the level of the R-sweep fixed at the center of the scope. Range can thus be very accurately measured on the calibrated control knobs.

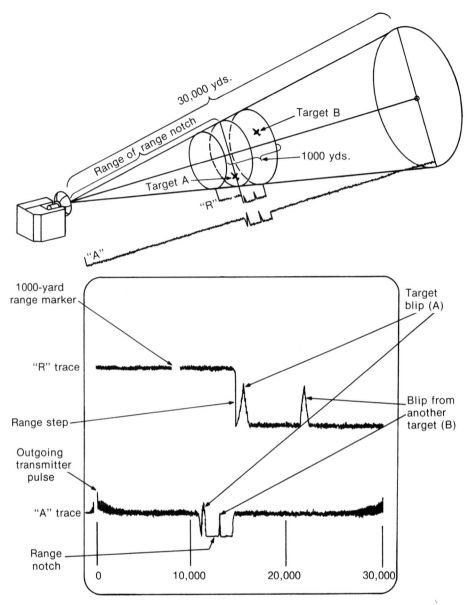

Figure 10-10. *The spatial relationship of targets shown by radar in the A/R scope presentation.*

B-Scope

The B-scope presentation (figure 10–11) shows bearing horizontally and range vertically. The trace appears as a vertical band, with its center always at the center of the scope. The trace width in bearing depends on the antenna scan. The range mark appears as a horizontal

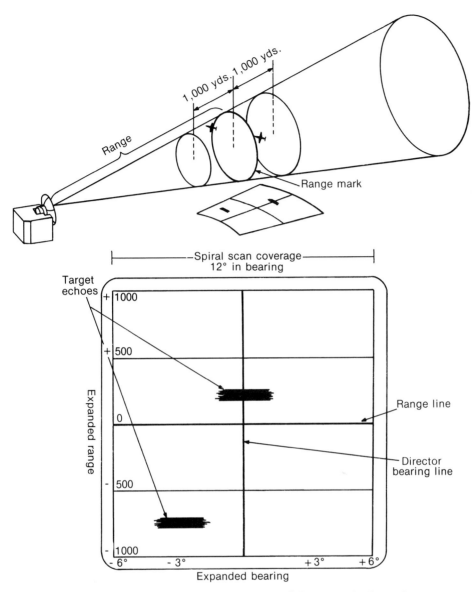

Figure 10–11. The B scope presentation of targets and their spatial relationship.

line at the center of the scope, extending across the entire width of the trace. Target blips appear as horizontal lines.

E-Scope

The type E-scope, shown in figure 10–12, is similar to the B-scope, except that it presents range horizontally and target elevation on the vertical scale. The target echo appears as a short vertical pip. The

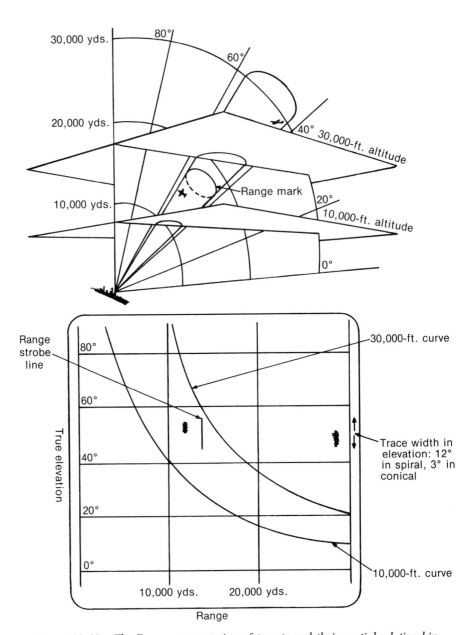

Figure 10–12. The E scope presentation of targets and their spatial relationship.

coverage or sweep of the radar beam is represented by a series of horizontal traces across the scope face between the elevation angles scanned by the radar beam. A vertical range mark is used in the same manner as the B-scope range line to measure range. Two curved lines on the scope face furnish an indication of target altitude. No measurement of target bearing is possible with this scope; it must therefore be obtained from a separate indicator, such as a B-scope.

Continuous Wave Radar (CW)

Continuous Wave (CW) radar is used as a speed-measuring device and for missile guidance. Figure 10–13 illustrates an elementary CW radar. The transmitter continuously radiates RF energy of a constant frequency. There is no timing circuit because the transmitter operates continuously. Targets in the radar beam reflect some of the RF energy back to the receiver antenna. A separate receiver antenna is used because the receiver operates continuously and simultaneously with the transmitter. If a target is moving toward, or away, from the radar, the reflected signal is shifted in frequency. The shift in the frequency of the reflected energy is due to a characteristic of wave motion called the Doppler effect or Doppler shift. The difference between the transmitted frequency and the echo frequency is used to track the target. Since the radar operates continuously, it can theoretically detect targets down to almost zero range. But the radar has no time reference and therefore cannot measure range. The change in the echo frequency because of the Doppler shift is proportional to the target's velocity and thus can be used to obtain range rate.

The transmitting antenna of the radar set beams uninterrupted energy of a constant frequency towards the target. The target reflects the energy, and becomes in effect a second emitter of waves. If target motion is in the radar line of sight, the frequency of the returning echoes differs from that of the outgoing signals. The echoes are picked

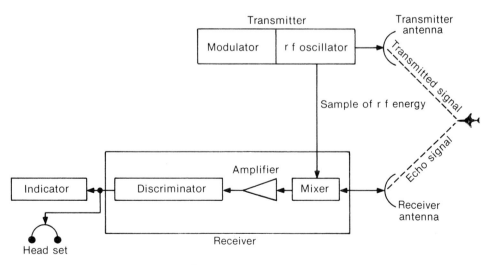

Figure 10–13. Continuous wave radar.

up by the antenna and are compared in the receiver with a small reference voltage at the frequency of the outgoing waves. The difference value, or beat frequency, which results from mixing the reference and echo voltages, is the Doppler signal. The presence of this signal indicates a moving target, and the Doppler value in cycles per second serves as a measure of the relative speed (range rate).

Continuous wave radar and pulse radar systems can be combined to measure a target's velocity toward or away from the ship and also measure the distance and transit time. This is known as pulse-doppler radar. This radar combines the best features of CW and pulse radar. The pulse-doppler method uses high frequency CW, in the form of short bursts, or pulses. The pulse repetition rate (PRR) is much higher than that of a conventional pulse radar, and the pulse length is longer. A measure of the target's velocity toward or away from the radar can be obtained by means of the Doppler shift. This can be accomplished in the same manner as in CW radar.

Scanning

The systematic movement of a radar beam while searching for or tracking a target is referred to as scanning. The type and method of scanning used depends on the purpose and type of radar and on the antenna size and design. Two basic methods of accomplishing scanning are mechanical and electronic. In mechanical scanning, the radar beam can be moved in various ways. The entire antenna can be moved in the desired pattern; the feeder can be moved relative to a fixed reflector; or the reflector can be moved relative to a fixed source. Air search, surface search, and gun fire control radars are examples of this type of scanning. In electronic scanning, the beam is effectively moved by such means as switching between a set of feeder sources, varying the phasing between elements in a multi-element array, and comparing the amplitude and phase differences between signals received by a multi-element array. An example of this type of scanning is the monopulse tracking radar used in missile fire control systems.

Mechanical Scanning

A common form of scanning for target tracking is conical scanning, where the beam is moved in a circle. This type of scan will be described here; the other types, such as spiral scan, are similar in principle.

The radiated RF energy is concentrated by the antenna's reflector to form a very narrow beam. Once the radar is on target, this beam pattern is ideal for establishing target position. But it is very difficult to acquire the target because of the narrowness of the beam. Furthermore, when the target is in the beam we would receive an echo but no indication of target motion. We could wait till the target's motion carried it out of the beam, then bring the beam back on. The direction and amount we moved the antenna could then be used as an indication of target motion. Obviously this would not be very satisfactory.

Fire control radar has a high PRR and can "look" at the area surrounding a target over a thousand times per second. The radar takes advantage of this feature and moves the beam in a systematic pattern about the target area. This is called scanning. The radar compares the echoes from the pulses to detect any change in the target's position with respect to the center of the area scanned by the beam. Since a target cannot move very far in the short period of time between the radar pulses, a smooth flow of tracking information is obtained.

In conical scan the radiated beam is deflected by the antenna to produce a rapidly rotating beam that forms a small cone. The apex (point or tip) of the cone is located at the center of the antenna as shown in figure 10–14. Conical scanning is accomplished by nutating* the feedhorn while the reflector remains fixed. The reflector dish is the center of nutation. This assembly is shown in figure 10–15. As a result of the nutation of the feed, the beam spins in space in the manner indicated in the figure.

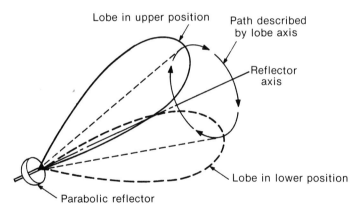

Figure 10–14. Conical scanning.

Also shown in figure 10–15, during automatic tracking the beam points at an angle of a few degrees with respect to the antenna axis. A target located exactly on the antenna axis continuously receives a constant amount of the radiation, in this case about 80 percent of it. However, a target situated away from the axis receives radiation that varies in strength from 100 percent of maximum to less than 30

---

* To nutate is to move back and forth in a nodding or rocking pattern.

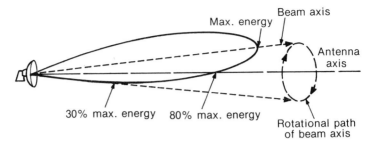

Figure 10–15. Appearance of an antenna beam in conical scanning.

percent, depending on its displacement from the line along which the antenna is pointing. This is shown more clearly in figure 10–16, in which the return signals from a target that is $1\frac{1}{2}$ degrees off the antenna axis are contrasted with the echoes from a target on the axis.

Electronic Scanning

Electronic scanning (used in missile fire control radar directors) can accomplish lobe motion more rapidly than, and without the inherent disadvantages of, the mechanical systems. For target tracking, the radar discussed here produces a narrow circular beam of pulsed RF energy at a high pulse repetition rate. Each pulse is divided into four signals which are equal in amplitude and phase. The four signals are radiated at the same time from each of four feed horns grouped in a cluster as shown in figure 10–17. The radiated energy is focused into a beam by a microwave lens. Energy reflected from targets is refocused by the lens into the feedhorns. The amount of the total energy received by each horn will vary depending on the position of the target relative to the beam axis. Be sure to notice, and remember, that a phase inversion takes place at the microwave lens similar to the image inversion in an optical system. The amplitude of returned signals received by each horn is continuously compared with those received in the other horns, and error signals are generated which indicate the relative position of the target with respect to the axis of the beam. Angle servocircuits receive these error signals and correct the position of the radar beam to keep the beam axis on target.

Identification Friend or Foe (IFF)

Although technically not radar equipment, an electronic system that is employed with radar permits a friendly craft to identify itself automatically before approaching near enough to threaten the security of other naval units. This system is called identification, friend or foe (IFF) (figure 10–18). It consists of a pair of special transmitter-receiver units. One set is aboard the friendly ship; the other is aboard the friendly unit (ship or aircraft). The IFF system operates as follows: An air-search radar operator sees an unidentified target on his radar scope. He turns on the IFF transmitter-receiver, which transmits an interrogating or "asking" signal to the airborne transmitter-receiver. The interrogating signal is received by the airborne unit, which automatically transmits a characteristic signal called an identification

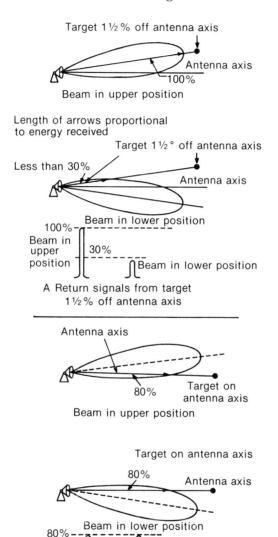

Figure 10–16. The signal echoes in conical scan.

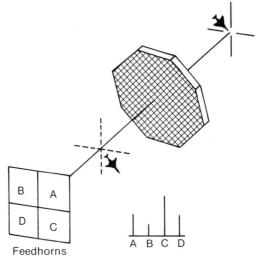

Figure 10–17. *The monopulse technique radiating four signals simultaneously.*

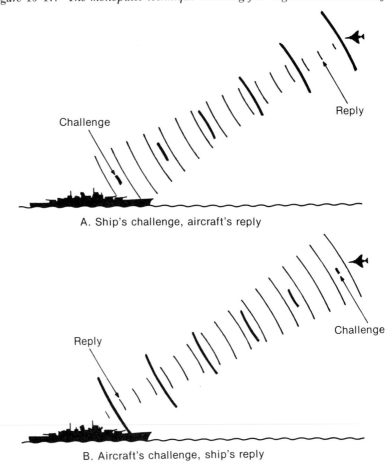

A. Ship's challenge, aircraft's reply

B. Aircraft's challenge, ship's reply

Figure 10–18. *The IFF principle of operation.*

signal. The shipboard system receives the signal, amplifies it, decodes it, and displays it to the air search radar repeater. When the radar operator sees the identifying signal and identifies it as the proper one, he knows that the aircraft is friendly.

If the aircraft does not reply when interrogated, however, or if it sends the wrong identifying signal, then the ship must assume that the target is an enemy, and defensive action must be taken.

Electronic Warfare

Although radar is widely used, there is a separate technological approach in electronics to provide weapon systems with information about the target. This development in modern weaponry is called electronic warfare (EW), and results from the heavy reliance by all navies on electromagnetic emissions brought about by the invention of radio and radar. Electronic warfare has become a highly developed, sophisticated field in weaponry in the areas of detecting the enemy, locating the enemy, and obstructing his fire.

Electronic warfare has been defined as the means by which your own forces attempt to nullify the advantages of the enemy in employing his electronic devices as well as to obtain all possible information concerning the enemy's electromagnetic radiations. EW may be either passive (ESM) or Active (ECM).

ESM refers to measures that are not detectable by the enemy. One use of ESM is an intercept search by a very sensitive receiver, of all electromagnetic wavelengths that the enemy might use. When electromagnetic radiation has been detected, a determination of its source and characteristics is made. Intercept searches detect radiation from such types of electronic equipment as radars, radios, electronically controlled weapons, and electronic navigational aids. ESM equipment can show the direction from which radiation in the radio and radar frequencies is coming, and it also displays and records the radiation so that it can be analyzed. ESM is used in some weapon systems for the direct guidance of weapons.

ECM includes any methods that are detectable by the enemy. ECM's purpose is to impair the operation of the enemy's electronic devices by either noise jamming to mask his target detections or by feeding them false but realistic targets or signals that confuse enemy operators and equipment, called deception jamming. Weapon systems incorporate ECM when gun and rocket projectiles are designed to scatter radar-reflective material.

Summary

Radar is the most widely used means of detecting the presence of and pinpointing the location of surface and air targets. It is widespread because it can function effectively day or night and in most weather conditions. Electronic warfare as it relates to weapons, like radar, is used to warn of hostile ships, missiles and aircraft, and it is also used to provide bearing information. It is further used to protect one's ship from any enemy weapon that depends on electronic emission.

11

Sonar and Magnetic Anomaly Detection

Introduction

Unlike radar and electronic warfare equipment, sonar and magnetic anomaly detection (MAD) equipment are principally employed to detect, locate, and track submarines. Sonar uses acoustic energy, while MAD detects differences in magnetic fields that may betray the presence of a submarine in the water. Sonar can be installed on ships or aircraft, but MAD is only used in aircraft, where there is less interference from the metal. Sonar is used both in the detection of targets and in the control of weapons; MAD is used to pinpoint (localize) the location of an underwater target after it has been detected by other means and to classify the target (determine what it is). MAD and sonar do not actually guide weapons from the launching ship or aircraft, as does radar. Instead, they provide enough information to make it possible to place the weapon (torpedo or depth bomb) near the target.

Sonar

Sonar uses sound energy to locate such submerged objects as enemy submarines and mines. Certain types of sonar can also detect surface ships. Sonar equipment may be either active or passive. Active sonar equipment transmits a sound pulse into the water and then detects the portion of the sound reflected from a target in order to determine bearing and range. Passive sonar depends upon the sounds generated by the target (i.e., screw cavitation and machinery noise) for bearing information. Moreover, passive sonar can detect sound at very long distances (hundreds of miles) with the right equipment and water conditions. Active sonar has been relatively restricted in range to the local operating area of a ship.

To understand sonar and its uses, it is necessary to know the principles of sound in air and water.

Sound

Theoretically, anything that produces sound can be detected by sonar. Noise generated above water as well as in a body of water can be detected by a submerged sonar. Sound travels in the form of energy

Figure 11-1. *Two methods for detecting submarines with sound are shown:* top, *a bow mounted sonardome in unfamiliar surroundings;* bottom, *sonar buoys being loaded on an aircraft going out on ASW patrol.*

Figure 11–2. The three conditions of sound.

waves, which vary in length, depending on the frequency employed. A wave length is measured from one point on a wave to a corresponding point on the next wave. A sound has a low pitch if it has a long wavelength and a high pitch if it has a short wavelength. A complete wavelength is called a cycle, and is measured in Hertz, where Hertz = 1 cycle per second. Normally, sounds between 20 Hertz (Hz) and 15,000 Hertz are within the range of human hearing.

In this text, sounds that can be heard will be called *sonics*. Sounds below 20 Hz are called *subsonics* and those above 15,000 Hz are known as *ultrasonics*. It will be assumed that sound exists when three conditions are met—when an audible vibration is (1) caused by a source, (2) transmitted through a medium, and (3) detected.

The *source* for a sound can be anything that vibrates, thereby disturbing the medium around it (for example, bells, radio-loudspeaker diaphragms, or stringed instruments). A sound *medium* is any material substance through which sound vibrations will travel, such as air, water, or steel. The *detector* simply acts as a receiver of the sound vibrations. Figure 11–2 gives an example of these three conditions. The sound source vibrates when activated. The vibrating transmitter moves the particles (medium) that are in contact with it. The sound then travels through the medium to the detector.

Sound Waves

Sound waves, as stated above, are caused by a vibrating object—for example, the vibrating sonar transducer with water particles lying against it. The outward motion of the transducer produces an initial area of high pressure (compression). In the opposite motion of the vibration, the water particles move apart to produce an area of low pressure (rarefaction). Next, the particles in the first compression expand and push the water particles immediately in front of them which causes a second compression wave farther out. As this action continues, a spreading series of compressions and rarefactions are set up. In figure 11–3 the compression waves are shown as the rings that are close together. As the sound waves spread out, the energy is spread through an increasingly larger area.

Another way of showing the compression and rarefaction sound waves in water is illustrated by the diagram in figure 11–4. The

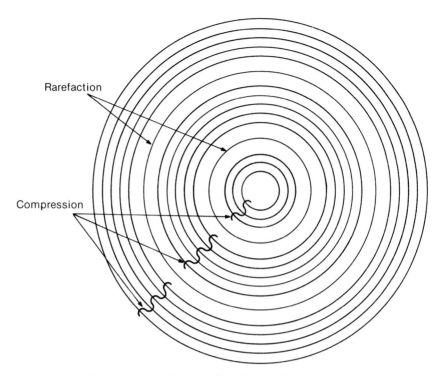

Figure 11–3. Compression/rarefaction. Sound waves in water.

compression wave with its higher pressure goes up the graph while the rarefaction wave (lower pressure) goes down. Also shown in the graph are *wavelengths*, a *wave cycle*, and a *wave amplitude*. As previously stated, a wavelength could be measured as the distance from one pressure point along the sound wave to the same point on the next sound wave. A cycle occurs each time one complete set of changes

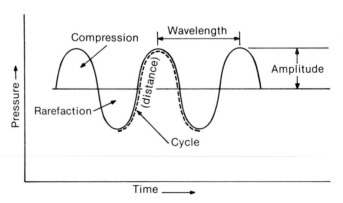

Figure 11–4. Graph of compression/rarefaction in a sound wave.

(compression and rarefaction) has taken place. The wave's amplitude is determined by taking one-half of the total vertical movement of the sound wave. Amplitude is the factor which determines the intensity (loudness) of the sound. As amplitude increases, the sound also increases. Using figure 11–4, the frequency of the sound wave may be determined. Sound frequency is measured in terms of the number of Hertz, as previously discussed.

The speed at which sound will travel is another factor that must be determined. The speed of sound is directly affected by the density of the medium in which it will travel. The denser the medium, the quicker the transmission of sound. A sound wave is transmitted from particle to particle as it passes through the medium. If the particles are far apart, they have a greater distance to move to transmit the sound energy to successive particles. The distance between particles determines the density of a medium or, phrased another way, the density of a substance is determined by the number of particles contained in a given volume measurement. Density is one of the factors which causes a sound wave to travel through air at one speed, pure water at another speed, and sea water at still another speed. For example, at approximately the same temperature, the speed of sound is 1,134 feet per second in air, 4,708 feet per second in pure water, and 4,800 feet per second in sea water.

Characteristics of Sound

Sound can be divided into two types—sound with a pattern of regular vibrations and sound with irregular vibrations. For example, a musical note has regular vibrations, while an explosion of projectiles has irregular vibrations. A sound with no regular pattern is called noise.

Pitch is determined by the frequency of the sound vibration. The high-pitched notes of a piano, for example, are obtained from wires that vibrate much faster than the wires that produce low-pitched notes. Loudness is determined by the wave amplitude, which is a function of power. Quality is determined by creating distinctive wave forms made up of a combination of pure or fundamental tones in suitable proportions. On the other hand the explosion of many projectiles is called noise, because the sound has so many instantaneous sources that it has no regular pattern of vibrations.

Marine Noises

Some of the kinds of sound that will have an adverse effect upon sonar reception are *marine* ambient noise, *flow* noise, and *cavitation* noise.

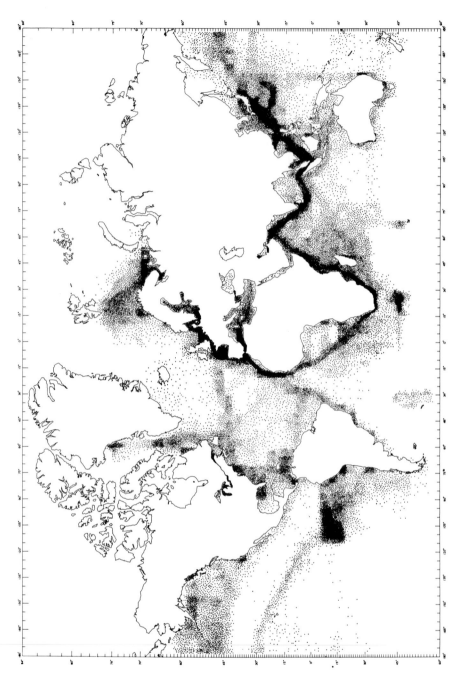

Figure 11–5. Worldwide merchant ship distribution (including fishing vessels), projected to 1980.

Marine Ambient Noise

This is a background noise that is always present. One of the major contributors to ambient noise in the higher frequencies is surface agitation. As the wind rises, the ocean's surface becomes more and more agitated thereby raising the ambient noise level. Even more troublesome for sonar search operators is the lower frequency ambient noise primarily generated by ocean shipping. The Maritime Administration estimated in 1972 that there were about 20,000 oceangoing vessels in the world. The scope of daily traffic at sea, about 10,000 vessels underway on any given day, may be appreciated from this estimate. Figure 11–5 illustrates the pattern of this traffic projected to 1980, and shows by implication where the man-made noise problems are the greatest.

Flow Noise

As an object moves through water, there is a relative flow between the object and the medium. If the object is reasonably streamlined and the object's surface is relatively smooth, a flow pattern, known as a *laminar flow*, is set up at low speed. Such a flow pattern is shown in figure 11–6. The lines represent the paths followed by the water as it flows around the object. Laminar flow does not produce noise. It occurs at very low speeds and depends on the shape, smoothness, and length of the underwater hull.

If the speed of this same object were increased, whirls and eddies would appear in the flow pattern (figure 11–7). This phenomenon is referred to as *turbulent flow*. Within these eddies occur points where the pressure varies greatly from the static pressure in the medium, and an internal noise field is created within the area of the turbulence.

Figure 11–6. Pattern of laminar flow.

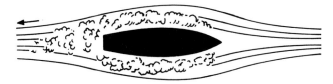

Figure 11–7. Pattern of turbulent flow and self-noise.

The average pressure of the whole eddy differs very little from the static medium pressure. Therefore, there is very little noise radiated outside the area of turbulence. Should a hydrophone be placed in this field of intense flow noise, it would pick up the noise. Should another hydrophone be placed at some distance from the flow noise field, it might not be able to detect the noise at all. Flow noise is almost exclusively a self-made noise problem.

Cavitation Noise

Cavitation takes place when a solid object moves through a liquid medium fast enough to reduce the pressure behind the object, causing the water to vaporize into bubbles. The liberated gas forms thousands of very small bubbles. In general, the greater the speed of the object as it passes through the liquid, the larger the bubbles will be. After bubbles have formed and passed away from the object, they start to rise to the surface. But in the absence of the moving object, the pressure returns to normal, and the bubbles collapse. It is this collapse that causes the acoustic signal known as cavitation noise. Each bubble, as it collapses, produces a sharp noise signal.

In a rotating propeller, cavitation will first show up at the tips of the blades where the speed of rotation is greatest. This type of cavitation is called *blade tip cavitation*. A propeller producing this type of cavitation is shown in figure 11–8.

As the propeller revolutions increase, more and more of the propeller's surfaces start moving fast enough to cause cavitations. The cavitating areas move down the trailing edge of the blade. As the speed of the propeller continues to increase, the whole back face of the blade

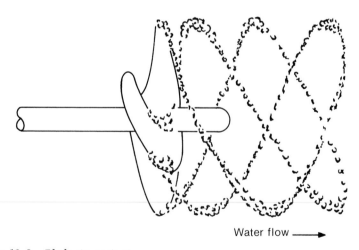

Water flow ⟶

Figure 11–8. Blade tip cavitation.

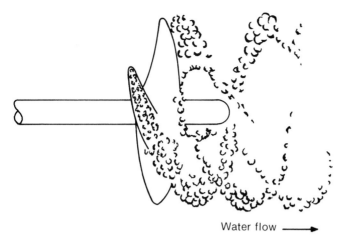

Water flow ⟶

Figure 11–9. Sheet cavitation.

begins cavitating, while pressure on the face of the blade continues to increase with increasing RPM. This phenomenon is called *sheet cavitation* (figure 11–9). In general, sub-cavitating blades develop the most efficient propulsive force, while cavitating and super-cavitating blades make more noise and are less efficient. Therefore, cavitation is a price of higher speed.

Machinery Noises

Machinery noises are produced on board ship by the main propulsion and auxiliary machinery. Machinery noise is usually produced by the rotating or reciprocating action of the pistons, which causes a vibration within the machine. This vibration may then be transmitted through the machine mounts to the hull and radiated out into the water as acoustic energy. Since every machine has a characteristic and repetitive cycle, the machine can be identified by the noise it makes. This is called a *signature.* The Navy is continually involved in efforts to design and build ships and submarines that emit the least possible amount of engine noise, using such methods as noise-absorbent lining of engine compartments, shock mountings for vibrating equipment, and the like.

Underwater Transmission

The usefulness of an active sonar depends on the transmission of an underwater sound, the recognition of the returning echo from an object, and the factors affecting the sound wave velocity. Recognition of the returning echo depends on the quality, relative strength (loudness), and character of the echo compared with the other underwater sounds that tend to mask it.

Absorption

Some sound is absorbed while it passes through the water. Loss of strength because of absorption is directly related to the frequency of the pulse. Lower frequencies are not absorbed as easily as high frequencies. The amount of sound lost this way depends a great deal on the sea state. For example, on the surface, absorption is great when winds are high enough to produce whitecaps and cause a concentration of bubbles near the surface of the water. Absorption is also much greater in ship wakes and strong currents.

Scattering

Sound waves are weakened when they pass through a region of sea water that contains foreign matter (i.e., seaweed, silt, animal life). This foreign matter scatters the passing sound wave and causes it to lose energy. The overall result of scattering is that it reduces the echo strength. The sound strength lost because of absorption and scattering is referred to as *attenuation*.

Reflection

Echoes occur when the sound wave strikes an object in such a manner as to reflect the sound back to its source. If sound waves sent

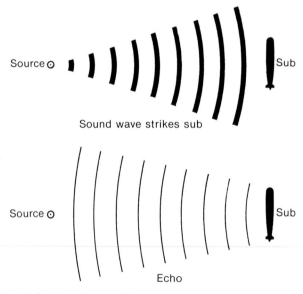

Figure 11–10. Reflection of a sound wave.

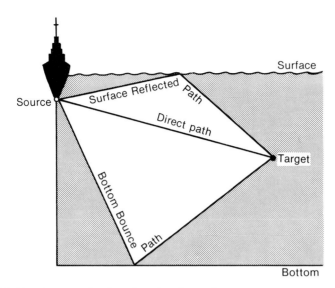

Figure 11–11. Direct and reflected paths of sound waves.

out by an echo-ranging sonar transducer hit a submarine (figure 11–10), the sound waves are reflected back as an echo.

Unfortunately, the reflection of sound waves also takes place when there is a change in the medium density. As an example, a sound wave traveling through sea water is almost entirely reflected at the boundary (sea surface) between the water and the air. Sound is reflected better from a smooth sea than a rough one. Rough seas tend to scatter the sound waves (reflecting them in different directions). A calm or smooth sea has a reflection quality similar to a mirror and the sound wave is reflected in one general direction. Furthermore, the ocean bottom also reflects sound waves (figure 11–11). In deep water this effect is not common. In waters of less than a hundred fathoms, the sound waves may be reflected from the bottom. The echo will be a confusing factor when searching for submarines.

Spreading or Divergence

A sound wave acts much like a beam of light. If it were not subject to other physical influences, such as salinity, pressure, or temperature, it would travel approximately in a straight line, and its speed would be uniform throughout the water column. The spherical wavefront of the sound wave would just spread and weaken with distance by absorption at a relatively constant rate (figure 11–12). Since the area of this wavefront grows during its travel, the intensity of the sound decreases as the wave moves over an increasingly large area. This effect on signal intensity is called *spreading loss* or *divergence*.

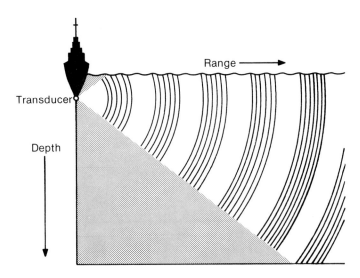

Figure 11–12. Sound travel in constant temperature.

Refraction (Bending)

Unfortunately, in addition to the spreading loss other factors affect the sound signal and the path it follows. For example, the speed of sound is not the same at all water depths. The velocity of sound in sea water goes from 4,700 feet per second to 5,300 feet per second as temperature increases from 30° to 85°F. The effects of salinity and pressure on sound speed usually are small compared with the large effects commonly produced by temperature changes in the sea. Because of the varying temperature differences in the sea, the sound wave follows curved paths which results in bending, splitting, and distortion of the directed sound. When the beam of sound is bent it is said to be *refracted*. Sound beams bend away from high temperatures and bend toward lower temperatures (figure 11–13 a and b).

Quenching

In strong winds and heavy seas, the ship's rolling and pitching make it difficult to keep the sound directed on the target. Also, the presence of air bubbles in the water weakens the sound waves. Sometimes this envelope of air bubbles completely blankets or quenches the sound transmitted by the transducer.

Shadow Zones and Multi-Path Propagation

When the transmitting ship is in shallow water (smooth ocean bottom), the sound wave bends down from the transducer to the bottom, then back up to the surface, and down to the bottom again

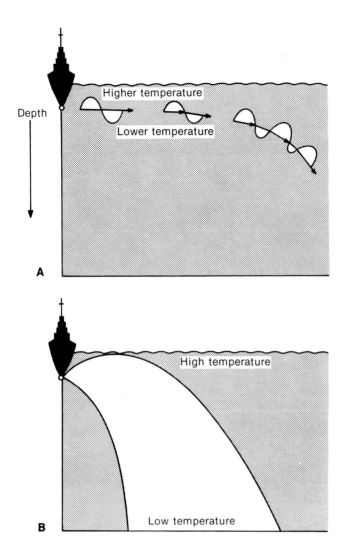

Depth

Figure 11–13. *(a) Bending effect of cold water on sound path in a thermoline; (b) The refracted sound wave path.*

(figure 11–14). When the transmitted sound acts in this manner, there are areas where there is no sonar coverage. A submarine can pass into these "shadow zones" and be undetected. Sonar echoes are regained when the submarine enters the wave path again. Note the example in figure 11–14 of making contact at long range (point A), losing it (point B), and regaining it at short range (point C). Without the reflection, the maximum detection range would have been the short range at which the contact was regained at point C.

The reason for the loss of contact at short range (point D) is that the submarine passes beneath the original sound beam. The distance

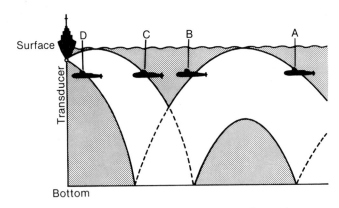

Figure 11–14. The effect of shallow water on transmitted sound.

at which contact is lost at short range depends directly on the depth of the submarine. A rule of thumb for this situation is that the range in yards at loss of contact is roughly equal to the depth of the submarine in feet. Therefore, a contact lost at 400 yards would thus be presumed to be at a depth of 400 feet.

Sound Propagation in Water

Since water is the acoustic medium, it also has an effect on the transmission of sound. Three factors control the speed of sound and the direction of the sound wave in water—temperature, pressure, and salinity.

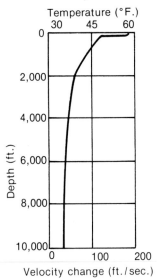

Figure 11–15. Temperature versus depth changes in sound velocity.

Temperature

Temperature is the most important factor affecting the speed of sound in water. Temperatures of the waters throughout the world vary greatly according to location and depth. The speed of sound decreases or increases at a rate of four to eight feet per second per degree of temperature change. The sea temperature varies from freezing in the polar seas to more than 85° F in the tropics. Sea temperature can also decrease by more than 30° F from the surface to a depth of 450 feet. As a result, there are dramatic geographic differences in the conditions for sound propagation in ASW operations.

Figure 11–15 shows on a graph a normal change of temperature in a given depth of water. The water temperature at the surface is 60° F. The water temperature at 10,000 feet is approximately

34° F, or 26° lower. The change of speed of the sound wave is approximately 200 feet per second. In other words, in this graph, the speed of sound, considering temperature alone, will be lower at a 10,000-foot depth than at the water surface.

Pressure

Sound waves will travel faster as the water pressure increases. This effect on the speed of the transmitted sound is smaller than the effect that temperature has on sound. The pressure effect (figure 11–16) is represented by a straight line from the surface down, because the increase in sound velocity is linear (in a line) with depth. Note from the graph that sound velocity increases 180 feet per second at a depth of 10,000 feet.

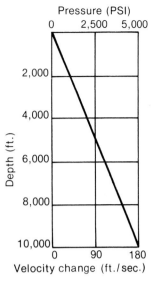

Figure 11–16. Pressure versus depth changes in sound velocity.

Salinity

Seawater contains many elements and compounds in solution. This is referred to as salinity. Salinity is defined as the amount of solid material dissolved in a body of water.*

In the open ocean away from fresh water, the salinity values run between 30 and 35 parts per thousand. In the sea, close to the outlets of rivers and other fresh water sources, the salinity values approach zero. Salinity plays a minor part in changes of sound velocities. In figure 11–17, the salinity effect takes place almost entirely in the first 500 feet below the surface of the water. A total of six feet per second change in sound velocity normally takes place in a water depth of 10,000 feet. Because the temperature, depth, and salinity of the water are conditions that always occur in some combination, it is useful to consider them together.

Figure 11–18 shows the velocity graph combining the above graphs on temperature, pressure, and salinity. Notice that temperature and salinity have their greatest effect on the composite graph in the first 500 feet below the sur-

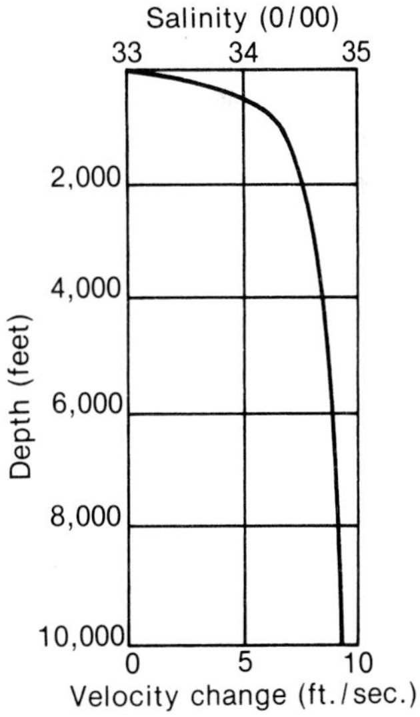

Figure 11–17. Salinity versus depth changes in sound velocity.

* The American Practical Navigator, H.O. Pub. 9 (Bowditch), Wash. D.C., 1962, p. 695.

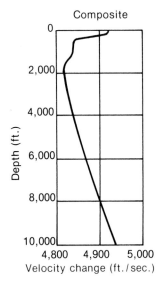

Composite

Figure 11-18. A composite of temperature, pressure, salinity versus depth changes in sound velocity.

face. Another factor to observe is that the composite curve resembles the temperature curve for the first 2,000 feet.

Sound Paths in Water

The individual routes that sound will follow through a body of water is a subject of paramount interest to those who employ sonar in ASW. Having described the roles of temperature, pressure, and salinity in determining sound velocity, we can now view the effect of these variables on the path a sound will follow with an eye to our being able to predict sound conditions in a local situation, encountered in sound propagation, which will affect the underwater delivery of antisubmarine weapons.

The Effect of Pressure

Pressure in the ocean is always present and acts in a predictable way. With the ocean temperature remaining constant, the speed of the sound wave will increase with depth as a result of the effect of pressure which will cause the sound beam to bend upward. This occurs because the molecules, under higher pressure at low depths, transmit the sound more rapidly than the molecules under less pressure in the upper water levels. The slower transmission at the top bends the sound wave upward around the lower upper strata (figure 11–19).

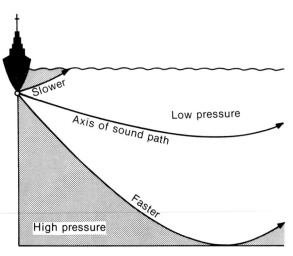

Figure 11-19. Effect of pressure on a sound path.

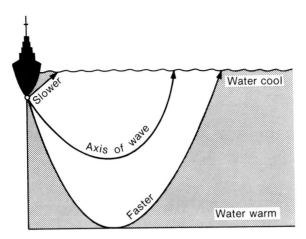

Figure 11–20. Effect of a positive thermal gradient on a sound path.

Temperature/Pressure Effect

If the temperature of the ocean increases as the water depth gets greater, the water is said to have a positive thermal gradient. The speed of the sound wave will greatly increase with depth, causing the sound beam to bend sharply upward (figure 11–20).

If the temperature of the ocean decreases as the water depth increases, the water is said to have a negative thermal gradient. The effect of the temperature change will greatly outweigh the effect of the pressure change. As a result, the sound beam will be bent downward (figure 11–21).

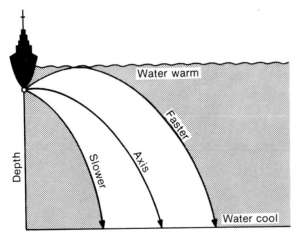

Figure 11–21. Effect of a negative thermal gradient on a sound path.

Sonar and Magnetic Anomaly Detection   **153**

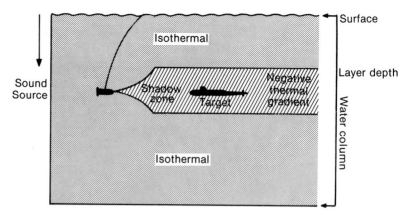

Figure 11-22. Combination thermal gradient effect.

Normally, the ocean temperature will not be just one of the above situations, but instead a combination of them. Where a large change in temperature takes place, the depth at which the change begins is called the *layer depth*. The intermediate zone in which there is a markedly different temperature is called the *layer*. Figure 11-22 shows the paths of the sound wave when the water is isothermal above the layer depth, and the water has a negative thermal gradient in the layer. The sound wave splits and bends upward above the layer and downward below it, causing a shadow zone. Should a target get into a shadow zone, the sonar would not be able to detect it. This phenomena has led to the development of the *variable depth sonar* (VDS). A variable depth sonar is usually mounted aft in the stern of or on the fantail of destroyer-type ships. It can be lowered into the suspected shadow zone to cover the areas being missed by the hull-mounted sonar.

Sound Channel

An underwater sound channel is formed when a body of water that has a negative thermal gradient meets a body of water that has a positive thermal gradient in a layer (figure 11-23). If a sound is transmitted at this layer depth, all of the sound beams that travel in an upward direction would be bent back down and those that travel downward would be bent back up. The beam that started out downward will rise as high above that depth as it went below it and then will be bent downward again, assuming equal gradients of opposite sign. Sound that is bent back and forth within this channel will remain in the channel as long as the thermal gradient exists. The sound will suffer very little loss as it progresses through the channel.

A sound channel is rarely formed in water less than 100 fathoms

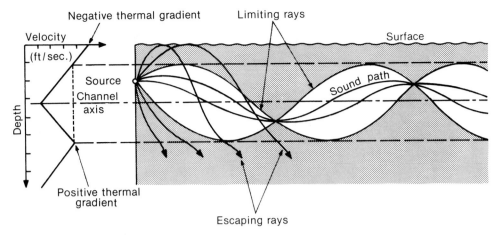

Figure 11–23. Negative and positive thermal gradients forming a sound channel. Note the location of the sound source.

deep. Sound channels are, however, always present in the deep water areas of the world. The depth of the sound channel in the central Pacific Ocean is about 350 fathoms, and somewhat over 500 fathoms in the Atlantic. Where the surface water is materially colder, such as in the polar regions, the axis of a channel is nearer the surface.

Convergence Zone

The convergence transmission path is based on the principle that in a negative thermal gradient, sound energy from a source near the surface of the water (ship's sonar) travels downward in the ocean. As the sound wave moves downward, the bottom edge of the sound wave will increase in water pressure with depth. Since sound travels toward the slowest medium and a sound wave tends to maintain a coherent front, the sound will bend upwards toward the surface. The upward path that the sound wave takes will be sufficiently steep to penetrate the layer and reach the surface. When the sound signal reaches the surface, it will be reflected downward once again. A convergence zone, then, is the water area covered by the sound signal where it reaches the surface again after initial transmission (figure 11–24 a and b).

A second and third convergence zone may occur, and under peculiar water conditions, several more may be identified. Generally, the first zone will occur between 15 and 40 miles from the source, and any subsequent zones will appear at approximately equal intervals thereafter.

If a target is to be detected applying this principle in active sonar search it will have to be located in the sound path. Convergence zone searches are normally conducted in water over 2,000 fathoms deep.

Sonar and Magnetic Anomaly Detection   **155**

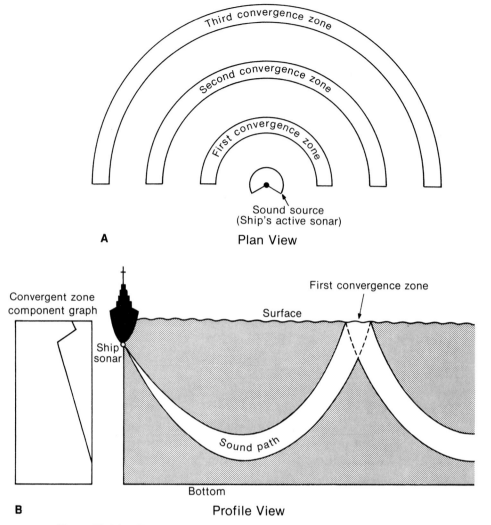

Figure 11-24. *Convergence zones in active sonar search (a) plan view; (b) profile view.*

With proper bathythermograph information, it is possible to predict where this convergence zone lies at any given time or place.

Bottom Bounce

For long-range search in water depths over 1,000 fathoms, a bottom reflection or bottom bounce effect may be used with some sonars. The bottom bounce effect is obtained by selecting a transmission angle that will reflect from the ocean floor. This effect is illustrated in figure 11-25.

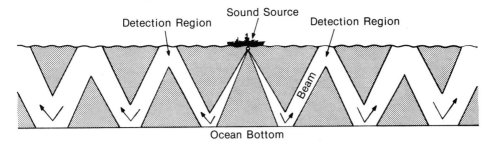

Figure 11–25. *The bottom bounce effect.*

Bathythermographs

A *bathythermograph* (B/T) is an instrument which is used during ASW search operations to help the sonar operators make the most intelligent use of the sonar in their search procedures. It is designed to record temperature at various depths. In so doing it is the primary source of such ASW environmental information as the depth of the mixed layer, the thermocline, and special conditions affecting sonar search.

Figure 11–26 shows the parts of a typical bathythermograph. As the B/T is lowered to a desired depth and then raised back up to

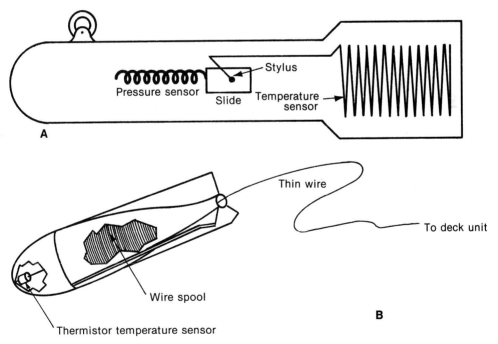

Figure 11–26. *(a) The internal parts of a bathythermograph* (BT); *(b) The expendable bathythermograph (XBT).*

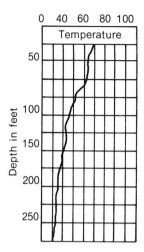

Figure 11–27. A partial reproduction of a B/T slide as seen through a viewer.

the surface, water depth (pressure) is measured by a pressure-sensitive bellows similar to the bellows used in a barometer to measure air pressure. The bellows is anchored to one end of the B/T, which allows the other end, holding a piece of coated glass, to move as the water depth (pressure) changes.

Water temperature is measured by a temperature sensitive element called a *bourdon tube*. The bourdon tube moves a stylus point horizontally across the same coated piece of glass. The water temperature at each water depth is then read from the scratched glass by mounting it in a special viewing instrument. This instrument superimposes a coordinate system on the mounted glass. A partial reproduction of this with the coordinate system and temperature in relation to depth is shown in figure 11–27.

Figure 11–28 shows one method by which a B/T is lowered and raised from a moving ship. The B/T is placed on the end of a wire which comes from the power winch. The gate swings out away from the side of the ship to keep the B/T from hitting the ship's side or being sucked into the ship's propellers. After the B/T has been lowered to the desired depth, which can be gauged by a counter that shows the amount of cable that has been payed out, the B/T is brought back to the surface by the power winch. The gate is brought back to the side of the ship and secured there. The B/T is disengaged from the cable, taken below for removal of the slide, and stowed until the next B/T drop. For best results in streaming a mechanical B/T, a ship should steam at ten knots; 15 knots is an approximate upper limit.

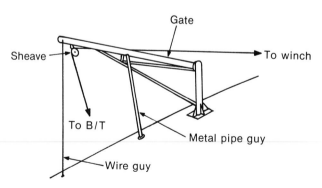

Figure 11–28. B/T handling equipment.

The Expendable Bathythermograph (XBT)

Many ships in the Navy are equipped with an installation which permits the use of throw-away B/Ts. The instrumentation installed in the ship records the same data shown on the composite slide in the mechanical version. The recorder prints out a record while the B/T is transmitting. The B/T itself is a rather light composite plastic cylinder, which contains a reel of thin copper wire as well as sensing devices and a battery pack for power. It may be dropped from a tube mounted on the stern and will sink while recording its observations through the copper filament to the recorder. The expendable B/T is a useful version of the mechanical instrument because it can be dropped from aircraft and it can be used from a ship steaming at any speed. However, it can become a relatively expensive way to observe water conditions if frequently used on a ship, and a large enough supply of expendable B/Ts for a full deployment takes stowage space. As a result the expendable version is used only where its special mechanical advantages recommend it.

Doppler

Doppler effect is the term for a comparison in sound between a moving object and the medium in which it moves.

In echo ranging sonar, three audible sounds are generated: (1) the sound that is actually sent into the water; (2) the sounds or reverberations that are heard as an echo from all the particles in the water (i.e., seaweed, fish); and (3) the sound of the target echo. Since the actual outgoing pulse signal is seldom heard, there are actually only two sounds that must be dealt with in the Doppler effect—reverberations, echoes returning from all the small particles in the water, and target echoes.

The stationary particle will not change the pitch of the traveling ping and the reverberations. The Doppler effect then is determined by comparing the pitch of the reverberation and the pitch of the target echo. Doppler is classified in one of three ways: no Doppler, up Doppler, and down Doppler. It can be determined by the transmitting ship regardless of whether she is under way or stationary.

When the target is not going toward or away from the sound beam, its echoes will have the same pitch as the echoes from particles in the water (figure 11–29). When there is no difference in pitch between the echo pitch from the target and the echo pitch from the reverberations, there is said to be "no Doppler."

When the target is coming toward the sound beam (figure 11–30), the target reflects back a higher echo pitch than the particles in the

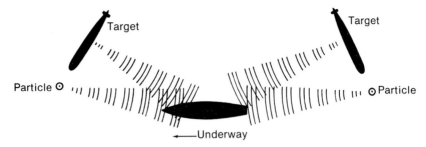

Figure 11–29. No Doppler.

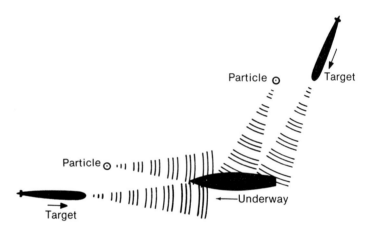

Figure 11–30. Up Doppler.

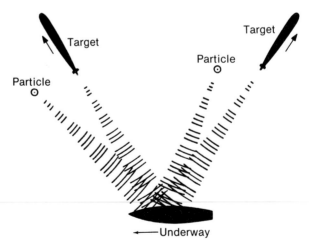

Figure 11–31. Down Doppler.

water. When the echo pitch from the oncoming target is higher than the reverberations, this is called "up Doppler." This indicates that the submarine is moving through the water, headed toward the receiving ship.

The opposite form of Doppler occurs when the moving submarine is heading away from the receiving ship. Figure 11–31 shows that the echo pitch from the submarine is lower than the echo pitch of the reverberations. This is called "down Doppler."

Uses of Doppler

Two of the major uses of the Doppler effect are classification and tracking. Because underwater objects that reflect the transmitted sound cannot be seen, classification of the contact is a major problem. An up or down Doppler is a clear indication that the contact is moving and is not a stationary object, such as kelp or seaweed. Doppler is also used during target tracking to compare the fire control solution with what is actually being heard from the target echo and the reverberations.

Sonar Contact Classification

When a contact is detected by sonar, every effort is made to determine what the contact is in order to be able to take further intelligent action. A contact may be classified as follows:

1. non-submarine
2. possible submarine
3. probable submarine
4. positive submarine

As described, Doppler is one principle which can be effectively applied in the efforts to identify the contact. However, as the newest sonars transmit at very low frequencies (VLF) to achieve better range, the round trip sonar ping will take longer to cover the longer range made possible by VLF, making Doppler discrimination a difficult task. Nevertheless, newer sonars will provide an automatic Doppler readout, even at low frequencies for classifying targets. Other characteristics of echo ranging are also employed, such as audio echo strength. If the audio echo is sharp and clear, the contact is likely to be metallic. If the echo is fuzzy, the contact is likely to be vegetation or a school of small fish. The video image on the cathode ray tube display is similarly examined for good resolution in echo size, strength, and brightness. Another significant factor in distinguishing submarines from most natural contacts is the consistency of the movement of the track and if this track is within the capability of a submarine. Finally, if any engine or propeller noise is overheard by the sonar, a submarine may be readily identified by its characteristic vibrations.

Magnetic Anomaly Detection (MAD)

Another method of employing energy to detect the presence of an object at sea is by using equipment which senses a change in the earth's magnetic field induced by the presence of a large body of steel, such as a ship hull or a submarine. This application is called *magnetostatics* and the airborne equipment is called magnetic anomaly detection equipment (MAD) (figure 11–32). Additionally, metal hulls develop their own electric field which can be detected at short range by appropriate electrode sensors. The principle is called *electrostatics*, and the theory is applied in mine, torpedo, and depth bomb fuzing. Neither magnetostatic or electrostatic detection devices depend on energy radiated at a frequency and are therefore not included in the frequency spectrum discussed above.

The electronic portion of MAD equipment is normally carried within the aircraft. A probe extending from the antisubmarine aircraft (fixed-wing or helicopter) contains the highly sensitive MAD equipment (figure 11–33). MAD is used for area searches to locate a previously detected target and for classification of the target.

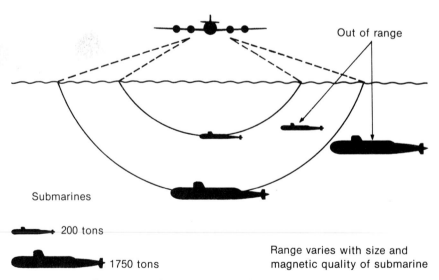

Figure 11–32. The concept of magnetic anomaly detection.

Figure 11–33. MAD sensors on (a) land-based and (b) carrier-based antisubmarine aircraft.

PART 3

Guns

The student has gained some familiarity in the preceding sections with sensors and fire control equipment of the three major categories of weapon types described. It remains for him to become acquainted with the launcher part of the gun system and with missile and ASW systems. In this Part, guns are first discussed in general terms. Then some examples of the newest guns in service with the Fleet are given. It is hoped that an understanding of gunnery and the present state of that science will be gained in this section. The next sections will present missiles and torpedoes in the same way.

12

Gun Mounts

Figure 12–1. This five-inch gun firing on board the USS Turner Joy (DD-951) is representative of contemporary design in medium caliber, dual-purpose naval gun mounts. As gun crews have been reduced or entirely removed from serving in the gun mounts, the shielding has become lighter, twin barrels have been replaced by single barrels, and the degree of automation has increased. The calibers of the guns in the Fleet are typically becoming smaller and the barrels are getting longer. Nevertheless, many basic design features of naval guns have not changed.

Introduction

Although gun mounts vary considerably in detail, they possess many common features.

It will be recalled from Chapter 1 that guns are usually described by their caliber—measurements of bore width and barrel length. First, the bore width is expressed in inches or millimeters, followed by the barrel length in calibers for three-inch and larger guns. The description can show the gun as 5-inch 54 caliber, or simply as 5″/54. This signifies a gun of five-inch bore width and 54 calibers in barrel length, giving a total barrel length of 270 inches (the width times the length) (figure 12–2). The calibers are followed by the U.S. Navy mark and model number—e.g., 5″/54 Mark 42 Mod 10.

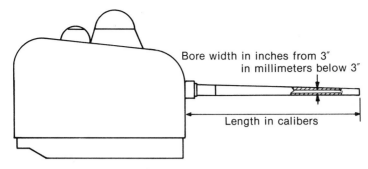

Figure 12–2. Gun measurement.

Guns smaller than three inches are described by their bore width in millimeters and sometimes a name—the 20mm Vulcan-Phalanx gun—or by the name of the manufacturer and the function of the gun—35mm Oerlikon antiaircraft gun.

Guns are additionally classified according to bore diameter as: major caliber—eight inches or larger; intermediate caliber—greater than four and less than eight inches; minor caliber—greater than 0.60 inch but not more than four inches; and small arms—0.60 inch or smaller.

Structural Arrangements of Typical Naval Gun Mounts

Figure 12–3 shows the "skeleton" structure of a typical intermediate caliber naval gun mount.

Serving as the mount foundation is the stand, which is a steel ring bolted to the deck. The training circle is the internal gear inside the stand. Supported by the stand, and capable of rotating in train on roller bearings, is the base ring. The base ring has a weldment on top of it with a groove to allow the barrel maximum elevation. The weldment and base ring together make up the lower carriage assembly. The lower carriage assembly may also have a platform welded to it which supports the gun crew and the surrounding splinter shield of an enclosed gun mount. On top of the lower carriage assembly is bolted the trunnion brackets which support the gun and slide assembly. These elements are called the upper carriage assembly. Resting in the trunnion bearings is the gun slide which holds the gun and its housing. Contrary to its name, the slide does not slide. It supports the moving parts, in recoil and counterrecoil, and the loading system. These parts include housing, breechblock, gas ejection vents, firing circuits, recoil, and counterrecoil mechanisms.

The base ring (figure 12–4) can turn on the stand in two large-diameter roller-bearing axes. One, the roller path, takes up vertical thrust, the other, the horizontal thrust.

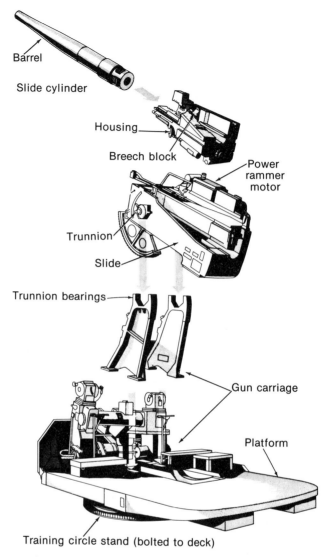

Figure 12–3. *The main assemblies of an intermediate caliber mount.*

Holding-down clips (figure 12–5), bolted to the base ring, fit under the stand so that the carriage will not tip when the gun fires or when the ship pitches and rolls.

A pinion in the carriage engages the training circle gear teeth to train the mount, as illustrated in figure 12–3.

The elevating arc is bolted to the forward part of the slide (figure 12–6). It has gear teeth which engage the elevating pinion. The mount elevation and train drives are attached to the carriage assembly. The

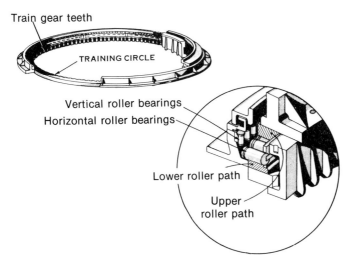

Figure 12–4. *Roller bearings in the stand.*

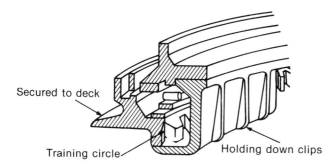

Figure 12–5. *Holding-down clips.*

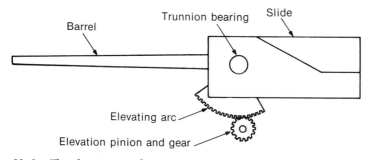

Figure 12–6. *The elevating mechanism.*

automatic loading equipment, such as ammunition hoists, are also bolted to the carriage assembly and train with the mount.

The gun barrel itself is secured to the housing with a bayonet joint (figure 12–7). The most common method of attaching a gun barrel to

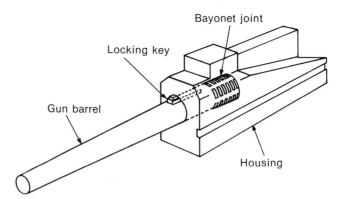

Figure 12–7. The gun barrel secured in the housing. The slide is not shown.

a housing is by using an interrupted screw joint, with a key to lock the barrel against the possible rotation. During recoil and counterrecoil the housing moves in guides in the gun slide.

Major Parts of a Gun Barrel

Figure 12–8 shows the cross section of a typical gun barrel. The breech housing provides support for the breechblock, which can be opened for loading and closed for firing.* Just forward of the breechblock, and inside the barrel, is an enlarged chamber for the propelling charge. It should be noted that the bulkiest part of the gun is at its breech end, where the metal has to be thick to withstand the initial high propellant gas pressures.

The barrel tapers (this tapering part is the chase), then thickens to form a bell, which discourages any tendency for the metal to split. The narrow part of the barrel just abaft the bell is the neck.

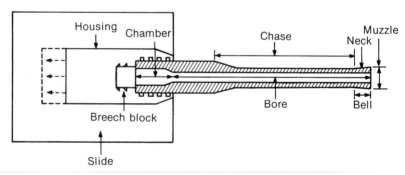

Figure 12–8. The slide shown enclosing a cross-sectional view of the barrel and the housing.

* The operation of a typical breechblock is discussed in the following chapter.

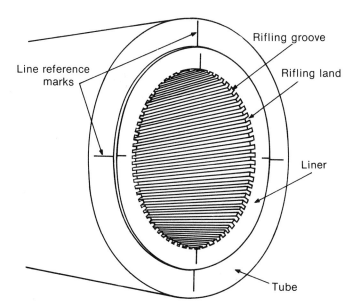

Figure 12–9. Gun barrel rifling showing the lands and the grooves.

Barrel Rifling

The bore of the gun is rifled with helical or spiral grooves (figure 12–9) to make the projectile spin on its long axis and to prevent the projectile from tumbling. In all naval guns and small arms, except the .45 caliber pistol,* the rifling has a right-hand twist. The twist is usually uniform throughout the length of the bore (generally around 1 in 15 or 20 times the bore diameter). The caliber of a rifled gun is measured from the top of one land (the high surfaces between grooves) to the land on the opposite side of the bore.

The rotating band for the projectile is made slightly larger than the gun bore diameter. The rifling cuts into or engraves the softer metal of the rotating band when the projectile is rammed into the barrel (figure 12–10 a). When the gun is fired, the projectile spins at an increasing rate as the propellant gas accelerates it (figure 12–10 b). Moreover, because of the close fit between rotating band and rifling, the propellant gas is sealed behind the projectile.

Firing Systems

This description will be limited to intermediate and large caliber guns using fixed and semifixed ammunition. Bag ammunition is not used in the active Fleet.

---

* The .45 caliber has a left-handed twist so that the pistol will tend to rest in the right hand, rather than twist out of it when fired.

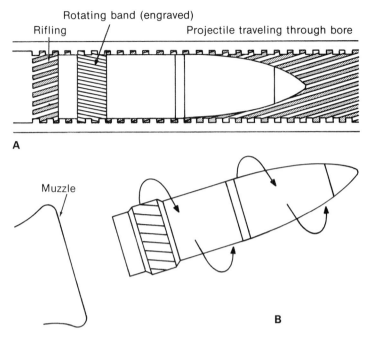

Figure 12–10. The rotating band engraved by the rifling (a) causes the projectile to spin in the bore (b).

The firing mechanism (figure 12–11) that is common to all firing systems for case ammunition is secured in the breechblock, but is not considered part of the breechblock. It is easily removed for servicing or replacement. The firing pin makes contact with the primer of the propelling charge case when the gun is loaded and the breech is fully closed. The pin is withdrawn into the breechblock whenever the breech is not fully closed. In the combination electric and percussion and the simple percussion firing systems, the firing pin, when actuated by a mechanical firing linkage, delivers a blow to the primer, provided the gun is in battery and the breech is fully closed.

In combination and electric firing systems, the firing pin is normally electrically insulated and is part of the electrical firing circuit.

Electrical Firing Circuits

A sequence of actions takes place in firing. This sequence can be followed in figure 12–12, which shows a schematic drawing of the elements in the circuit of a typical five-inch gun mount. The drawing does not show the physical locations of the parts.

Number 1 is the power source. Under normal service conditions, the gun-fire electricity is provided by the ship's primary 115 volt AC

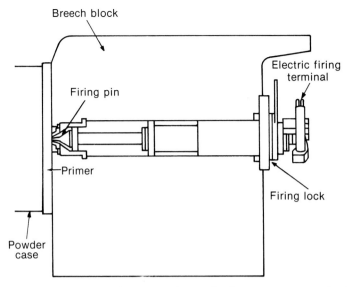

Figure 12–11. Relationship of the cartridge to the firing pin in a standard breech firing mechanism for percussion and electrical firing.

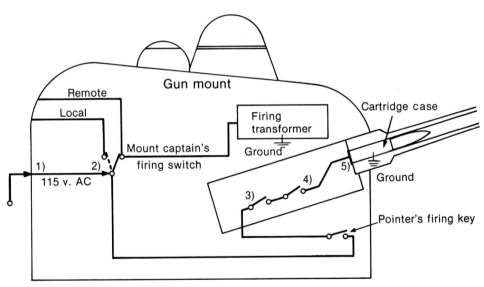

1) Power source
2) Mount captain's selector switch
3) Firing stop mechanism switch
4) Interlock switch or relay
5) Firing pin

Figure 12–12. A basic electrical firing circuit.

supply. Should the primary source of power be interrupted for any reason—for example, from battle damage—secondary methods are available for obtaining electrical power.

Number 2 is the mount captain's selector switch. As the mount captain is in overall charge of the gun mount, he determines who will be in control of the mount's firing circuit—be it a remote station or local firing. In *remote*, a station outside the mount, such as a director or the plotting room, fires the mount. In *local*, the gun is fired by the *pointer** in the mount. In either position of the selector switch, the pointer's firing key must be closed to complete the firing circuit. This safety measure allows the man on the spot where the ammunition is being loaded to control the situation.

Number 3 is the firing stop mechanism switch. The firing stop mechanism is explained in detail in the next section of this chapter. It keeps the gun from firing when the barrel is pointing at part of the ship. The switch must be closed if the gun is to be fired.

Number 4 shows the place of interlock switches or relays. There may be six or more of these, each of which confirms that a certain mechanism is in a safe position for firing. The interlock that registers when the breechblock is closed is a common example of these interlocks. The breechblock holds the round in the barrel and must be closed for firing. The interlock insures that this critical function has taken place.

Number 5 is the firing pin. The last part of the circuit is the firing pin's contact with the electric primer. The circuit is completed through the filament in the primer, the carriage case, and ground return to the firing transformer.

Firing Stop Mechanism

Normally, the axis of a gun's bore (line of fire) differs from the line of sight to the target. This makes it possible, particularly in enclosed mounts, for a pointer or trainer looking through a telescope to see no obstacle in the line of sight, while the line of fire may be in line with some part of the ship's structure. Firing the gun will cause the projectile to hit the ship. It is, therefore, necessary either to prevent pointing the gun bore toward the ship's structure or to prevent it from firing under these conditions. The latter is the more common method. The function of the firing stop mechanism is to disable the firing system when the gun is so aimed that the projectile would hit the ship if it were fired.

The firing stop mechanism (figures 12–13 and 12–14) is essentially

* The pointer also elevates and lowers the gun using the sight.

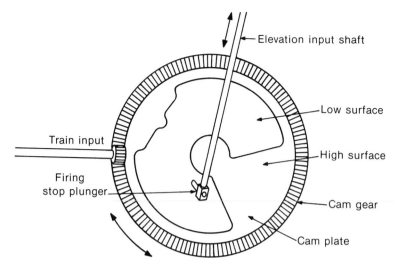

Figure 12–13. *Mechanical inputs in the firing stop mechanism.*

a plate or disc cam, in which the inputs are the gun train (which rotates the cam) and gun elevation (which moves the cam follower approximately radially across the cam). The elevation input shaft moves toward the center of the cam plate when the gun elevates, and toward the edge when it depresses. At the end of the elevation input shaft is a spring-loaded plunger which contacts the cam plate.

Each point on the surface of the cam plate corresponds to a specific position (in train and elevation) of the gun barrel. The complete cam surface is a profile map of the gun's safe and unsafe firing areas in relation to its position on the ship.

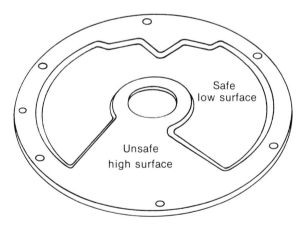

Figure 12–14. *The profile of the cam plate in the firing stop mechanism.*

Recoil and Counterrecoil Systems

Just as a naval gun is secured to the deck so that it can be trained and elevated, some provision for the recoil must be made, or the force of it would tear the mount from its foundation. This is accomplished with recoil brake cylinders and counterrecoil mechanisms.

A recoil brake's primary function is to absorb the force of recoil and "spread" it so that the sudden shock is converted to a thrust exerted over an appreciable distance through which the recoiling parts of the gun are permitted to move. A secondary function of all recoil brakes in naval gun mounts is to bring to a smooth stop the forward movement (counterrecoil) that follows recoil.

The function of a counterrecoil mechanism is to store some of the energy of recoil and use it to force the recoiling parts forward into battery after the projectile has left the gun muzzle.

Recoil and counterrecoil mechanisms are normally designed to work together, Figure 12–15 shows in a general way how the recoil and counterrecoil systems are opposed to each other in their design.

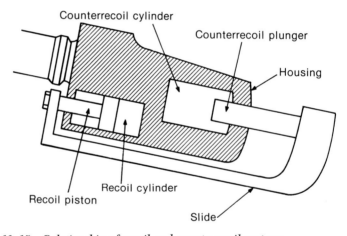

Figure 12–15. Relationship of recoil and counterrecoil systems.

Gun-Positioning Drives

On most mounts, the method of positioning the gun bore axis is by electric or electric-hydraulic power drive. Gun mounts will also have one or more control systems for these elevation and train driven movements—automatic, local, and manual controls. In automatic control, the power drives are under complete remote control from the computer or director. In local control, the power drives are controlled electrically by the mount crew. In some five-inch, electric-hydraulic mounts, the hand control provides the gun crew with the capability

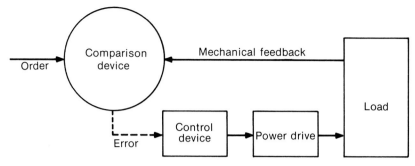

Figure 12–16. Diagram of a simple servo system.

of directly moving the hydraulic elements of the power drive. Furthermore, many mounts can be trained and elevated mechanically by hand wheels, mostly for maintenance or repairs.

Servo Systems

The entire system of devices used to transmit gun orders and to train and elevate the gun itself is called a *servo* system (figure 12–16). The servo system has principal component devices called *synchros* and *power drives*.

Synchros

Synchros are used in servo systems for transmitting gun angle positioning data between remotely located units in a weapon system (figure 12–17). Synchros resemble small electric motors in appearance. They

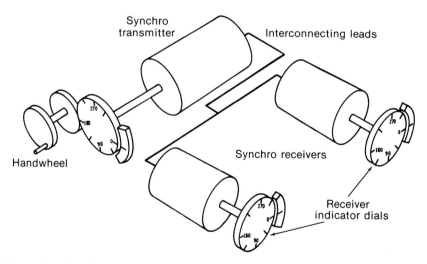

Figure 12–17. The principle of synchro operation.

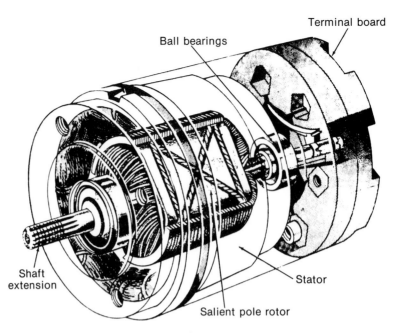

Figure 12–18. Cutaway view of a synchro.

consist of a rotor (R) and a stator (S) (figure 12–18). The letters *R* and *S* are used to identify rotor and stator connections in wiring diagrams and blueprints.

Synchros are, in effect, transformers whose primary-to-secondary coupling may be varied by physically changing the relative orientation of the two windings. This is accomplished by mounting one of the windings so that it is free to rotate inside the other. The inner movable winding is called the rotor (R) and the outer stationary winding is called the stator (S). The windings of the rotor core are stacked together and rigidly mounted on a shaft which contains slip rings. The ends of the coil are connected to these slip rings. Brushes riding on the slip rings provide continuous electrical contact during rotation, and low friction ball bearings permit the shaft to turn easily. The leads coming off the rotor are labeled R1 and R2. The stator consists of three coils wound in internally slotted laminations on which three *Y*-connected coils are wound with their axes 120 degrees apart (figure 12–19). These leads are labeled S1, S2, and S3. When an AC voltage is applied to the rotor leads of the synchro transmitter (R1 and R2), the resultant current produces an AC magnetic field. The lines of force vary in amplitude and direction. They induce voltage by transformer action into the stator coils. The voltage induced in any stator coil depends upon the angular position of that coil's axis to the rotor axis. Synchro

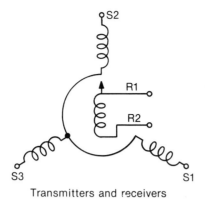

Figure 12-19. The winding of a stator.

receivers are electrically identical to synchro transmitters of the same size.

A simple synchro transmission system consists of a transmitter connected to a receiver as shown in figure 12–20. The transmitter rotor is positioned to a certain bearing. The angle through which the transmitter rotor is mechanically rotated is called a signal. Current immediately flows along the S1, S2, and S3 connections between the transmitter stator and the receiver stator. A torque is developed in the receiver rotor, causing it to attempt to follow through the same angle. When the receiver and the transmitter are in alignment (the same angle), the torque is reduced to zero.

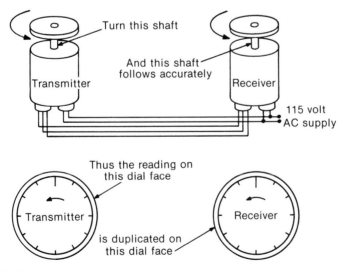

Figure 12–20. A synchro transmission system.

Power Drives

The Navy employs electric-hydraulic power drives to control the movement of heavy gun mounts from the five-inch guns up through the major caliber guns. Smaller guns such as the three-inch will use an emplidyne generator power drive. The desired end result in both kinds of gun drive is to transmit gun order signals promptly to the gun so that the movements of the gun will be synchronized with the signals from the computer or director. Gun order signals are always changing, not only because of changes in the relative position of target and ship, but also because of the roll and pitch of the ship. The problem of transforming gun order signals to mount movements is solved by the power drive portion of the servo system.

Electro-Hydraulic Power Drives The electro-hydraulic transmission consists essentially of a hydraulic pump (*A* end) and hydraulic motor (*B* end) transmission. The hydraulic pump (*A* end) (figure 12–21) is driven at a constant speed by an electric motor. The output pressure of the pump is determined by the angle of the tilt box. The pistons that are connected to the tilt box provide the driving force behind the hydraulic fluid. The hydraulic fluid travels to the *B* end, another motor similar to the *A* end. The fluid under pressure exerts force in the face of the *B* end pistons. Because the *B* end tilt box has a fixed angle, a rotational motion is created. The rotating tilt box thus causes the output shaft of the *B* end to rotate clockwise or counterclockwise. This rotary motion is used to train or elevate a gun mount.

Amplidyne Power Drives The second kind of power drive used in servo systems is called an amplidyne generator (figure 12–22). It

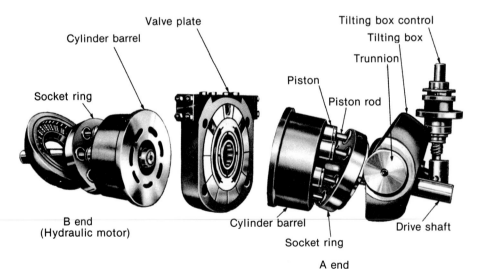

Figure 12–21. Hydraulic pump (exploded view).

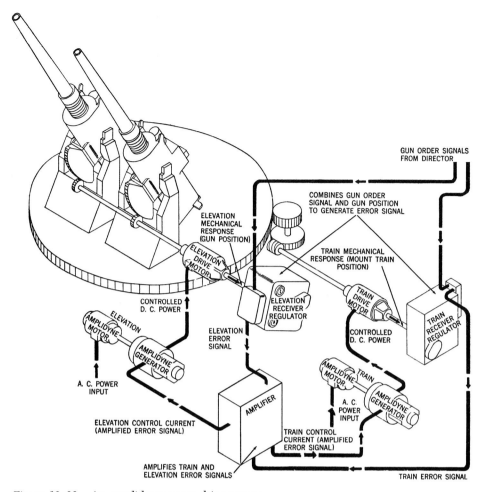

GUN ORDER SIGNALS
FROM DIRECTOR

COMBINES GUN ORDER
SIGNAL AND GUN POSITION
TO GENERATE ERROR SIGNAL

ELEVATION
MECHANICAL
RESPONSE
(GUN POSITION)

ELEVATION
DRIVE
MOTOR

TRAIN MECHANICAL
RESPONSE (MOUNT TRAIN
POSITION)

TRAIN
DRIVE
MOTOR

TRAIN
RECEIVER
REGULATOR

CONTROLLED
D. C. POWER

ELEVATION
RECEIVER
REGULATOR

CONTROLLED
D. C. POWER

AMPLIDYNE
MOTOR

ELEVATION

AMPLIDYNE
GENERATOR

ELEVATION
ERROR
SIGNAL

AMPLIDYNE
MOTOR

TRAIN

AMPLIDYNE
GENERATOR

A. C. POWER
INPUT

AMPLIFIER

A. C.
POWER
INPUT

ELEVATION CONTROL CURRENT
(AMPLIFIED ERROR SIGNAL)

TRAIN CONTROL
CURRENT (AMPLIFIED
ERROR SIGNAL)

AMPLIFIES TRAIN AND
ELEVATION ERROR SIGNALS

TRAIN ERROR SIGNAL

Figure 12-22.   An amplidyne power drive system.

employs both AC and DC motors and an amplidyne generator power
drive system. The control amplifier amplifies the error signal and
converts it from AC to DC to bring current into the field windings
of the amplidyne generator. The amplidyne generator is a power
amplifier on a large scale, capable of multiplying the input error signal
as much as 10,000 times. The output of the amplidyne generator is
applied to the DC drive motor on the mount and turns it in the proper
direction to reduce the original error. The DC drive motors, located
on the mount, train and elevate the gun by means of its gearing. The
direct current to generate the drive motor is supplied by the amplidyne
generator (figure 12–23). The direction in which the motor rotates
depends on the polarity of the output of the amplidyne generator. The
direction of this output, in turn, depends on the direction of the error

Gun Mounts   **181**

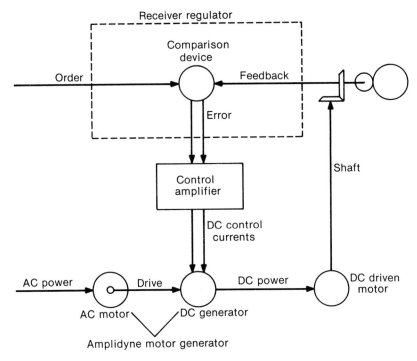

Figure 12-23. Schematic plan of an amplidyne generator.

signal. Consequently, the motor moves the load in the proper direction to reduce the error. As long as there is an order signal present, there will be an error signal. Without an error signal, no power would be supplied to the DC drive motor to move the mount.

Ammunition Transfer Equipment

There are three basic ways in which the ammunition reaches the breech from the magazine (1) entirely by hand, (2) by hand to dredger hoists° and then hand loaded, or (3) by dredger hoists and automatic power loaders.

The Manual Loading Cycle

The ammunition is carried from the magazine (below deck) to ready service lockers in the immediate area of the gun. When the gun is to be fired, the ammunition is taken out of the ready service locker and carried to the gun-loading mechanism. A 3″/50 gun is loaded this way.

° Dredger hoists are so named because of their resemblance to dredger shovel belts.

Dredger Hoists and Manual Loading

The ammunition is carried by hand from the magazine to dredger hoists. The dredger hoists (figure 12–24), which are electric-hydraulic units, pass the ammunition up through the decks to the gun (figure 12–25), and then the ammunition is hand loaded. Fuze setters in the projectile hoists will automatically set time-fuzed projectiles during hoisting. It is important to notice, from a damage control point of view, that the tubes containing hoists only penetrate one deck. A new hoist is installed for each deck through which ammunition must pass from magazine to gun mount. This prevents a fire or explosion from spreading throughout the ship's structure.

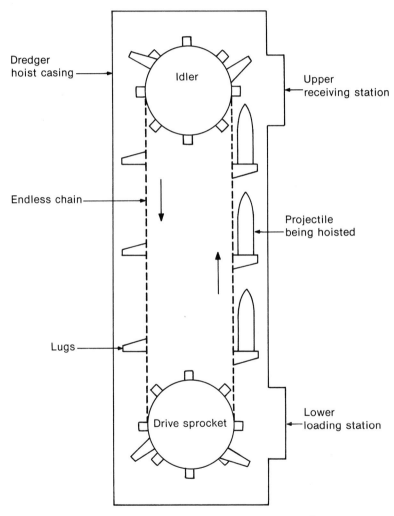

Figure 12–24. Cutaway view of a dredger hoist lifting projectiles.

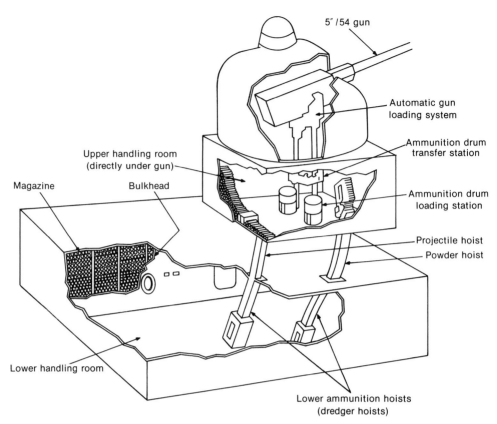

5″/54 gun

Automatic gun
loading system

Ammunition drum
transfer station

Upper handling room
(directly under gun)

Magazine

Bulkhead

Ammunition drum
loading station

Projectile hoist

Powder hoist

Lower handling room

Lower ammunition hoists
(dredger hoists)

Figure 12–25. The magazine stowage and loading installation for a five-inch gun mount.

Dredger Hoists and Automatic Power Loaders

If the magazines are not located near the loader drums of the gun, the ammunition is carried by hand from the magazine to the dredger hoists as in most five-inch mounts (figure 12–25). The ammunition is then taken from the dredger hoists and placed in the loader drums. When the gun is fired, the ammunition is mechanically removed from the drums and conveyed up through the deck where it is rammed into the breech.

Figure 13–1. A new barrel is fitted to one of the USS Taussig's 5″/38 caliber gun mounts.

Gun Barrel Requirements

The gun barrel may be thought of as a tube, designed to withstand a given pressure from within in order to expel the projectile. The gun tube must be made strong enough to withstand the pressures exerted at various points along its length to insure safe operation. The gun bore (internal surface of the tube) must also be of a material that will stand up to the wear and tear of having many projectiles fired through it.

Gun Barrel Stresses

Considering a gun only as a cylinder, the two principal stresses to which such a cylinder is subjected upon firing tend to split the gun open longitudinally and radially. The inertia and the friction of the projectile traveling in the bore cause longitudinal stress (figure 13–2a). Radial stress is set up by the propellant pushing outward from the center against the sides of the bore (figure 13–2b).

Experiments have shown that the greatest stress on the metal of the gun is the tensile stress against its internal circumference by the pressure of powder gases. These experiments have also shown that the longitudinal stress is minimal.

Lame's law concerning radial stresses applies as follows: at any point whatever, in a cylinder under fluid pressure, the sum of the tangential tension and the radial pressure varies inversely as the square of the radius. This law says that in a simple hollow cylinder under internal pressure, the metal close to the gun bore experiences a larger proportion of the stress than the metal at a greater radius. As a result, in a hollow cylinder of homogenous metal, there is a limit beyond which any thickness of wall is of little help in enabling the cylinder to withstand the overall pressure. Therefore, a gun barrel must be built to withstand more internal pressure than is possible with simple cylinder construction. This is accomplished by making the outer layers of metal take a greater proportion of the stress than normal in a common cylinder.

Gun Barrel Construction Methods

Prestressing the gun tube makes it possible for the outer layers of metal in the gun barrel to bear a greater share of the pressure. The two types of gun construction using this principle are the *built-up* construction and the *radially expanded* construction.

The built-up method of prestressing starts by heating steel ring-shaped jackets or hoops to a high temperature. The hoops are then

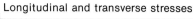

Longitudinal and transverse stresses

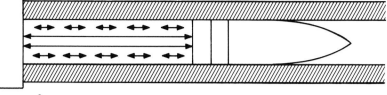

A

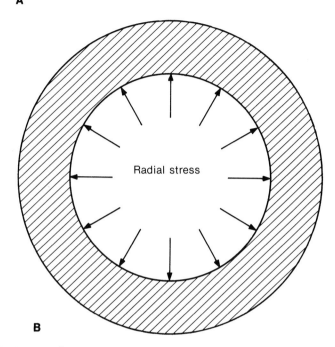

Radial stress

B

Figure 13–2. Gun bore stresses.

slipped over the gun tube and allowed to cool. As the hoops cool, they contract and squeeze the gun tube with a pressure of thousands of pounds per square inch. Guns of over six-inch caliber are usually constructed in this manner.

In the radial-expansion process, a gun forging is first bored to a diameter slightly smaller (about one-half inch) than the caliber desired; then the cold tube is expanded by hydraulic pressure. When the hydraulic pressure is released, the outer layers of the tube tend to return to their original dimensions. The enlarged inner layers tend to remain at their enlarged size. This condition is called *autofrettage*. As a result, the inner layers of metal are severely compressed by the contraction of the outer layers. This provides the same prestressing condition as if a hoop had been shrunk on the gun tube.

Smaller guns of three-inch caliber or less are usually made from a single steel forging with neither radial expansion nor hoops.

Gun Bore Deterioration

The interior surfaces of the gun bore and chamber are "working surfaces" of the gun. As time passes and rounds are fired, these surfaces will work out of proper alignment and will deteriorate. The major causes of deterioration are corrosion, dirt, erosion, constriction, and copper fouling. Maintenance is required to ensure a gun bore's continued usefulness.

Corrosion and Dirt

The burning of the propelling charge produces great heat, great pressure, and complicated chemical changes. Some, but not all, of the propelling powder residue is blown out of the muzzle after the projectile is ejected. The standard procedure to remove the remaining residue is to wash out the bore with a hot soda solution and apply a thin film of oil at the completion of the firing period. The corrosive effect of powder fouling has been reduced by plating gun bores with chromium.

Dirt in a gun bore not only encourages corrosion but also can be a source of danger if it causes sufficient resistance to the passing projectile. A solid plug called a tompion (pronounced *tom-kin*), is inserted into the muzzle opening of the gun when it is not in use to prevent the accidental intrusion of dirt, water spray, or moisture into the bore.

Tompions cannot be used in combat because of the danger of a tompion being accidentally left in a gun bore. If the gun were fired, the nose fuze could be damaged and the escaping gases would expand before the tompion was blown out. In combat, to protect the gun bore from the elements, canvas or plastic muzzle covers are used. In an emergency, the projectile can be fired through such covers without bursting the barrel. It should be remembered that projectiles with supersensitive nose fuzes cannot be fired through any type of muzzle cover.

Erosion

Erosion is the deterioration and wearing away of the bore surface caused by the passage of projectiles through it. The following actions and reactions are recognized as the principal causes of erosion:

As the projectile passes through the bore, the direct effect of friction erodes the surfaces.

The bore surface becomes intensely heated during firing, and the rush of hot gases and residue across this hot metal has a scouring effect.

The hot powder gases react with the metal, which changes the carbon content on the surface of the bore. Since this surface is designed with an optimum carbon content, this change results in a weakening of the metal.

The alteration of intense heat and rapid cooling affects the metal temper.

The propellant gases are forced into and out of the pores in the metal surface as the pores open and close during the rapid expansion and contraction which accompanies such drastic temperature changes.

Heat cracks may develop.

Gases escaping around the projectile in the heat cracks act as high-velocity jets which scour the bore and cause more damage.

Furthermore, erosion is always the greatest at the origin of rifling (figure 13–3), because the rotating band is forced into the rifling at this point and the propellant gases build up there. The tops of the lands also wear away faster than do the bottoms of the grooves. As the lands wear, more gas escapes around the projectile, and the rifling engraves the rotating band less deeply. This reduces both the initial forcing propellant pressure and the resistance of the projectile to the gas pressure. The overall effect is a great drop in projectile velocity at the muzzle.

Remedy for Erosion

All erosion factors are directly related to the expanding gas temperatures and the duration of the hot gases' confinement in the bore. In

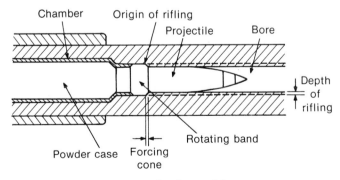

Figure 13–3. Erosion areas in a gun chamber and bore.

larger guns with their slower powders and longer barrels, there is more erosion per round fired than in smaller guns. Smaller guns, however, having a higher firing rate, also have an erosion problem, because there is less cooling time between rounds.

Chromium plating of the gun bore has reduced these effects of erosion to some extent. Also, cooler propellants are under development that will reduce the heat of the propellant gases and thereby aid in erosion control.

Loss of IV

For each class of gun there are data sheets that show the relationship between the enlargement of the bore and the initial velocity to be expected from the gun. These data sheets show this information in the form of plotted curves. If the bore diameter is frequently checked, the velocity loss can be determined. Proper allowance for the current IV can be made for the fire control problem. It can also become apparent when barrels or liners must be replaced.

Measurements of bore enlargements in some minor caliber guns are made at the origin of rifling with a wear gauge. A wear gauge is a truncated cone that can be inserted directly into the breech for the measurement of erosion. Erosion is measured in larger guns at several points in the bore with a star gauge (figure 13–4).

Velocity Loss Estimation

Star gauging is performed in port by highly skilled workers on tenders or at shore-based facilities. When the amount of erosion is measured along the bore, and especially at its origin, the corresponding predicted loss in IV can be included in the fire control solution. There are ordnance publications for each type of naval gun.

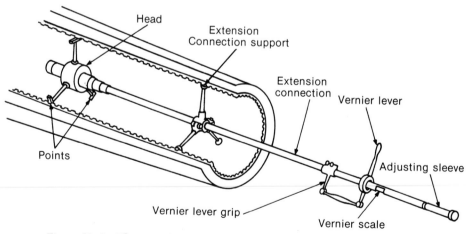

Figure 13–4. The star gauge.

Since star gauging is done in port, and guns are fired at sea, a method is needed to update the corrected IV. This is done by the use of the *Equivalent Service Rounds* (ESR). Immediately upon receipt of the star gauge data at the ship, the data is converted into an ESR for each individual gun bore. The total gun bore ESRs for the battery are then averaged and the applicable ordnance publication is consulted for the correct conversion factors. The resultant IV, once computed, is set into the fire control computer. It should be realized that this IV is only correct until the gun has been fired. As soon as projectiles are fired from the gun, another quantity must be added to the original IV computation. That quantity is called *Pseudo Equivalent Service Rounds* (PESR). The PESR is determined from estimates which are based on the fact that each round fired causes a certain amount of gun bore erosion. It is normal procedure for a projectile that is propelled by a full-service powder charge to be counted as one PESR. Reduced powder charges are equivalent to about one-sixth of a PESR. The PESR is added to ESR for the updated IV computation. The PESRs are kept separately in records so that comparison can be made with the ESR at the time of the next star gauging. This ensures that the PESR is an accurate estimate of the actual gun bore erosion. Without periodic star gauging, the ESR and PESR procedure is not accurate because the PESR quantity does not reflect the rate of fire. It is known that rounds fired with very short cooling intervals between shots cause more erosion than the same number of rounds fired at a slower rate. In practical gunnery this method of estimating has proven to be sufficiently reliable for use at sea.

Figure 13–5. Plug gauge (left) and lapping head (right).

Constriction

When constriction occurs it is more immediately dangerous than corrosion or dirt. Before and after each firing mission, gun barrels must be tested for constriction with a plug gauge (figure 13–5). A plug gauge is a steel cylinder accurately machined to have a slightly smaller diameter than the gun bore. If the plug gauge will not pass through the bore without undue forcing, the constriction must be investigated. The most likely cause is an accumulation of copper. Distortion of the steel surface of the bore can also cause metal constriction. This has been known to occur in some built-up guns. Minor steel constriction can be removed by lapping (filing) and polishing.

Copper Fouling

Copper fouling is basically a form of constriction. The copper rotating band of the projectile leaves a small amount of metallic deposit on the bore, which impedes the projectile and affects the projectile's accuracy. Metallic lead foils have been used in some powders to control this coppering. The lead, when melted with the burning of the propellant charge, serves as a lubricant for the next round, and discourages any new copper deposits. The existing copper deposits are generally removed by the passing projectile. Copper residue can also be removed with an acid treatment. This treatment may not be performed by crew members, but is done during tender or yard periods. The use of a wire bore brush or lapping head (figure 13–5) is the approved mechanical means for decoppering a gun barrel aboard ship. The lapping head is covered with a fine abrasive material and is drawn back and forth through the constriction until the plug gauge can be passed through without forcing it.

14

Propellants

Components of Gun Ammunition

The principal components of any full round of gun ammunition are a *propelling charge* and a *projectile*. The propelling charge develops the thrust that ejects the projectile at the desired velocity from the muzzle (IV). The propelling charge assembly includes a fire ignition system as well as the propellant and the container. The payload or projectile assembly includes the fuze containing a detonator, the booster, and the burster.

Kinds of Charges

In a naval gun, the charge is packed behind the projectile either in bags or in metal cartridge cases. If the propellant is packed in bags, the ammunition is called bag ammunition; if it is packed in a case, it is called case ammunition.

Figure 14-1. Expended cases litter the deck after the propellant has sent the projectile on its way.

Propelling charges or propellants are chemical substances that burn at a given rate rather than detonate. The rate of burning, though rapid compared with the burning of combustible materials (e.g., wood), is much slower than detonation. An important characteristic of any propellant's rate of burning is that, under a given set of conditions, it will always burn at the same rate.

Thrust and Reaction

Propellants, in a liquid state or in solid form, will burn to produce a hot, high-pressure gas that will have two major applications. In the first application, such as in rockets and JATO units, the thrust is developed within the engine as burning gases escape through a nozzle. The second application is indirect and reactive, as in guns and mortars. In these instances a burning gas is enclosed by a tube and, in seeking to escape, develops sufficient propulsive force to eject a projectile from the tube.

Cool Propellant

The term *cool propellant* is used to describe a propellant that burns at a relatively low temperature. This is an advantageous characteristic which increases bore life. It is explained in Chapter 2, "Interior Ballistics."

Practically all propellant units contain two or more types of propellants, arranged so that they function in sequence when the unit is actuated. The action of the series within a propellant unit is called a propellant train (figure 14–2).

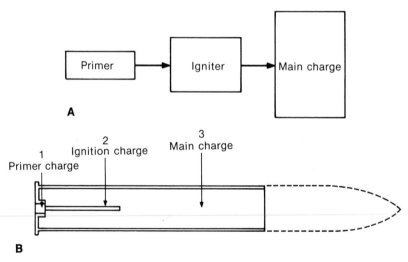

Figure 14–2. The propellant train: (a) concept; (b) location.

Propellant Train

The initiating stage in a propellant train is called a *primer,* and it produces a hot flame which sets off the next stage, called the *igniter.* The igniter in turn sets off the main charge.

Basically, two kinds of chemical reactions account for the functioning of propellants. One is combustion (the combination of oxygen with other atoms or atomic groups) that releases heat and gases. The second type is a molecular breakdown or disintegration (followed by some recombination) of the relatively unstable nitrogren compounds which are the basis of most propellants used by the Navy.

In propellants, much of the energy developed by the reaction comes from internal oxidation; no significant proportion of the oxygen comes from the atmosphere. As an example, in black powder the oxygen comes from potassium or sodium nitrate, which yields oxygen when heated; the oxygen combines with the other two components of the mixture (charcoal and sulfur). In all other propellants, the oxygen is part of the original composition, and it recombines with other elements when the composition breaks up.

Propellant powders are normally ignited by heat. The resulting reaction is a burning process occurring on the exposed surfaces of the substances and progressing through the mass as the grains are consumed.

As stated earlier, the primary function of a propellant is to produce gases under pressure to develop propulsion. The degree of control over the speed of an explosion determines the type of explosive compound that can serve as a propellant.

Powder

There are three main classes of propellant powders: (1) *single-base,* (2) *double-base,* and (3) *multi-* or *triple-base* powders.

In single-base powders, cellulose nitrates (nitrocellulose) form the only ingredient of the propellant powder. Single-base nitrocellulose powders have lower burning temperatures and cause less wear in the gun bore than double-base powders.

Double- and multi-base powders include nitroglycerin to assist in dissolving the nitrocellulose during manufacture and to add to the propellant qualities. Present multi-base powders, with a large proportion of the cool-burning explosive nitroguanidine, produce temperatures close to those of single-base powders.

U.S. Navy guns, larger than small arms, use propellants composed either of a single-base or multi- (triple) base powder. Double-base powders are usually used as rocket and missile propellants.

There are two types of propellant powders in standard Fleet use—

smokeless and flashless. Smokeless powder, used during daylight engagements, keeps the target from being obscured by the firing ship's own smoke. Flashless powder is used at night to hide the firing ship from the target.

Bag and Case Propelling Charges

Naval gun propellants are manufactured in two types: bag and case. The difference lies in the way the charge is assembled. The most common type of naval gun ammunition in service with the Fleet is case ammunition. There are two kinds of case ammunition—semifixed and fixed. Semifixed ammunition is a service round which consists of a projectile and case charge loaded in sequence, and is commonly used in five-, six-, and sometimes eight-inch guns. Fixed ammunition is a service round which is manufactured as a preassembled unit with the case charge fixed to the projectile, and it is stored and loaded as a single unit. Fixed ammunition is commonly employed in three-inch guns and guns of smaller caliber. However, in the largest caliber naval guns, such as some eight-, and all sixteen-inch guns, bag ammunition is required.

Bag Ammunition Propelling Charges

A complete round of bag ammunition as shown in figure 14–3 has three different parts:

> A lock combination primer (so-called because it fits into a firing mechanism called a firing lock and has a combination arrangement which enables it to be initiated either on an electric firing impulse or by percussion).

> Two or more powder bags.

> A projectile.

Large guns must burn large quantities of propellant powder to propel the projectile at the initial velocity required. In an eight-inch

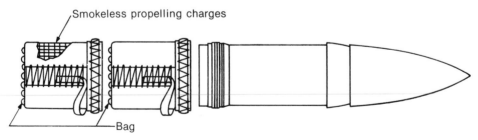

Figure 14–3. Bag ammunition propelling charges.

gun, several hundred pounds of propellant are needed for one full service round. The gun can be loaded in a relatively brief time by dividing the propellant into several silk bags, each of which can be handled by one man. Silk is used because it burns without leaving a smoldering residue.

The use of bag ammunition is restricted to ships in the reserve fleet that carry large caliber guns.

Case Propelling Charges

Gun ammunition which has its propellant charge in a metal case or cartridge instead of a silk bag is called *case* ammunition. Both semifixed and fixed ammunition are of this type. The primer in case ammunition is inserted into the base of the case and is not removed or changed aboard ship.

The designs of various sizes of case ammunition are similar, as may be seen in figure 14–4. The case assemblies are similar except for the seal used for the cartridge case. In fixed ammunition the base of the projectile is the seal, while in semifixed ammunition a plug is used at the open end of the case.

The case is cylindrical but tapers slightly from base to top. It has

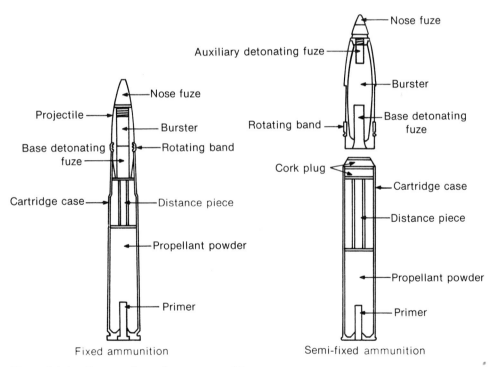

Figure 14–4. Cross sections of case ammunition.

a rim at the base end, like 40mm cases and, depending on the caliber, it may have an annular groove. The groove and the rim at the base are needed to engage the loading mechanisms on guns. Cartridge cases have in the past been made of brass. Steel cartridge cases have now replaced the brass cases in most guns. However, any brass cases, as well as containers and fuze nose plugs, all classed as "retrograde" items, must be retained on board until the ship can return them to a replenishment ship or an ammunition depot to be used again.

Primers

The primer in case propellant ammunition is always secured to the center of the base of the case. Figures 14–5 through 14–7 show the three types of case primers. There are percussion, electrical, and combination primers.

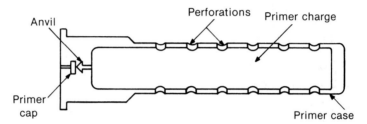

Figure 14–5. *A percussion primer. Perforations allow the ignition charge to ignite the main charge.*

In percussion primers (figure 14–5), the impact of a firing pin on a primer cap imparts a blow to a sensitive initiating mixture located between the cap and a metal anvil. This initiates a burning reaction that ignites the remainder of the primer charge.

In electric primers (figure 14–6), a brief pulse of firing current heats a small bridge wire that ignites the initiating mixture; the flames thus

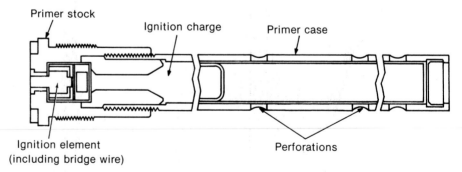

Figure 14–6. *An electric primer.*

produced are transmitted to the ignition charge, which in turn sets off the propelling charge.

The combination primer (figure 14–7) has both a bridge wire and the anvil arrangement; either one can start the reaction. (Electric firing is preferred with combination primer ammunition, because most firing takes place from a remote control station.)

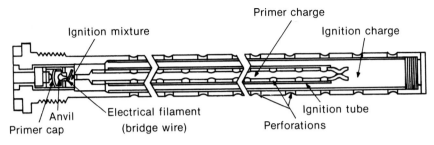

Figure 14–7. A combination primer.

A percussion primer is used when there is no electrical firing circuit. Normally an electrically actuated primer is used to ignite the propellant charges on ships currently in commission. U.S. Navy five-inch guns preceding the 5″/54 caliber Mark 42 can be fired either electrically or with percussion (combination primer). The Mark 42 and later models cannot be fired with percussion because they are basically automatic guns and are not equipped with a percussion circuit. For a description of firing circuits refer to Chapter 12.

Once the ignition charge has caught fire by the action of the primer, the main work-producing propellant charge begins to burn, thus completing the propellant train.

15

Explosives

Introduction

In strictly technical usage, the term *explosive* includes only those substances that *detonate*. This means that when the reaction is initiated, it produces a sharp shock wave that releases all the stored energy almost instantaneously. In this textbook, the term explosive will be used in this sense only.

Explosives are divided into two classes—*primary explosives* and *high explosives*.

Primary explosives are very sensitive to shock and heat. They are therefore used in initiating devices (such as the primers and detonators described in the previous chapter) to set off chemical reactions in less sensitive substances.

High explosives are comparatively insensitive to shock or heat. They are normally detonated by the initiating devices previously mentioned. High explosives may be used as projectile burster charges to damage the target by blast, by heat, or with fragments from the container (the projectile body).

Basic Chemistry of Explosives

Like propellants, explosive substances include a very large number of chemical compounds and mixtures, few of which have characteristics that make them practical for military use. Explosive substances discussed in this section are those used in the Navy.

Most explosives are organic compounds or mixtures of explosive organic compounds based on nitrogen (hence the word "nitro" in the chemical names of most Navy explosives). One explosive, black powder, is a simple mechanical mixture (not a chemical compound) of chemicals which individually are not explosives.* Very few inorganic compounds are used. (Lead azide is an inorganic compound that is used as the sensitive initiator in detonators.)

---

* Ingredients are potassium nitrate, sulfur, and charcoal. Black powder is used variously as an igniter powder or in fuzes as well as in special purpose projectiles as above.

Figure 15–1. Projectiles fired from North Vietnamese coastal batteries straddle the USS St. Paul (CA-73) in 1967. In the exchange, projectiles from the cruiser destroyed one coastal gun and damaged two others.

In high explosives, the important energy source is the breakup of the chemical bonds of the original composition and the recombination of the elements into simpler compounds.

The products of detonation or burning may include the usual products of complete combustion (carbon dioxide, water vapor), products of incomplete combustion (carbon monoxide, free hydrogen), products of molecular breakdown and partial recombination (free nitrogen, oxides of nitrogen, methane, hydrogen cyanide), and unburned residue of the original composition. Some of these products are harmless, some are suffocating, some are combustible or explosive, and some are dangerous poisons even in fairly low concentrations. Since these products are dangerous in enclosed gun mounts, the mounts are fitted with gas-expelling air supplies and fans. If such gases are not promptly expelled, they could ignite while the gun is being reloaded and the breechblock is open, causing a burst of flame into the inside of the mount. This is called a *flareback*.

Characteristics of Explosive Reactions

Velocity

An explosive will differ from a propellant in its reaction speed, depending upon the type and physical state of the substance. For example, the burning rate of colloidal, cellulose nitrate powders, used as propellants, is about 24 centimeters per second. The velocity of the reaction of high explosives will range from 2,000 to 8,500 meters per second.

Heat

A rapid liberation of heat always accompanies an explosive reaction. The amount of this heat represents the energy of the explosive and hence the extent of its ability for doing work.

Gases

Other products of explosive reactions include hot gases and a small amount of solid residue. In gun barrels, propellant gases and solid residue have an erosive effect, contributing significantly to the wear of the gun bore. The effects of such wear on gun performance are detailed in Chapter 2, "Interior Ballistics."

Pressure and Shock Wave

The high pressure accompanying a propellant or explosive reaction is a result of the formation of gases which are expanded by the heat liberated in the reaction. The work which the reaction is capable of performing depends upon the volume of the container, the volume of gases produced, and the amount of heat liberated. The rapidity with which an explosive develops its maximum pressure determines its *brisance*. A brisant explosive attains maximum pressure so rapidly, its shock wave shatters material surrounding it.

Explosive Train

The explosive train (figure 15–2), typically consists of an initiating device called a *detonator*, which contains a relatively small quantity of primary explosives; a *booster*, which contains a larger quantity of less sensitive explosives; and a *burster*, which contains a large quantity of comparatively insensitive explosive. The function of the detonator is, when initiated, to detonate the booster, which in turn detonates the burster. In some devices there are variations on this basic sequence of stages. In small gun projectiles where the explosive train is simpler, the booster is omitted or combined with the initiating device.

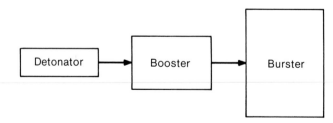

Figure 15–2. The explosive train of a projectile.

Initiation of Explosive Reactions

Explosive reactions are initiated by application of a stimulus. This provides the energy required to get the reaction started.

High explosives normally require the application of a strong shock or detonation to initiate the explosion. This shock or detonation is usually obtained by exploding a smaller charge of a more sensitive high explosive in contact with or in close proximity to the main charge.

The amount of energy necessary to initiate the explosive reaction is the measure of the sensitivity of the explosive. The degree of sensitivity can be important in selecting an explosive for a particular purpose. For example, the explosive in an armor-piercing projectile must be relatively insensitive to the shock of impact or it will detonate before penetration. An explosive with a high sensitivity can be undesirable because minor shocks or temperature variations could initiate the reaction.

Classification of Navy Explosives by Use

High Explosives

A "high" explosive used in bursters will ideally have the following qualities:

Relative insensitivity to shock in handling, gunfire, and impact against armor.

Maximum power.

Good fragmentation characteristics (i.e., ability to break up its warhead into lethal fragments upon detonation).

Low cost of manufacture and handling.

Maximum stability for durability and resistance to such adverse conditions as moisture and heat.

No single high explosive meets all of these requirements, so the Navy uses a number of explosives. The more important ones that will be presented here are TNT, RDX, HBX, tetryl, and Explosive D.

TNT (trinitrotoluene)

This is probably the best known of the high explosives and is made by treating the organic compound toluene with nitric acid. At temperatures below about 170°F, TNT is a crystalline substance that is chemically stable and quite insensitive to shock.

Cast TNT can be used as a bursting charge in gun projectiles (other than armor-piercing), torpedoes, rockets, missile warheads, and mines.

In granulated form it is more sensitive and can be used as a booster in the explosive train.

RDX (cyclonite)

RDX is made by nitration of a complex organic compound. It is substantially more powerful and more sensitive than TNT or Explosive D. In its pure crystalline form it is too sensitive for use as a military explosive. To make it usable, other materials must be added as follows:

Composition A is a semi-plastic combination of RDX and nine per cent wax. This composition is a little more sensitive than Explosive D but is more powerful. It is used as a projectile filler in place of Explosive D.

Composition B is a mixture of about 60 percent RDX, 40 percent TNT, and less than one percent wax. It is used as a projectile and bomb burster charge.

Composition C is a plastic mixture of about 90 percent RDX and ten percent emulsifying oil. It is used as a demolition explosive.

Explosive D (ammonium picric) is a phenolic compound in crystalline powder form, chemically stable up to 150°F, when not exposed to unprotected metal. It is a combination of high power (nearly that of TNT) with sensitivity so low that an armor-piercing projectile containing an Explosive D as a burster can be fired through armor plate without being detonated. It is commonly employed in armor-piercing rounds. Burster cavities in armor-piercing projectiles must be protected by varnish before Explosive D can be loaded.

HBX (high brisant explosive)

This is a mixture of chemicals without a name, and is manufactured in two varieties for naval service—HBX-1 and HBX-3. HBX-1 is a cast explosive, consisting of a mixture of RDX, TNT, aluminum powder, and a desensitizer (mainly wax). Stable, relatively insensitive to impact, and more powerful than TNT, it is used as a rocket and missile head burster. HBX-1 is used in rockets. HBX-3 has a much larger proportion of aluminum powder to increase brisance. It is used in depth bombs and other underwater explosive devices such as torpedo warheads.

Tetryl (tri-nitrophenyl-methyl-nitramine)

Tetryl is produced by nitration of an aniline-based organic compound. It is used as a booster in small gun projectiles (40mm and

3-inch). It is more generally employed as a detonator when mixed with a primary explosive, and it is 30 percent stronger than TNT.

Pyrotechnics

Pyrotechnics are a combination of chemical elements that produce (1) light for illumination, (2) light for signaling, and (3) smoke for signaling.

The Navy uses a large variety of pyrotechnics, but only a few common examples, all used on surface vessels, are given here.

Illumination Service

The illuminating projectile (called a *star shell*) is a bright-burning flare. The flare is conveyed to the desired location within the body of a gun projectile. A timing device (mechanical time fuze) causes the flare to be ejected from the rear of the projectile and ignited. It falls slowly, supported by a parachute.

Signaling Devices

The three pyrotechnic signaling devices used by the Navy are signal lights, Navy lights, and distress signals. Signal lights (often called by their older name of Very lights) are contained within a cartridge that looks like a shotgun shell. They are fired from a special hand-held projector (called a Very pistol) to a height of about 200 feet. At that height red, white, or green "stars," or small flares, ignite and burn for five to seven seconds. The Navy light is a blue or red, hand-held flare, which burns steadily for one to three minutes. The distress (day/night) signal is also a hand-held flare. It is a double-ended flare which from one end produces smoke (orange colored) for daytime use, and from the other end, a bright light for use at night.

Demolition Agents

The last kinds of explosives to be introduced here are demolition agents. Tetrytol, which is a cast mixture of tetryl and TNT, is used in the form of demolition block charges. These explosives are issued and used in specialized demolition equipment for the destruction of obstacles or hazards to navigation, blasting preparatory to construction, or the destruction of enemy targets.

16

Gun Projectiles

Introduction

Having explained gun ammunition and its division into propellants and projectiles, and having reviewed the composition of propellant and explosive charges for naval gun ammunition, we are ready to look at the makeup and individual parts of a projectile.

A projectile is the part of a complete round of service ammunition that is expelled at the highest possible velocity from the gun bore by the burning propelling charge.

Projectiles are cylindrical with pointed noses. Such a shape gives stable ballistic performance to the projectile when it spins about its long axis in flight. The bores of modern guns are rifled so that the projectile will develop this spin as it travels through the bore. The need for imparting a spin to a projectile after it leaves the barrel is explained in Chapter 3, "Exterior Ballistics."

Figure 16–1. North Vietnamese gun projectiles approach a U.S. destroyer.

Projectiles in small weapons often consist of solid metal; projectiles used in larger guns, however, are assemblies of several components. The three essential projectile parts are (1) the metallic body, (2) the fuze which sets off the charge, and (3) the explosive bursting charge.

The solid bullet damages by impact alone. Assembled projectiles inflict damage primarily by the blast of their high-explosive contents and fragmentation. A projectile is cast so its body will break up into many fragments of specific dimensions.

External Features of Projectiles

The external shape of a shell is designed to achieve the desired stability in flight with a minimum resistance to air. The *ogival curve* is the form of the forward end of the projectile which best fulfills these conditions (figure 16–2). In small caliber projectiles, a cone is sometimes used instead, but this part of the projectile is still called the *ogive.*

In back of the ogive the projectile is cylindrical. The cylindrical shape may continue to the base, making a base the same diameter as the rest of the cylinder, or the after portion may be slightly tapered, making it boattailed.

Near the after part of the projectile is the *rotating band;* forward of this is the *bourrelet* (figure 16–2). These two surfaces, slightly larger in diameter than the body, support and steady the projectile in its passage through the bore. In small shells the entire body forward of the rotating band may be finished to bourrelet diameter.

The rotating band, generally made of copper, is actually slightly larger than the bore diameter. Its main functions are to seal the bore,

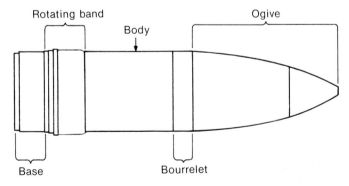

Figure 16–2. *External features of a gun projectile.*

* See glossary.

to position and center the rear end of the projectile, and to engage the rifling grooves in the gun bore to rotate the projectile. New projectiles use plastic in their rotating bands.

Projectile Classifications

All gun projectiles, other than small arms, share the characteristics described above. Projectiles must differ in design, however, because the targets they have to destroy differ in character. There are three general classes of projectiles: penetrating, fragmenting, and special purpose.

Penetrating Projectiles

Penetrating projectiles include *armor-piercing* (AP) *projectiles,* designed to penetrate heavy armor such as a ship's armor, and *common* (COM) *projectiles,* designed to penetrate light armor such as aircraft armor. Explosive D is usually the bursting charge for these penetrating projectiles, because it is insensitive enough to permit penetration without premature detonation.

Figure 16–3 shows the cross section of an armor-piercing projectile. The body has thick walls, a small burster charge cavity, a nose cap, and a thin metal windshield. To be effective, an armor-piercing projectile must keep its burster charge intact until it has penetrated the target. The projectile body of tough steel backs up the hardened, but somewhat brittle, steel nose cap, which is shaped to dig into and cut through a heavy, armor-plated target. The windshield, which collapses upon impact with the target, is screwed onto the blunt nose cap and gives the exterior of the projectile nose a satisfactory ogival shape and improved flight characteristics. The projectile has a delayed fuze to burst after penetration.

In the common projectile, used for lightly armored targets (figure 16–4), the armor-piercing cap is replaced by a hood. The common projectile has a larger burster and thinner walls.

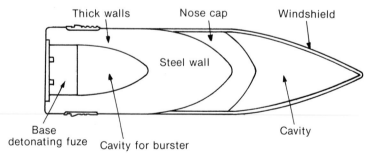

Figure 16–3. A cross section of a projectile for piercing heavy armor.

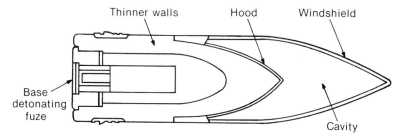

Figure 16–4. A cross section of a common projectile for piercing light armor.

Fragmenting Projectiles

Fragmenting projectiles are designed to damage by blast effect and/or fragmentation. Fragmentation is the breaking up of the projectile walls into high-velocity fragments. These projectiles characteristically have relatively thin walls and large cavities for the burster. There are two kinds of fragmenting gun projectiles—*high capacity* and *antiaircraft.*

High Capacity (HC) Projectiles (figure 16–5) are used against such lightly armored surface targets as torpedo boats, shore objectives, or personnel. Since no penetration ability is required, such explosives as Composition A that are more sensitive than Explosive D may be used as the burster charge.

Antiaircraft (AA) Projectiles (figure 16–6) are designed for use against aircraft in flight. Except for the lack of a base-detonating fuze, the antiaircraft projectiles are substantially the same as high capacity projectiles. In smaller sizes (20mm and 40mm), the explosive contained in the projectile body is often an incendiary element.

Antiaircraft Common (AAC) Projectiles have a dual-purpose design (figure 16–7). They combine the qualities of antiaircraft projectiles

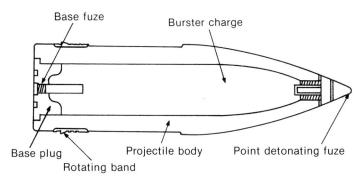

Figure 16–5. A cross section of a high capacity projectile.

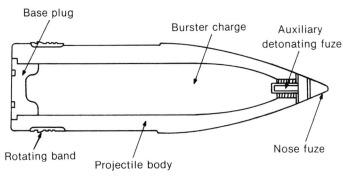

Figure 16–6. A cross section of an antiaircraft projectile.

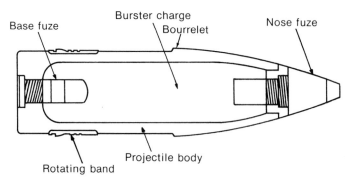

Figure 16–7. A cross section of an antiaircraft common projectile.

with the capability of penetrating steel plating that is not as thick as armor-plate. The type of fuzing will depend on the use, with the mechanical time nose fuze used against unprotected aircraft and personnel, and the base-detonating fuze used against lightly armored surface/land targets. The projectile body walls are heavier than those of the other fragmenting projectiles. The burster charger is usually Explosive D.

Special Purpose Projectiles

The special purpose classification of projectiles includes shells that are not intended to inflict damage by blast or fragmentation. If the projectile body cavity contains any explosive, it is a small charge designed to expel the contents of the projectile. The five common varieties of special purpose projectiles are: *illuminating, smoke, chaff, nonfragmenting,* and *target.*

Illuminating (ILLUM) Projectiles (figure 16–8), often called star shells (SS), contain within the projectile body cavity a bright flare attached to a parachute. At a preset time, the mechanical time fuze ignites a small black-powder charge which expels the flare and parachute back through the projectile base plug. The black-powder charge also ignites the flare. The target is illuminated as the parachute slowly lowers the flare.

Smoke Projectiles (figure 16–9) contain tubes of white phosphorus (WP) within the projectile body cavity. The point-detonating fuze (a nose fuze which detonates upon impact with the target) or mechanical time fuze ignites a small black-powder charge that expels the tubes out the base plug, where upon they scatter and burst. The white phosphorus produces a screening smoke which is useful in such applications as spotting the fall of shot during shore bombardment, and can be used as an incendiary.

Chaff (W) Projectiles (figure 16–10) contain metal foil strips within the projectile body cavity. (The letter *W* stands for window, the former name for this special purpose projectile.) The mechanical time fuze ignites a small black-powder charge which expels the metal

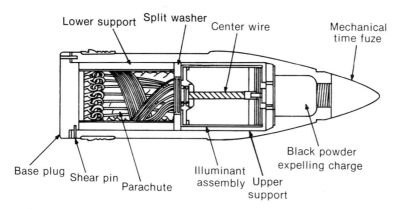

Figure 16–8. *A cross section of an illuminating projectile.*

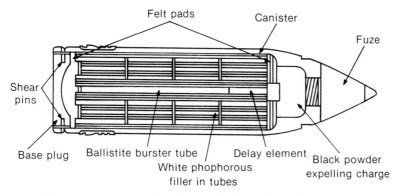

Figure 16–9. *A cross section of a smoke (white phosphorous) projectile.*

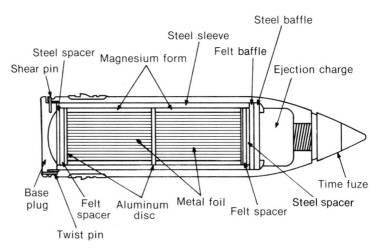

Figure 16-10. A cross section of a chaff projectile.

foil strips high into the air. The foil strips confuse enemy radar by causing false echoes that look like targets on a radar scope.

Nonfragmenting ("Nonfrag") Projectiles are commonly used for antiaircraft gun practice. They contain chemicals which produce various colors of smoke, making observable bursts without destroying the target.

Target or *Blind-loaded (BL) Projectiles* contain sand or other inert substances to simulate the weight and balance characteristics of burster charges. They are used for gun practice against surface targets.

Lightweight, Subcaliber, and Rocket-Assisted Projectiles

This is a group of projectiles designed to achieve a higher speed or a longer range than is possible with standard equipment. Higher speed is desirable in antiaircraft fire, while longer range is desirable in surface action. Some of these projectiles can be, or are designed to be, fired from special guns called hypervelocity guns.

In hypervelocity guns, a higher muzzle velocity is obtained by using lightweight or subcaliber projectiles, which effectively reduce the amount of propellant required. This requires less gun bore strength, thereby reducing the weight of the gun for the equivalent velocity. Alternatively, higher muzzle velocity can also be obtained by increasing the propellant gas pressure (force) applied to the projectile, but this has the disadvantage of requiring greater gun bore strength, hence more weight. Of the various means tried to achieve higher muzzle velocities, the following ideas have proven to be the most practical.

Lightweight Projectiles

By firing a lightweight projectile from a conventional gun, the projectile muzzle velocity can be greatly increased. This type of projectile is useful only at short ranges. It is greatly affected by air resistance, because of its light weight. It has a further limitation in the smaller payload it can carry compared with a conventional round of the same caliber. The considerations of ballistic factors, such as mass and air resistance are explained in Chapter 3, "Exterior Ballistics." Each advantage gained in velocity must be weighed against disadvantages in size and range. In general, higher velocities sacrifice range and payload. The following formula governs: Force = Mass × Acceleration (deceleration).

Subcaliber Projectiles

When using a projectile smaller in caliber than the bore of the gun, the weight and the air resistance encountered during the projectile's flight are reduced; thus, a higher muzzle velocity acts to increase the speed and range of the round. In order to seat a subcaliber projectile firmly in the gun and guide it through the barrel, the projectile is fitted with a lightweight bushing which is called a *sabot* (figure 16–11). The sabot falls away from the projectile after the projectile leaves the muzzle. The disadvantage of this projectile is the danger which the falling sabot presents to any friendly forces that might be in the vicinity of the projectile flight.

To obtain the high muzzle velocity advantages of a subcaliber projectile without endangering friendly forces, guns with tapered bores have been used (figure 16–12). The projectile is fitted with skirts (flanges) which act as a gas seal, preventing the propellant gases from going around the projectile.

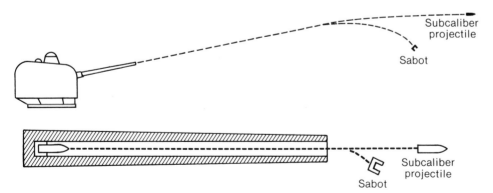

Figure 16–11. Subcaliber projectile and sabot being fired from a conventional gun.

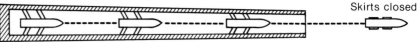

Figure 16–12. *A skirted projectile being fired from a gun with a tapered bore.*

Rocket-Assisted Projectiles

Another method of achieving higher projectile velocities and ranges is through the use of an additional propelling charge contained in the projectile, with the rocket action being initiated during flight (figure 16–13). Although higher velocities and greater ranges are achieved, the destructive potential of the projectile must be decreased, because part of the payload has to be eliminated to make room for rocket propellant. Rocket-assisted projectiles (RAP) have the advantage of needing lighter gun barrels and mounts. RAP projectiles fired from 8-inch guns have increased the range of such guns by an average of 33 percent.*

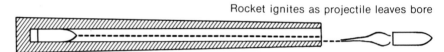

Figure 16–13. *A rocket-assisted projectile being fired from a conventional gun.*

All of the projectiles mentioned, except lightweight and subcaliber projectiles, are available to the weapons officer either as a part of the ship's ammunition allowance or from the ordnance depots. These projectiles cannot be guided once they leave the gun barrel.

Terminal Guided Projectiles

A new projectile, still under development at the time of writing, can guide itself toward a target in the terminal part of its flight as it approaches the target area. The terminal guidance projectile can be shot through a standard gun bore (figure 16–14). The rotating band is free to turn during firing as it engages the rifling so the projectile does not spin. It carries stabilizing fins in the back of the projectile, which unfold after the projectile leaves the barrel (figure 16–15), providing stabilization instead of the spin imparted by the rifling of the bore. The fins are also needed to provide the control surfaces for the guidance system, which will alter the flight path to hit the target. Several types of guidance systems with internal power supplies can

* See report of trial in 1970 on the *St. Paul* (CA 73) in *Les Flottes de Combats*, 1971.

be used in the projectile. Some are active and some passive. An active system might radiate electromagnetic energy such as a laser beam, and steer toward the echo. A passive system might include an infrared homing system or one that homes on the electromagnetic radiation of the target. The projectile will be able to carry the same payload as a normal round.

The projectile may use rocket-assisted propulsion, or it may not. Generally the projectile would alter its course during free fall at the end of its trajectory, steering like a glide bomb toward the target. The projectile would not be able to significantly alter its flight path as would a missile, because it would not be powered at the end of its flight. However, it would have the advantage of being placed very close to the target by the gun fire control system. Because the projectile has a greater mass for the same payload, it would be limited by increased air drag. Unless RAP were employed, this would result in shorter range compared with a standard round.

The introduction of this system, coupled with RAP in the Fleet, could give the naval gun the same ability to fire at targets over the horizon that some surface-to-surface missiles now have. It would be an extremely difficult gun system for an enemy to foil.

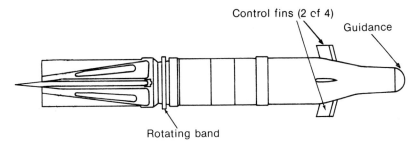

Figure 16–14. *A terminally guided projectile with the stabilizing fins folded.*

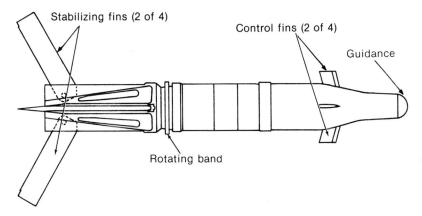

Figure 16–15. *A terminally guided projectile with its stabilizing fins extended.*

17

Fuzes

Introduction

Once a projectile has reached its target, a device is required to set off its burster charge. Some of these devices, called *fuzes*, are quite simple. Some are remarkably complex.

A projectile fuze is a mechanical or electronic device which will detonate or ignite the explosive train in a projectile. Detonating fuzes contain within themselves a high-explosive charge sufficient to set off a high-order explosion in the burster. Ignition fuzes contain sufficient powder to ignite the burster charge in small projectiles. In larger projectiles, ignition fuzes function indirectly through an auxiliary detonating fuze which is normally located directly behind the nose fuze.

Fuzes are classified according to their function (impact, time, auxiliary, or proximity), the position of the fuze in the projectile (nose or base), the mechanism or principle (mechanical or variable time), and specific action at time of functioning or initiation (ignition or detonation). Figure 17–1 illustrates locations of typical fuzes.

A fuze is said to be armed when it is set to permit initiation of the explosive train. It is unarmed when set to prevent initiation.

A satisfactory fuze must be safe to handle; that is, the fuze must not arm if dropped or jarred, and it should remain unarmed after firing until it is at a safe distance from the gun bore. A fuze with these

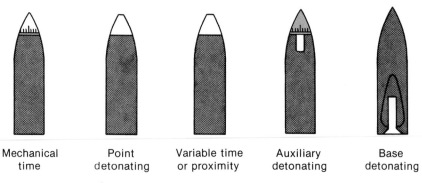

| Mechanical time | Point detonating | Variable time or proximity | Auxiliary detonating | Base detonating |

Figure 17–1. Fuze locations.

characteristics is said to be *boresafe*. A satisfactory fuze must also be dependable; it should initiate the explosive train at the proper instant.

Forces that Arm Fuzes

From the instant of firing until it strikes its target, a projectile and its components are subjected to five forces which can be used to move a fuze's mechanism. Many fuzes use more than one of these forces.

Setback

When the propelling charge is fired, the projectile is accelerated forward and twisted clockwise (as seen from the base). Because of their inertia, movable parts of the projectile consequently develop, during the period of projectile acceleration and twist, a rearward force called *setback* (figure 17–2), and a rotational force or torque in the counter-clockwise direction (i.e., in the direction opposite to the twist). This torque is called *angular setback*, because the net effect of both forces is a movement by the movable part at an angle to an imaginary fore-and-aft axis.

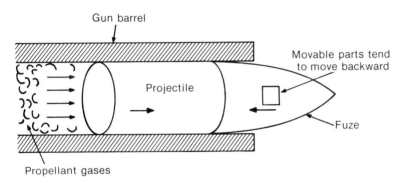

Figure 17–2. Setback.

Centrifugal Force

Newton's laws of motion say that any moving particles tend to keep moving in a straight line. Consequently, because of its inertia, a revolving particle develops a radial thrust (*centrifugal force*) away from the center of revolution. As shown in figure 17–3, the fuze parts therefore develop a continuous outward thrust from the rotating projectile's centerline as long as the projectile is spinning in flight.

Creep

While the projectile is in flight, it is gradually slowed by air resistance acting on its exterior surface. Since the parts inside the projectile

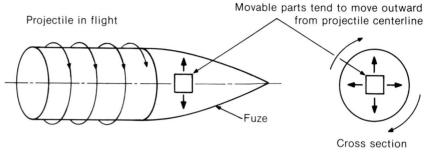

Figure 17–3. Centrifugal force.

are not in contact with the air and do not meet this resistance, the projectile's internal parts tend to continue in motion at the same velocity. Thus, as illustrated in figure 17–4, they exert a continuous forward thrust, called *creep*.

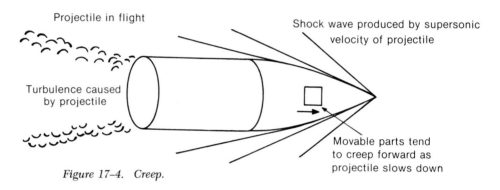

Figure 17–4. Creep.

Impact

When a projectile strikes, its internal parts (figure 17–5) tend to continue moving forward, developing considerable force.

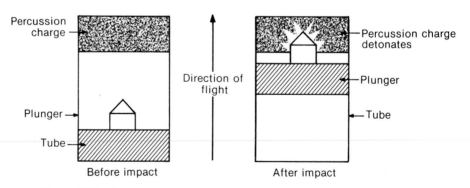

Figure 17–5. Impact.

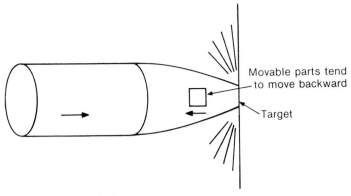

Movable parts tend to move backward

Target

Figure 17–6. Contact with the target.

Target Contact

When a firing plunger or other part of a projectile contacts the target, it is driven toward the rear of the projectile (figure 17–6).

Types and Applications of Fuzes

Nose Fuzes

Mechanical Time Fuzes (MTF) contain a gear train and an escapement mechanism which start to operate immediately after the inertial force of setback has ceased. Centrifugal force acting on weights, with or without the aid of coiled springs, supplies the energy to run the clock mechanism.

After the predetermined interval has elapsed, which was set into the fuze by the loading mechanism just before firing, a spring-loaded firing pin is released and strikes the initial element of the fuze explosive train. Mechanical time fuzes are used in high explosive, illuminating, and various other special purpose projectiles. When used in high explosive projectiles, these fuzes work in conjunction with auxiliary detonating fuzes.

Point Detonating Fuzes (PDF) are placed in the projectile nose in an unarmed position. In this unarmed condition (figure 17–7a), the fuze explosive train is separated by a mechanical stop, called an *interrupter*. The interrupter prevents an accidental detonation of the primer in the fuze nose from igniting the other fuze explosives, and the warhead, by protecting the relay detonator from the primer's flash. When the round is fired, the interrupter is locked clear of the explosive train by centrifugal force (figure 17–7b) and the fuze is armed. Point detonating fuzes are designed to function on target contact. They have the advantage of acting faster on impact than base detonating fuzes.

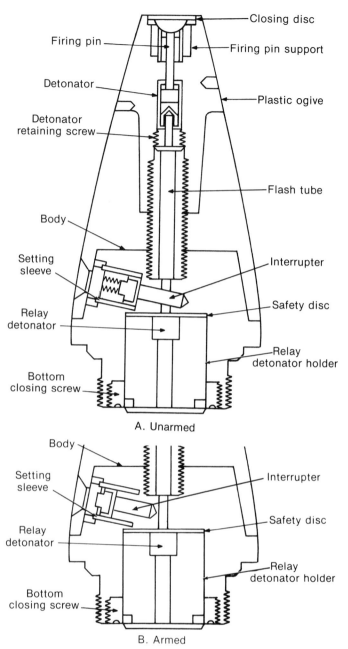

Figure 17–7. Cross section of a point detonating fuze: (a) unarmed; (b) armed.

Point detonating fuzes might be used in place of mechanical time fuzes for such firing missions as short bombardment with either high capacity, fragmenting, antiaircraft common, or white phosphorus smoke projectiles. There are also applications for these fuzes in projectiles fired against enemy ships.

Proximity Fuzes (VTF) are designed to detonate a projectile in flight at the position which will bring about the greatest damage to the target. The target may be metal, water, ground, or any other substance that will reflect electromagnetic waves. Proximity fuzes are most commonly found in antiaircraft projectiles. Essentially, the VT fuze is a rugged sending-and-receiving station containing mechanical and electronic devices (figure 17–8). When the projectile is fired from a gun, setback and centrifugal forces activate the fuze; that is, they release the safety devices and release and distribute an electrolyte to a battery. The battery becomes the source of electrical power for the fuze so the firing condenser can receive a charge and the transmitter

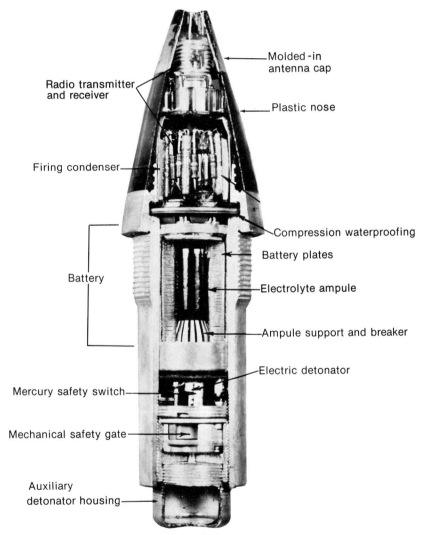

Figure 17–8. Cross section of a typical radio proximity fuze (variable time fuze).

can send out electromagnetic waves. When the firing condenser has been fully charged and the various safety devices have been released, the VT fuze is fully armed. The transmitter continues to send out electromagnetic waves which, when they strike a target, are reflected back to the fuze. When the projectile is close to the target, these impulses reach the required amplitude and trigger a switch which closes the electrical firing circuit. The firing condenser is discharged through an electric detonator. The latter detonates the auxiliary detonating fuze which, in turn, detonates the main charge of the projectile.

The Controlled Variable Time Fuze (CVT) the most recent improvement to the proximity fuze, has an adjustable delay before becoming active. This allows the weapons officer to choose the time at which he wants the projectile to arm and the radar to begin radiating. For example, if a ship were firing over other ships, the arming would be delayed until the projectile was well past friendly ships.

The proximity fuze is an important fuze to be familiar with, because it has wide application in the employment of ordnance.

The Auxiliary Detonating Fuze (ADF) completes the proximity fuze assembly and is discussed in general terms for all nose fuzes in the following paragraphs.

Auxiliary detonating fuzes (ADF) are inserted into the projectile in the unarmed position (figure 17–9a) and remain so until acted upon by the centrifugal force developed by the spinning projectile in flight. Centrifugal force causes withdrawal of detents° and movement of the rotor to align the explosive train. When armed (figure 17–9b), the auxiliary detonating fuze will allow the detonation of the main charge of the projectile instantaneously after the nose fuze has functioned. This fuze is intended to assure safety in handling and stowage, and to prevent detonation of the booster or the main burster charges in the event that the nose fuze functions prematurely. Because the detents are not withdrawn when the round is stowed, the primary fuze cannot set off the auxiliary. The round must be spinning before the auxiliary fuze can function. Auxiliary fuzes are used in combination with all types of nose fuzes in three-inch and larger caliber projectiles, except in special purpose rounds.

The Base Detonating Fuze

As in the auxiliary detonating fuze, arming of the base detonating fuze (BDF) is accomplished by the action of centrifugal force on the detents. The detents act as barriers between the firing pin and the

° Detents are interrupters, literally defined as mechanisms that unlock.

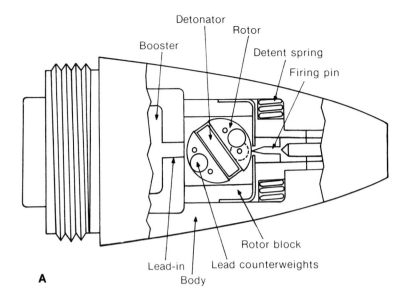

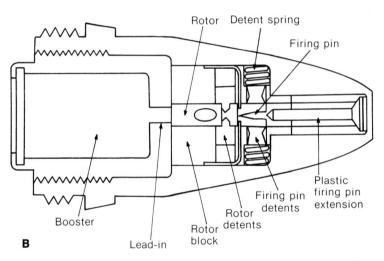

Figure 17–9. Cross section of an auxiliary detonating fuze: (a) unarmed; (b) armed.

initial element of the explosive train. An anticreep spring retains the detonator plunger in a safe position by counteracting the creep force resulting from projectile deceleration. The inertial force created by impact overcomes the resistance of the anticreep spring and causes the detonator plunger to move forward. The initiating element (sensitive percussion primer) strikes the firing pin, thereby initiating the explosive train of the fuze. All base detonating fuzes function on

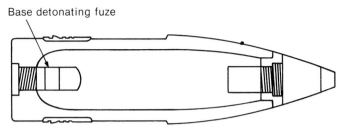

Base detonating fuze

Figure 17–10.   The base detonating fuze.

impact; some, however, have a delay time (0.02 to 0.033 second) after the projectile hits, to allow time for armor penetration. Base detonating fuzes are used alone in armor-piercing (AP and COM) projectiles (figure 17–10), and in combination with nose fuzes in such dual-purpose projectiles as AAC and HC. In the last variety, their functioning is completely independent of the nose and auxiliary fuzes.

18

The Intermediate Caliber Gun:
The 5"/54 Mk 42 Mod 10 Gun Mount

Figure 18–1. A 5"/54 caliber Mark 42 gun fires a routine naval gun fire support mission off the coast of Vietnam on board the USS Davis (DD-937).

Introduction

The 5-inch 54 caliber Mark 42 (5"/54 Mk 42, as it is written in abbreviated form) is rapidly becoming the most common naval gun in the Fleet today. The gun mount is a shielded, dual-purpose (antiair and antisurface), single-gun mount with an automatic firing rate of approximately 35 rounds per minute. The gun is trained and elevated (laid) by separate electrically controlled, hydraulically operated power drives. Ammunition is served to the gun by an automatic, dual-hoist gun loading system, which is hydraulically powered and electrically controlled. The 5″/54 gun mount is the most representative of current five-inch gun technology and capabilities; therefore this chapter will discuss it rather than the older and less complex 5″/38, which is still in service in some ships.

TABLE 18–1

Comparison of Mount Characteristics

Characteristic	5″/54 Mk 42 Mod 10	5″/54 Mk 45 Mod 0	5″/38 Twin Mk 32 Mod 2
Mount weight	139,000 lb.	47,820 lb.	117,000 lb.
Train limits	720°	350°	300°
Elevation and depression limits	−15°,+85°	−15°,+65°	−15°,+85°
Train velocity	40°/sec.	30°/sec.	25°/sec.
Elevation velocity	25°/sec.	20°/sec.	15°/sec.
Projectile weight	70 lb.	70 lb.	55 lb.
Initial velocity of projectile	2650 ft./sec.	2650 ft./sec.	2600 ft./sec.
Rate of fire (rounds/minute)	40 min.	15 min.	18–20 min.
Ready service rounds	40	20	0
Automatic loading	yes	yes	no
Personnel required	12	5	26
Personnel required on mount	2	0	13
ABC protection for gun crew	fair	good	poor
Regunning time	1 hr.	1 hr.	8 hr./gun
Automatic exercise	yes	yes	no
Solid-state logic	yes	yes	no
Misfired round removal	manual	automatic	manual
Target capability	antiship, shore bombardment, and anti-aircraft	antiship, shore bombardment, and anti-aircraft	antiship, shore bombardment, and anti-aircraft
Horizontal range	25,909 yds.	25,909 yds.	18,200 yds.

Table 18–1 shows the comparative characteristics of each of the three 5-inch U.S. Naval guns currently in service. The Mark 45 is briefly described at the end of this chapter.

The gun mount is composed of three basic systems: the gun mount structural system, the gun loading system and the gun laying system. These basic systems are supported by several auxiliary systems—the electrical power, heating, lighting, firing circuit, communication, and ventilation systems.

Gun Mount Structural System

The gun mount structural system provides physical support for and encloses most mount system components. This system consists of two major subsystems—the gun assembly subsystem and the mount structural subsystem.

Gun Assembly Subsystem

The gun assembly subsystem is composed of the slide, fuze setters, rammer, empty case ejector assembly, housing, breech mechanism, recoil and counterrecoil systems, gas ejector and gun barrel.

Slide

The slide (figure 18–2) is the framework that supports the parts of the gun assembly that move in elevation. The gun trunnions are welded to the outboard sides of the slide and allow the slide structure to rotate in elevation. The three main parts it supports are the gun barrel, the breechblock and the housing, which moves in recoil and counterrecoil.

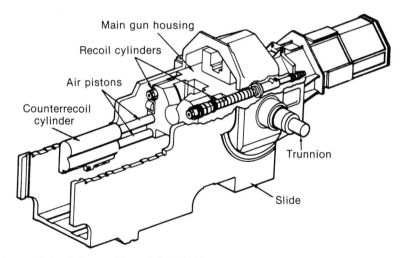

Figure 18–2. Subassemblies of the 5″/54 mount.

The Intermediate Caliber Gun: The 5″/54 Mk 42 Mod 10 Gun Mount   **227**

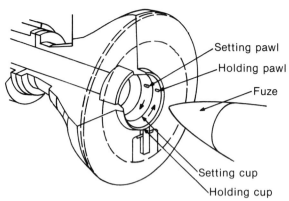

Setting pawl
Holding pawl
Fuze
Setting cup
Holding cup

Figure 18–3. Fuze (pot) setter.

Fuze Setters

When projectiles with mechanical time fuzes are being used, fuzes are automatically set by electrically controlled and hydraulically operated fuze-setting equipment mounted on the left and right sides of the gun slide structure. These fuze setters (pots) will extend to set the fuze on the projectile as ordered by the fire control computer and retract when the projectile is to be lowered and rammed into the gun bore (figure 18–3).

Rammer

The rammer is the last part of the gun assembly subsystem to control movement of ammunition. When either of the two transfer trays lowers a round into position in line with the bore of the gun, the rammer rams the round into the breech. As the breechblock closes, it pushes the rammer spade up to its latched position. In this position, the spade clears the top of the empty case tray during retract stroke. When the gun fires, recoil initiates the rammer retract stroke, and the spade retracts to its starting position.

Empty Case Ejector Assembly

After the gun has fired, recoil and extractor action move the empty powder case backward into the empty case tray. When either transfer tray lowers into the ramming position, the empty case tray is lowered, and the empty case is ejected through an open port in the forward part of the gun shield by an ejector, which moves forward with the rammer and starts a new cycle.

Housing

The housing is located and supported in the slide by six sets of roller bearings. These rollers (slide bearings) permit the gun housing, less the empty case ejector, to move forward and backward in the slide during recoil and counterrecoil. The gun barrel is attached to the housing with the interrupted-screw, bayonet fitting, which is secured by a locking key. The vertically sliding, wedge breechblock is attached to the housing at the breech end of the gun barrel.

Breech Mechanism

The breech mechanism is composed of a vertically sliding wedge breechblock*, a firing lock, extractors, and a breechblock mechanism.

The Breechblock

The breechblock (figure 18–4) is a rectangular, machined, steel block that moves vertically in forward sloping guide ways at the rear of the

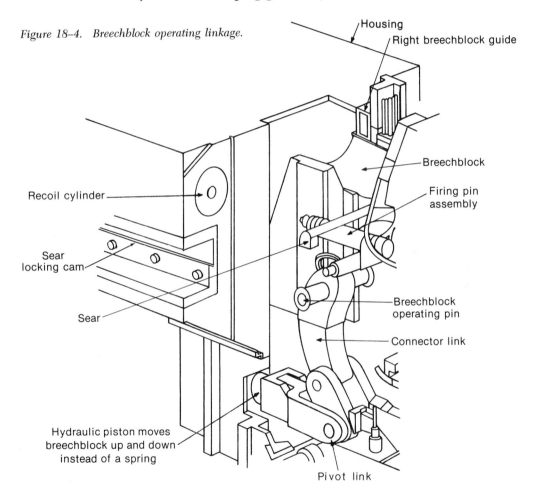

Figure 18–4. Breechblock operating linkage.

Housing

Right breechblock guide

Breechblock

Recoil cylinder

Firing pin assembly

Sear locking cam

Breechblock operating pin

Sear

Connector link

Hydraulic piston moves breechblock up and down instead of a spring

Pivot link

---

* So named because when the block slides up to close the breech, it wedges the round in the chamber.

housing. The forward face of the breechblock is also machined at an angle. Guides cause the block to move slightly forward as it rises to close. This action seals the chamber of the gun bore to ensure that no burning powder gases escape.

The Firing Pin

The firing pin fits into a cylindrical hole in the breechblock. It permits electrical or percussion firing of the propellant charge. When the breechblock starts to lower after a round is fired, the firing pin is pushed to the rear by a cocking bar. This action compresses the firing pin spring and holds the entire mechanism under tension. When the breechblock rises to close, the cocking bar is pulled away from the firing pin. This allows the contact spring to move the firing pin forward to the powder case primer. A smaller contact spring ensures positive contact between the firing pin and powder case primer. Electrical insulators and separators protect the firing pin against grounding.

The Extractor

This mechanism is mounted on top and at the rear of the gun housing. It consists of two extractor arms that extend down the breech face. When a round of ammunition is rammed into the breech, the extractor fingers are caught by the rim of the powder case. The face of the breechblock and gun breech both have recesses to prevent the extractors from interfering with breechblock movement. When the breechblock is lowered, the extractor fingers are forced backward by cams and levers and move the empty powder case out of the gun chamber into the empty case tray.

The Breechblock Operating Mechanism

This mechanism raises and lowers the breechblock by hydraulic pressure. Just before the rammer has completed its forward ramming motion, the rammer trips a hydraulic valve linkage that initiates the breechblock rising cycle. Hydraulic pressure is now applied against a mechanical linkage which causes the breechblock to rise. A breechblock lowering cycle starts when the housing moves backward in recoil. A camming surface on the slide causes a shift in hydraulic pressure which is applied to the other side of the mechanical linkage. This forces the breechblock down. As recoil ends and counterrecoil begins, the extractors function to extract the empty powder case. After the empty powder case has been extracted, the extractors retract into the face of the breech. The breechblock may be raised and lowered manually under power or with a hydraulic hand pump.

The Recoil and Counterrecoil Systems

As explained in an earlier chapter, this system absorbs the shock of the rearward moving housing assembly when the gun is fired, and then it returns the assembly to battery (figure 18–5).

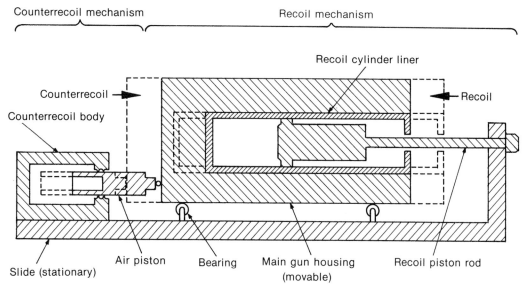

Figure 18–5. The recoil and counterrecoil system.

The main components of the recoil system are two recoil cylinders and two recoil pistons. The recoil cylinders are located inside the housing, one on the left and one on the right. The recoil pistons are attached to the slide and are placed inside the recoil cylinders. The pistons do not move during recoil or counterrecoil since the slide does not move. Each recoil cylinder contains recoil fluid, a solution of 80 percent water and 20 percent glycerin. Three longitudinal grooves on the inside surface of the cylinders taper toward the forward part of the cylinder and, in conjunction with the recoil fluid and pistons in the cylinder, hydraulically decelerate the gun housing.

The main components of the counterrecoil system are two air chambers and two air pistons. The air pistons are attached to and located on the left side of the housing and the air cylinders are located on the left side of the slide. The air pistons move with the housing during recoil or counterrecoil. During recoil, air in the air cylinders is compressed by the recoil pistons. At the completion of housing recoil, the force of the now compressed air is applied against the air piston to force the housing back in battery and hold it there until the gun is fired again.

The Gas Ejector Assembly

This assembly blasts compressed air into the breech of the gun when the breechblock lowers. This action expells hot propellant gases out through the barrel to prevent the gases from filling the gun house.

Gun Mount Structural Subsystem

The gun mount structural subsystem is composed of the stand, carriage, shield, and associated components. This subsystem was discussed earlier.

Gun Laying System

The gun mount laying system consists of the train and elevation subsystem. Each of these subsystems is electrically controlled and hydraulically operated to position the gun in response to gun train order and gun elevation order. The mount is normally operated in remote (automatic) control, gun orders being received from the fire control computer. In local control the gun is trained and elevated in response to the one-man control unit located in the gun mount and operated by the local control man.

Gun Mount Loading System

The gun mount loading system extends upward through the ship from the ammunition handling room (in the magazine) to the gun mount. The loading system consists of a lower gun loading subsystem and an upper gun loading subsystem that automatically serve rounds of semifixed ammunition to the gun breech from both sides of the slide (figure 18–6). All units of the loading system are electrically controlled and hydraulically operated.

Lower Gun Loading Subsystem

The lower gun loading subsystem consists of two loader drums, two lower hoists, hydraulic power units and control equipment necessary for their operation (figure 18–7). This portion of the gun mount loading system is stationary and does not rotate with the gun mount.

Ammunition Loaders

Two identical ammunition drums, located in the handling room and filled by members of the gun serving crew, supply an assembled round of ammunition to the lower hoists. Each loader operates independently of the other. A-loader supplies the C-lower hoist and B-loader supplies the D-lower hoists. Projectiles are loaded by hand through a projectile loading door into a cavity in the top portion of each loader drum.

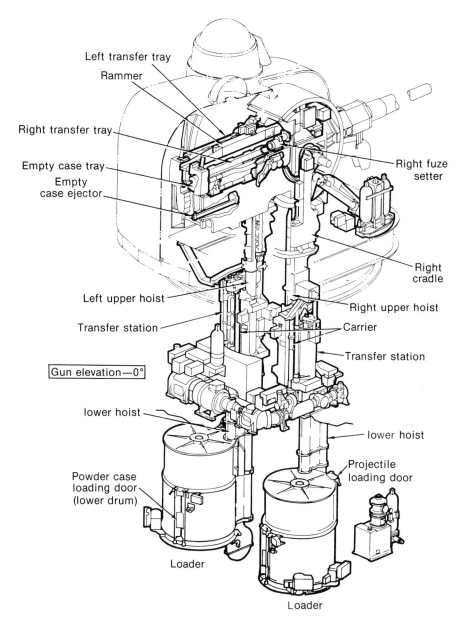

Left transfer tray
Rammer
Right transfer tray
Empty case tray
Empty case ejector
Right fuze setter
Right cradle
Left upper hoist
Right upper hoist
Transfer station
Carrier
Gun elevation—0°
Transfer station
lower hoist
lower hoist
Projectile loading door
Powder case loading door (lower drum)
Loader
Loader

Figure 18–6. The automatic gun-loading system.

Propellant charges are also manually loaded into a cavity in the bottom portion through a powder case loading door. Each loader drum will hold 20 complete rounds of ammunition (20 projectiles and 20 powder cases). The loader drums are rotated one cavity (step) at a time either manually or automatically, transferring a complete round into the lower hoist.

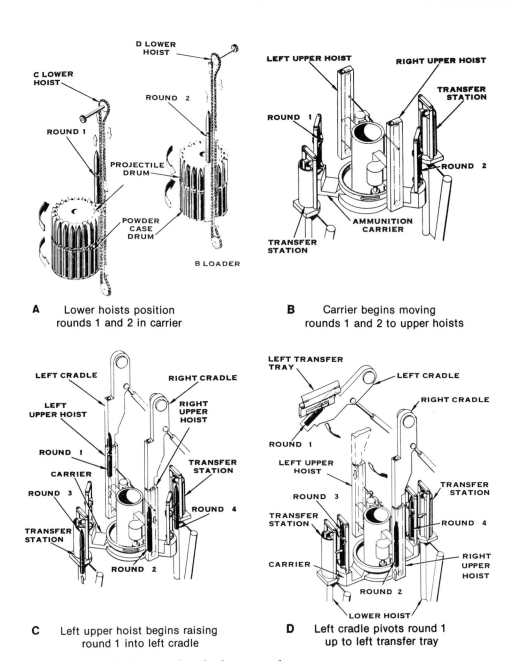

A   Lower hoists position rounds 1 and 2 in carrier

B   Carrier begins moving rounds 1 and 2 to upper hoists

C   Left upper hoist begins raising round 1 into left cradle

D   Left cradle pivots round 1 up to left transfer tray

Figure 18–7. Steps from loader to transfer tray.

Lower hoist

The lower hoists, C and D, move complete rounds of ammunition from the loader drums to the transfer station at the top of the hoist on the carrier deck. Ammunition is moved up through the hoist by lift pawls attached to an endless chain. The chain is synchronized with other gun loading components. Both hoists are used in automatic operation; however if one hoist is damaged or fails to operate, it can be cut out of the gun loading system. The lower hoist is then switched to single-sided operation, thus utilizing only one side of the gun loading system and reducing the firing rate by one-half.

Upper Gun Loading Subsystem

The upper gun loading system consists of the carrier, upper ammunition hoist, transfer trays and the empty case tray (figure 18–8). All the upper gun loading system components move with the gun mount in train.

Carrier

The carrier, located vertically beneath the gun house, is mounted around the center column. (The center column, part of the mount structural subsystem, is a cylindrical steel structure that hangs directly beneath the gun house. It supports the carrier and upper hoist and provides an access to the gun house for electrical cables.) Roller bearings allow the carrier to rotate around the center column regardless of gun mount train. The carrier transfers a round of ammunition from each fixed lower hoist transfer station to each one of the rotating upper hoists.

Upper Hoist

Each of the two upper hoists is divided into two parts; the lower part is usually called the "upper hoist," and the upper part is called the "cradle."

The upper hoists are located in the carrier room (located one deck below the gun house on DD hulls) and are secured to the center column, 180 degrees apart. When the gun loading system is in operation, the carrier will receive ammunition from the lower hoists, rotate, latch to the upper hoists and eject a round into each upper hoist. When the upper hoists are loaded, they alternate in raising rounds into the cradles by lift pawls attached to an endless chain. When the lift pawl on the *right* upper hoist raises a round into the *right* cradle, the *left* lift pawl lowers and engages the base of a powder case in the *left* upper hoist, and the cycle is ready to start again.

The cradles receive ammunition from the upper hoist and deliver it to transfer trays located on each side of the slide. The right cradle receives ammunition from the right upper hoist and the left cradle receives ammunition from the left upper hoist. Each cradle arm is mounted on a large journal bearing located on the gun trunnion.

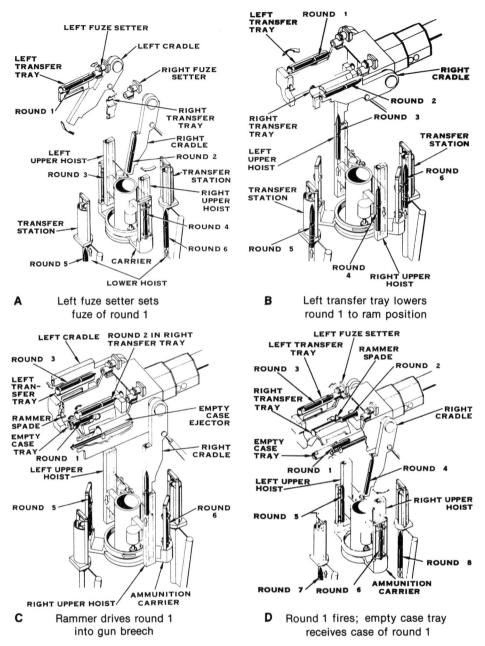

A   Left fuze setter sets fuze of round 1

B   Left transfer tray lowers round 1 to ram position

C   Rammer drives round 1 into gun breech

D   Round 1 fires; empty case tray receives case of round 1

Figure 18–8. The four steps from transfer tray to empty case ejection.

Transfer tray

The upper gun loading system uses two transfer trays to feed one gun barrel. Each transfer tray will receive, when in the up position, a round of ammunition from its cradle. The fuze setter will extend to set the fuze on projectiles requiring a fuze setting. The transfer trays will lower alternately down into the ramming position behind the gun breech. After the round has been rammed into the breech the transfer tray will raise to the up position to avoid the rearward recoiling gun housing. The loading cycle will repeat after the gun housing conterrecoils and returns to the in-battery position.

Empty Case Tray

There is only one empty case tray, but it will function with both transfer trays to receive the ejected empty powder case.

After the gun fires and the breech is opened, the extractors catapult the empty powder case rearward into the empty case tray. When a transfer tray lowers to the ram position, the empty case tray lowers into the empty case ejector which ejects the empty case forward and out through the gun mount shield. When the transfer tray raises to the up position, the empty case tray will raise to the firing position which will be far enough to the rear of the breech to avoid the recoiling gun housing.

Summary

A brief review of how ammunition moves from the magazine up through the gun loading system to the gun bore follows:

1. Loaders—20 rounds of semifixed ammunition are manually loaded into each loader.

2. Lower hoists—raise ammunition up to the transfer station at the top of the lower hoist on the carrier deck.

3. Carrier—transfers ammunition from the lower hoist (fixed to the ship's structure) to the upper hoists (fixed to the rotating structure of the gun mount).

4. Upper hoists—alternately raise rounds from the carrier to the cradles.

5. Cradles—alternately raise rounds from the upper hoist to the transfer trays.

6. Transfer trays—hold the rounds while the fuze setter sets the projectile fuze (only on mechanical time fuzes), then lower the round to the ramming position in line with the gun bore.

Gun Mount Crew

The gun mount crew consists of 12 men. Communications between the various mount stations are with sound-powered telephones. The following crew members are shown in figures 18–9 and 18–10.

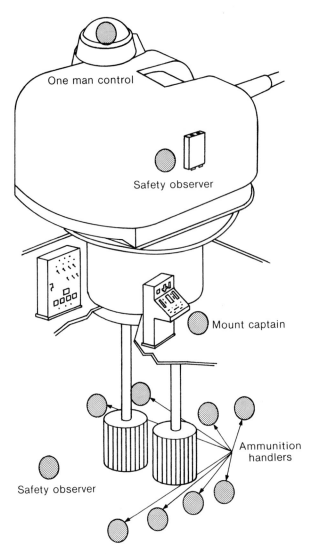

One man control

Safety observer

Mount captain

Ammunition handlers

Safety observer

Figure 18–9. Mount crew stations.

Mount Captain

The mount captain is the senior man in the crew, and he controls gun-laying, gun-loading, and fuze-setting operations. His station is at the EP2 control panel in the carrier room. Pushbuttons make control simple and rapid, and indicating lights permit him to monitor all phases of the mount's operation. Status lights at the rear of the panel will indicate a casualty to a specific area of the gun mount; therefore repairs can be accomplished rapidly. He exercises control over the entire mount crew by using a sound-powered telephone.

Gun Captain

The gun captain (safety observer) is stationed at the right side of the gun house. He is responsible for the safe operation of the upper gun-loading system. In the event of a casualty or safety hazard, he can stop the operation of the gun-loading system with a safety switch (SMX 17).

Local Controlman

The local controlman (assistant mount captain) is stationed at the local control station located on the left side of the gun house. Using

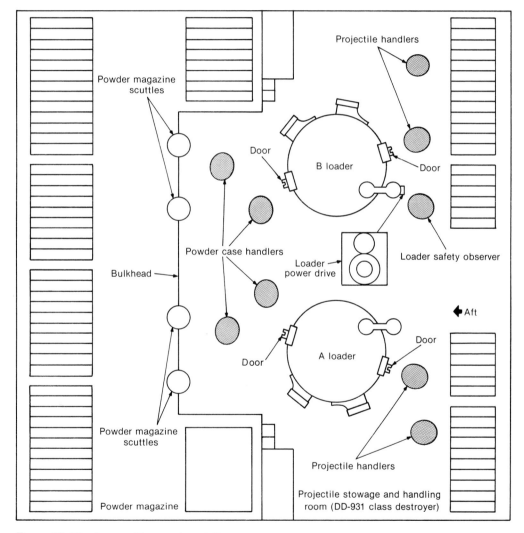

Figure 18–10. Ammunition-passing stations.

the one-man control unit (OMC), he can lay and fire the gun. By the use of sound-powered telephones he can exercise limited control over the gun-loading system.

Safety Observer

The loader deck safety observer exercises control over the ammunition handlers and controls the loading of the loaders in response to mount captain orders. In case of emergency, he can stop the loaders by the use of a safety switch (SMX14).

Ammunition Handlers

The ammunition handlers load projectiles and powder cases into the loaders on orders from the loader deck safety observer. They must work as a team to keep the loaders filled when the gun mount is in automatic operation. There are normally four projectilemen and four powdermen, but this number will vary from ship to ship.

5″/54 Mk 45 Mod 0

The 5″/54 Mk 45 gun mount reflects the application of some of today's technology and yesterday's experience (figure 18–11). This mount incorporates such design features as solid-state amplifier and logic circuits, plug-in replacement modules, and a trouble-shooting status board.* Proven attributes of the mount include accurate and reliable performance, ease of maintenance, safety, reduced space and installation requirements, a reduction in total weight of approximately one-half that of the 5″/54 Mk 42 mount, and reduced personnel requirements.

The mount is physically made up of two component groups (figure 18–12): the lower structure (below deck) and the upper structure (above deck). The lower structure delivers an uninterrupted flow of ammunition to the upper structure. The upper structure loads this ammunition, lays the gun, fires, and ejects the empty powder case. The lower structure (stationary) includes the lower hoist, loader, fuze setter, and upper hoist. The upper structure (rotating) includes the gun barrel, slide assembly, housing assembly, cradle, transfer tray, rammer, empty case ejector assembly, empty case tray, breech mechanism, breechblock operating mechanism, and recoil/counterrecoil system.

The major differences of the Mk 45 as compared with the Mk 42 mount follow:

---

* The tenth modification of the Mark 42 incorporates these improvements.

Figure 18–11. The Mark 45 undergoing firing tests on board the USS Norton Sound.

    1. The gun-loading system (figure 18–13) has been reduced to aid in weight reduction.

    2. The lower hoist is not present in all mounts. On those larger ships that require a lower hoist, the hoist moves projectiles and powder cases up to the loader drum.

    3. One loader drum is located immediately below the mount and holds 20 complete rounds of ammunition.

    4. The fuze setter is mounted on the loader drum next to

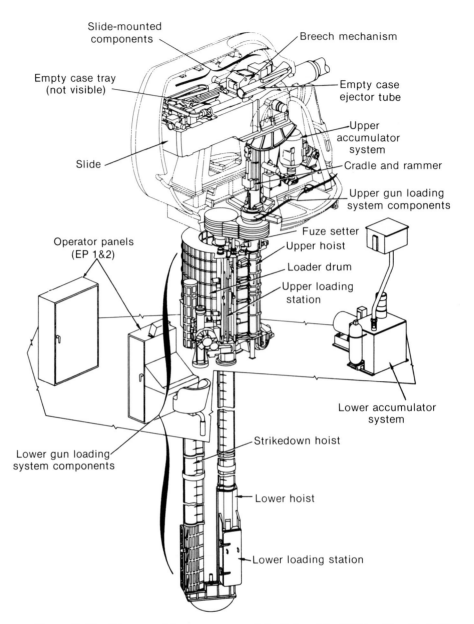

Slide-mounted components

Breech mechanism

Empty case tray (not visible)

Empty case ejector tube

Upper accumulator system

Cradle and rammer

Slide

Upper gun loading system components

Fuze setter

Operator panels (EP 1&2)

Upper hoist

Loader drum

Upper loading station

Lower accumulator system

Strikedown hoist

Lower gun loading system components

Lower hoist

Lower loading station

Figure 18–12. Diagram of the components of the lightweight 5″/54 caliber Mark 45.

the upper hoist and sets mechanical time fuzes (MTF) prior to the round entering the upper hoist.

5. The upper hoist has the capacity to bring the round that is in the cradle down to the projectile and powder case unloading door alongside the loader drum.

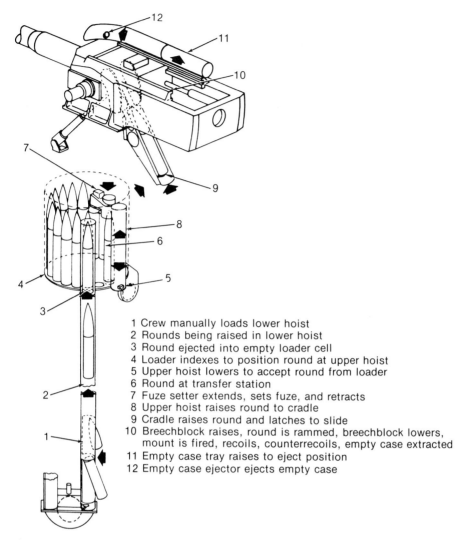

1 Crew manually loads lower hoist
2 Rounds being raised in lower hoist
3 Round ejected into empty loader cell
4 Loader indexes to position round at upper hoist
5 Upper hoist lowers to accept round from loader
6 Round at transfer station
7 Fuze setter extends, sets fuze, and retracts
8 Upper hoist raises round to cradle
9 Cradle raises round and latches to slide
10 Breechblock raises, round is rammed, breechblock lowers,
   mount is fired, recoils, counterrecoils, empty case extracted
11 Empty case tray raises to eject position
12 Empty case ejector ejects empty case

Figure 18–13. The Mark 45 gun loading system.

6. The strikedown hoist enables the gun mount crew to remove ammunition from the loader drum and return it to the magazine.

7. The cradle is a tubular-shaped structure that pivots inside the slide. When it is down, the cradle aligns with the upper hoist; when it is up, it aligns with the gun breech. The transfer tray has been eliminated.

8. The breechblock lowers to close and rises to open. This allows easy access to the breechblock and other components for maintenance and repairs.

9. The empty case tray and empty case ejector are mounted atop the right side of the slide. When the cradle swings up, the empty case tray pivots up to align with the empty case ejector. The empty case tray will pivot down when the cradle swings down.

10. A misfired round may be removed by the empty case tray and empty case ejector in case of emergency.

11. The mount can be trained and elevated by a remote signal or locally from the mount captains control panel EP2. There is no One-Man Control Unit for local control.

12. The firing rate has been reduced to 15 rounds a minute.

13. The maximum elevation angle is 65 degrees because of the position of the cradle between the slide.

14. The upper structure (gun house) is not manned. A normal operating crew consists of five men—a mount captain and four ammunition handlers. The mount captain controls the gun-loading and gun-laying systems as directed.

Summary

The 5″/54 Mk 42 gun mount has increased the firepower of a modern combat ship. Improvements developed in the Mk 42 have been incorporated in the Mk 45 to give better performance (except in firing rate and elevation), increased reliability, simplified logistic support, decreased training requirements, and reduced maintenance requirements.

19

Three-Inch and Smaller Caliber Rapid-Fire Guns

Introduction

Medium and small caliber rapid-fire guns are widely used in the Navy for the defense of both large and small ships. These guns are primarily designed to shoot down such air targets as cruise missiles and aircraft at close range. Their common characteristics are their high muzzle velocities, high rates of fire, and short ranges. The ones considered here are the standard Navy 3″/50 and two newer systems, the Italian 76mm 62 caliber Oto Melara compact and the Vulcan-Phalanx 20mm Gatling gun, Close-in Weapon System (CIWS). The newer systems are scheduled for new construction and may eventually replace the present 3″/50. There are other medium and small caliber gun systems available to the U.S. Navy. However, the three gun systems described here are representative of the gun system technology available today in a period of rapid technical development in gunnery.

Three-Inch 50 Caliber Guns and Mounts

The 3″/50 rapid-fire (RF) guns are semiautomatic with electric power-driven loaders, installed in open or enclosed twin or single mounts. They were primarily intended for air defense, but can be used against surface targets. The early single mounts had open sights on the mount and therefore had to see the target in order to fire on it. These mounts have a range of a little more than seven miles.

The 3″/50 rapid-fire mounts now serving in the Fleet are almost identical, the difference being in the slide. They are the twin Mark 27, the twin Mark 33, and the single-barreled Mark 34. The Mark 27 is an open gun mount found on board LPDs and other amphibious ships. The Mark 33 appears on the new auxiliaries and LKAs. The single Mark 34 is mounted on the *Asheville*-class PGs (figure 19–1).

All of the mounts use the same or similar gun loading mechanisms. The modifications of the Mark 33 have enclosed twin mounts with aluminum shield. The other mods are twins with modifications for

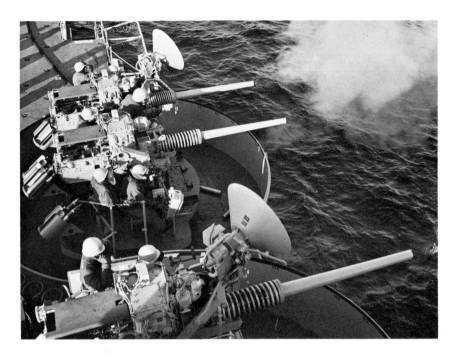

Figure 19–1. Top, *two 3″/50 open twin mounts firing at a surface target on board the USS* Guam *(LPH-9); bottom, a single enclosed version is found on board the* Asheville-*class patrol gunboats.*

installation of a fire control radar antenna or for substitution of aluminum platforms for steel.

The housing contains the vertically sliding, wedge breechblock mechanism. The slide supports the recoiling parts (gun barrel and housing) on bearings. Recoil and counterrecoil movement are controlled by a hydraulic recoil cylinder and a large counterrecoil spring surrounding the barrel.

Three-inch 50 Caliber

The foundation of a 3″/50 gun consists of the carriage and stand (figure 19–2). A heavy cast steel ring (the stand) is bolted directly to the deck. The training circle, a large worm wheel permitting the mount to be trained by means of a worm assembly, is bolted on top of the stand.

The bearing system with its chrome-plated ball or roller bearings, races, and bronze ring permits the gun to move in train and keeps the carriage from being rocked off the stand by gunfire or movements of the ship. Table 19–1 lists some of the significant specifications of the 3″/50 gun.

The principles of the 5″/54 sliding-wedge breech mechanism apply to the 3″/50 gun. The two different design features peculiar to the 3″/50 (figure 19–3) are a breechblock hold-down mechanism and a breech interlock mechanism.

Breechblock Hold-down Mechanism

This holds the breech open until the electric power-driven loader (described later) completes delivery of a round and, with a novel

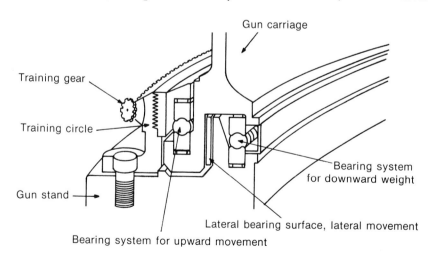

Figure 19–2. Foundation for the 3″/50 gun—inner and outer bearing systems of the stand.

TABLE 19–1

General Characteristics of 3″/50 Gun Mounts

Caliber	3″/50
Mount weight	31,000 lbs. (Mark 27, 33), 17,000 lbs. (Mark 34)
Maximum rate of fire	45
Ammunition feed system	semiautomatic, electric loaders
Muzzle velocity	2,700 ft./sec.
Ready to fire rounds	5 (no round in breech)
Range (horizontal/vertical)	14,200 yds./30,400 ft. at 85°
Number of barrels	1 or 2
Maximum train.	720° (limited by cable twist)
Maximum elevation	85°
Crew.	11 + additional men if ready service lockers need to be replenished
Cooling	air
Ammunition type	Fixed, electric primed
Fuze type (normal round)	proximity
Mission	dual purpose

extractor arrangement, increases the sensitivity of the breechblock unlocking action. Ammunition is normally fed into the chambers of most naval guns by ramming, which mechanically delivers a push that "follows through" until the projectile is seated in the chamber. In contrast, each gun on a 3″/50 mount is equipped with a loader which catapults the round into the chamber. Since there is no follow-through, the breech mechanism must be "triggered" into closing by the momentum of the catapulted round as it is thrown forward by the loader. This triggering function is performed by the hold-down mechanism. When the rim of the catapulted cartridge case trips one of the extractors, the extractors operate a push rod which triggers the breechblock hold-down mechanism. The triggering of the mechanism unlocks the breechblock and permits it to rise to the breech-closed position. The breechblock hold-down mechanism is interlocked with the breech interlock mechanism.

Breech Interlock Mechanism

The breech interlock mechanism (a part of the loader) is a system of mechanical linkages. These linkages function automatically to stop

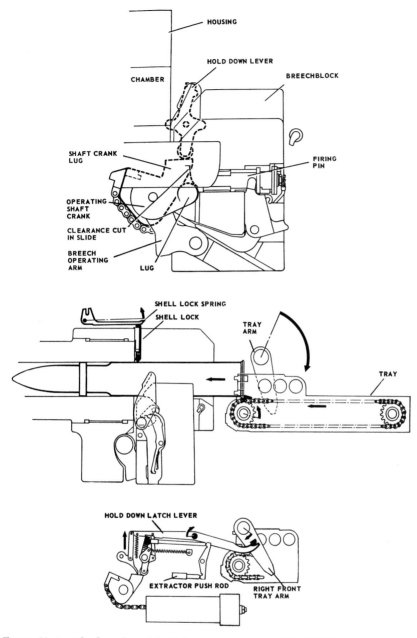

Figure 19–3. The breech and hold-down mechanism of the 3″/50 gun.

the loader from delivering another round to the breech whenever there is a round in the bore, the breechblock is up, or the gun is out of battery. When either a round is put in the breech or the block is raised, the interlock mechanism actuates the loader control lever, thereby preventing a repetition of the loading cycle until the round has been fired and the breechblock has dropped.

Loading System

The loader is an independent, electric, power-driven machine mounted on and bolted to the after part of the slide. It mechanically loads the gun at the rate of 45 rounds per minute. The loader is fed manually by two crewmen who insert the fixed ammunition, one round at a time, into the feed sprocket on each side (figure 19–4). The outer sprockets alternately shift the rounds to the center sprocket, which centers the round to be loaded above a gate mechanism.

When the breech is open, the gates admit the round to be loaded to a shell carriage mounted on a transfer tray which is in line with the gun bore axis. The loaded transfer tray swings down on its four arms until it is aligned with the chamber. The electric chain-driven shell carriage catapults the round into the breech (figure 19–5). After the round clears the carriage, the tray swings upward into position to accept another round.

The breech interlock automatically blocks repetition of the loader operating cycle until the gun has fired, recoiled, and returned to battery with breech open for the next round. All these functions are

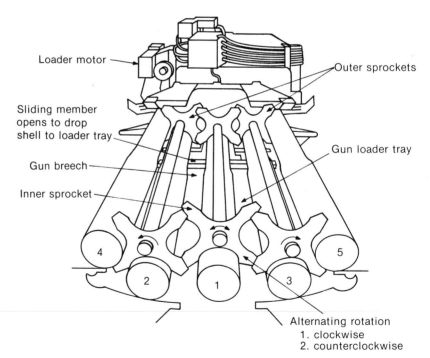

Figure 19–4. The loader sprockets of the 3″/50 being loaded.

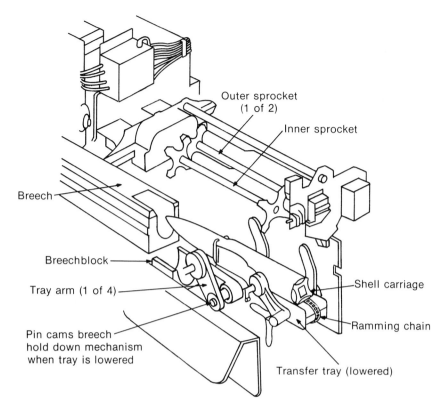

Outer sprocket
(1 of 2)

Inner sprocket

Breech

Breechblock

Tray arm (1 of 4)

Shell carriage

Pin cams breech
hold down mechanism
when tray is lowered

Ramming chain

Transfer tray (lowered)

Figure 19–5. Ammunition being catapulted into the breech in the 3″/50 loading cycle.

timed mechanically and electrically by control devices in the loader drive unit, and all are sequentially interlocked.

Mount Drives, Controls, and Sights

All 3″/50 rapid-fire mounts have amplidyne (electric) power drives for both train and elevation. There are no provisions for manual drive, except for handcrank arrangements which are intended only for stowing and servicing the mount.

There are two types of local control—*antiaircraft (AA) local* and *surface local*—plus automatic remote control from the director unit. Each side of the mount has a separate control station at which the gun layers are stationed to elevate and train the gun.

The antiaircraft and surface sights are mounted on a bracket extending from the side of the gun. In *automatic* control, which is the preferred type of control, sighting is done in the director unit—a separate unit especially made for fire control. Following chapters will explain gun fire-control directors.

Nevertheless, in some tactical situations it may become necessary to employ *local* control on the gun mount; for example, when battle damage has caused mechanical or electrical failure in the gun director unit.

AA Local

In AA local, the left gun layer (AA operator) controls the mount in train and elevation, using a ring sight and one-man gun-laying control unit with the firing key (figure 19–6).

Surface Local

The right-hand surface sight is a combination open sight and telescopic unit with provision for sight-setting (figure 19–7). The surface gun layer uses the open sight to get the target into the comparatively restricted field of view of the telescope. After shifting to the telescope, the mount position is adjusted with the controls to keep the cross hairs on the target. A sight-setter cranks in deflection and sight angle values at the mount in accordance with telephoned orders from the mount captain. The right gun layer has a firing key on his one-man control unit for firing the mount.

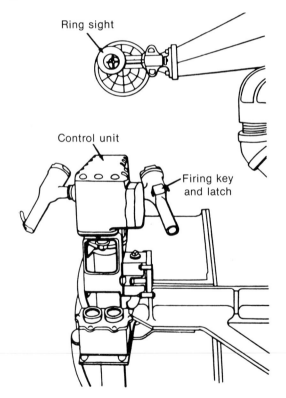

Figure 19–6. The left AA gun layer's station.

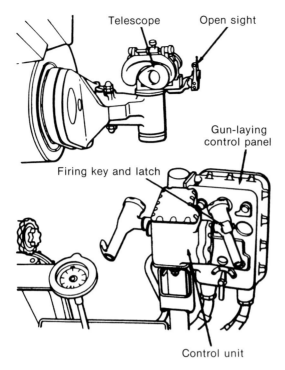

Telescope   Open sight

Gun-laying
control panel

Firing key and latch

Control unit

Figure 19–7. The right surface gun layer's station.

Three-inch 50 Caliber Rapid-Fire Twin Open Mount Crew

In addition to the AA and surface gun layers, and sight-setter already mentioned, the 3″/50 mount crew (figure 19–8) includes a mount captain, four shell* men (called "first loaders") and four shell passers (called "second loaders"). The mount captain is the supervising gunner. His operations are directed by phone by the director officer. The mount captain controls both barrels with controls designed for his use, which allow him to select the control station, switch to single or automatic fire, select the gun or guns to fire, and control the loaders. He also has power-drive emergency stop buttons, and two banks of neon indicators to enable him to check the loader mechanisms. His firing key must be closed before the loader mechanism will function and the gun will fire. The two shell men on each gun load ammunition into the hoppers of the loader mechanism. The second loaders keep the first loaders supplied with ammunition from the ready service lockers.

If the ammunition in the ready service lockers is expended, more men will be needed to carry ammunition from the stowage magazines

* A shell is the complete round of fixed ammunition.

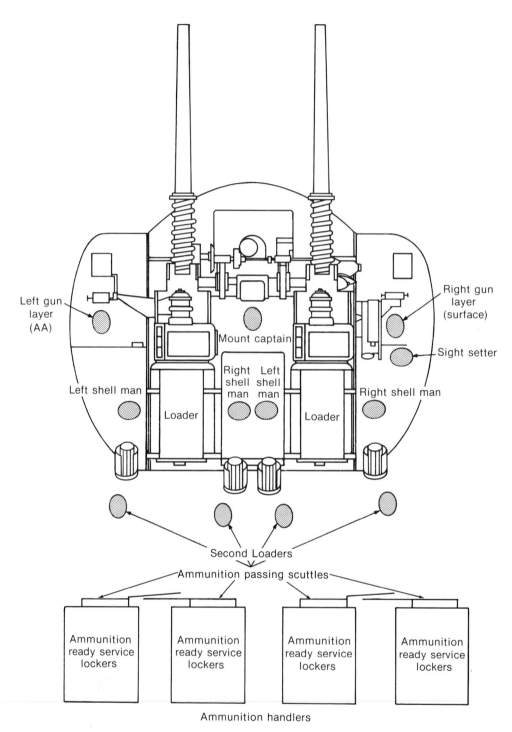

Left gun layer (AA)

Mount captain

Right gun layer (surface)

Sight setter

Left shell man

Right shell man

Right shell man

Left shell man

Loader

Loader

Second Loaders

Ammunition passing scuttles

Ammunition ready service lockers

Ammunition ready service lockers

Ammunition ready service lockers

Ammunition ready service lockers

Ammunition handlers

Figure 19–8. Mount crew stations in the twin barrel, open mount 3″/50.

below decks up to the gun mount to restock the ready service lockers. In this case the OOD will assign men from other General Quarters stations. Men assigned to damage control repair parties will often be detailed for this task.

76mm/62 Compact Gun Mount

Oto Melara, an Italian ordnance manufacturer in La Spezia, Italy, began work on the 76mm/62 compact gun mount in 1964 as a lightweight successor to the successful MM1 model. Production began in 1969. Since then the 76mm/62 has entered service in six navies and its technical evaluations were completed in the USS *Talbot* in 1975 (figure 19–9). Current plans are for installation on board the U.S. Navy's new Patrol Frigate (FFG) and Missile Hydrofoil Boat (PHM) classes for surface and air engagements. As can be seen from a comparison of tables 19–1 and 19–2, the Oto Melara is part of the new generation of rapid-fire, dual-purpose gun mounts that were developed for the AAW environment of the 1970s and 1980s.

Design Considerations

The need for the gun was a result of greatly increased aircraft target speeds and the cruise missile threat. The gun was built to meet the following criteria: it was to be light in weight, have a high rate of fire, and have large supplies of ammunition ready to use for long bursts of

Figure 19–9. The OTO Melara 76 mm/62 compact can be seen on the bow of the USS Talbot (FFG-4).

TABLE 19–2

Weapon Characteristics of the 76mm/62 gun

Mounting

Total weight without ammunition . . . . 7.35 tons
Rate of fire . . . . 85 rds/min.
Ready to fire rounds . . . . 80 (optionally 115)
Sweep radius of gun barrel 5,200mm
Sweep radius of turret 1,880mm
Diameter of deck opening for gun installation 1,800mm

Recoiling Mass

Barrel length . . . . 62 caliber = 4,700mm
Maximum pressure . . . . 3,600 kgs/cm²
Pressure at the muzzle . . . . 540 kgs/cm²
Muzzle velocity . . . . 925 m/s; 3,000 ft./sec.
Maximum recoil length 370mm
Recoil force . . . . 7 tons
Cooling . . . . Salt water, 40 liters/min.

Training

Arc . . . . unlimited
Maximum speed . . . . 60°/sec.
Maximum acceleration . . . . 72°/sec.

Elevation

Arc . . . . −15° + 85°
Maximum speed . . . . 35°/sec.
Maximum acceleration . . . . 72°/sec.

Ammunition (Fixed)

Cartridge weight . . . . 12.358 kgs./27 lbs.
Cartridge length 907.5mm
Projectiles in production . . . . IR (infrared) fuze for use
against low flying targets.
PD (point detonating) fuze for
surface targets.

Circuits

Power . . . . three-phase 440V — 60Hz
Signals . . . . biphase 115V — 60Hz
Synchro . . . . 115V — 400Hz
Crew . . . . 3 men + 1 in the mount if local
control option used

firing without the need of reloading; it was to be able to fire at short notice during an unexpected attack; it was to have high training and elevating speeds to obtain better tracking performance; and it was to be highly automated.

Description

The 76mm/62 is a shielded, dual-purpose (antiair and antisurface), Close-in Weapon (CIW), single gun mount with a rate of fire of from ten to 85 rounds per minute with either 40, 80, or 115 rounds respectively in one, two, or three revolving feed magazine drums (figure 19–10). The gun is trained and elevated by separate electrically controlled and operated power drives. The gun-loading system is geared together to provide continuous ammunition to the gun bore in a programmed sequence.

The gun mount is enclosed in a fiberglass shield which provides

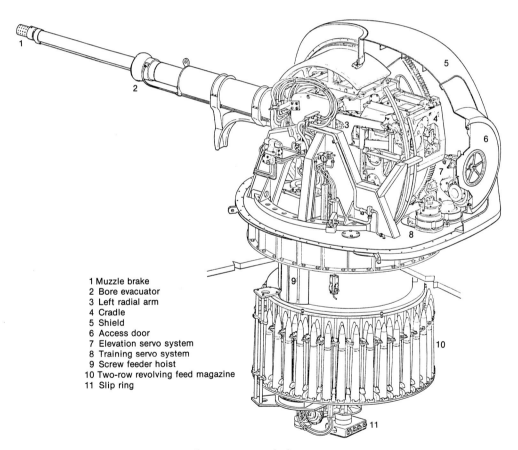

1 Muzzle brake
2 Bore evacuator
3 Left radial arm
4 Cradle
5 Shield
6 Access door
7 Elevation servo system
8 Training servo system
9 Screw feeder hoist
10 Two-row revolving feed magazine
11 Slip ring

Figure 19–10. Ready ammunition drums rotate with the mount.

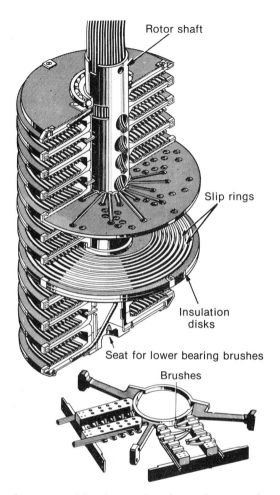

Rotor shaft

Slip rings

Insulation
disks

Seat for lower bearing brushes

Brushes

Figure 19–11. Slip rings and brushes used in the Mark 56 gun direction.

protection against the elements—seas, weather, and nuclear fallout.

Slip rings (electrical connections composed of brushes and contacts) allow the gun mount to have unlimited train (figure 19–11).

The gun house is not manned and there is no capability for local control except for maintenance by using controls at the control panel in the revolving feed magazine room.

By employing solid-state circuits, the time required to start the mount and shift to remote with the controlling fire-control system is within 2 to 4 seconds.

Gun Mount Structural System

The gun mount structural system is composed of the gun mount structural subsystem and gun assembly subsystem.

Gun Mount Structural Subsystem

The gun mount structural subsystem is composed of the stand, carriage, fiberglass shield, and associated components. The function of these components are similar to previously discussed gun mounts.

Gun Assembly Subsystem

The gun assembly subsystem is composed of the slide, housing, rammer, breechblock, recoil/counterrecoil system, muzzle brake, bore evacuator, empty case ejector assembly, gun barrel, and gun barrel cooling system.

The slide, housing, rammer, and breechblock are similar in design and function to the 3″/50 RF gun mount.

The Recoil and Counterrecoil Systems A muzzle brake is installed on the barrel which reduces recoil by approximately 35 percent. This consists of a short steel tube that extends out past the end of the barrel and has small holes that are angled back toward the gun mount. When a round has been fired, some of the propellant gas will pass through these holes and tend to push the barrel in the opposite direction from recoil. The remaining recoil energy is absorbed by the recoil and counterrecoil system. When the gun barrel recoils, energy is absorbed by a recoil piston and cylinder assembly located on each side of the housing. As the housing moves back in recoil, the pistons attached to each side of the housing move inside of their respective recoil cylinders, forcing recoil fluid out through a small hydraulic line. This action accommodates the remaining recoil energy. The recoil fluid, now under high pressure, is led to a counterrecoil cylinder on top of the slide, which contains a free-floating piston with nitrogen gas on one side. The force of the recoil fluid against this floating piston pressurizes the nitrogen gas which forces the housing back into battery after the out-of-battery locks release the housing.

This action reduces recoil by approximately 35 percent and aids the recoil system in reducing barrel travel during recoil.

The Bore Evacuator The bore evacuator, located on the middle portion of the gun barrel, has replaced the function of the gas ejection system of the 5-inch 54 caliber gun mounts. To prevent a flashback, the burning residual propellant gas must be removed from the barrel before the breechblock is opened. Six small holes are drilled in the grooves of the rifling at an angle to the barrel. They are placed in a circle all the way around the barrel, with a forward slope toward the muzzle. A bulb-shaped jacket is placed over the holes to form an expansion chamber. As the projectile passes the bore evacuator, a small amount of propellant gas flows through the holes into the chamber creating a high pressure area. When the pressure inside the barrel decreases, the gas in the expansion chamber of the bore evacuator rushes through the holes into the gun bore. Residual gases in the gun bore are drawn out of the entire length of the tube by the escaping bore evacuator gases.

The Gun Barrel Cooling System This is an open saltwater system that helps to keep the barrel at a reasonable temperature during rapid fire bursts. Seawater from the ship's firemain is fed through a small pipe into the cooling jacket surrounding the barrel. After one pass through the cooling jacket, the water exits through an open line and pours out onto the deck of the ship.

Gun Mount Loading System

The gun mount loading system is composed of a revolving feeding magazine, projectile hoist, two rocker arms, feeding drum, loading tray, out-of-battery securing locks, and an empty case tray.

Revolving Feed Magazine

The magazine is attached to and moves in train with the gun mount. The revolving magazine has one, two, or three rings that hold a total of 40, 80, or 115 rounds. The rounds are removed from the ammunition racks by the handlers and placed in an upright position in an empty section of the feed magazine, where they are held by spring-operated latches. As the mount fires, the magazine rotates clockwise to place a round in the hoist.

Projectile Hoist

This hoist is similar to the lower hoist in the 5″/54 and lifts rounds up to one of the two rocker arms.

Rocker Arms

Rocker arms are located on the left gun trunnion and each lifts one round up to the feeding drum located above the loading tray. The rocker arms work alternately; when one is up next to the feeding drum the other is down next to the projectile hoist (figure 19–12).

Feeding Drum

The feeding drum is located above the loading tray and acts as a waiting station. Four rounds are held here by a sprocket arrangement similar to the 3″/50 loader (figure 19–13).

Loading Tray

A loading tray, located under the feeding drum, is used to transfer rounds from the feeding drum to the gun bore (figure 19–14). This

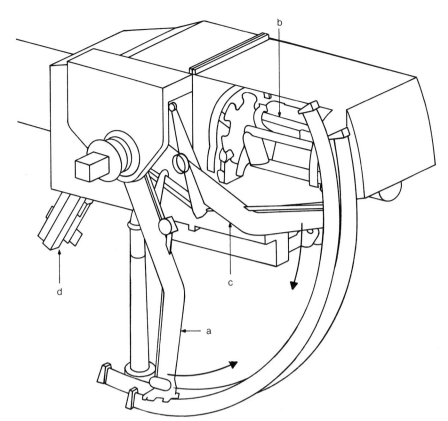

Figure 19–12.   The laden rocker arm (a) commences its transfer movement carrying the round to (b) the loading drum. Meanwhile the empty arm (c) moves downward to its receiving position at the screw feeder. The rocking arms are hydraulically driven by cylinder (d). In their ascending and descending movements the rocker arms cause the hoist to rotate one step.

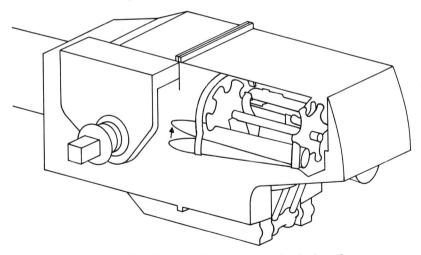

Figure 19–13.   The round is aligned with the bore in the feeding drum.

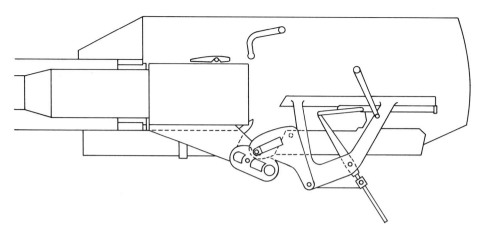

Figure 19–14. As the gun runs out into battery, the loading tray moves down and forward in line with the chamber of the gun.

tray pivots back and up to receive a round from the feeding drum, then swings down and forward to align the round with the gun bore (figure 19–15). The rammer rams the round into the bore from this position. When the gun fires, the loading tray swings up to avoid the recoiling housing and to receive another round.

Out-of-Battery Securing Locks

The out-of-battery securing locks engage the housing and hold the housing out of battery at the end of recoil. These locks are tripped as the breechblock rises to close. This action eliminates the time required for the housing to counterrecoil before a round is loaded into the bore, thus enabling a high rate of fire.

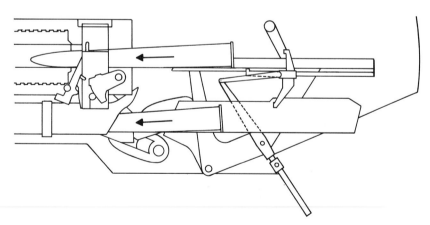

Figure 19–15. While the new round is rammed home from the loading tray, the empty case of the previously fired round is ejected by the rammer mechanism into an exit tube, which permits empty cases to fall outside the gun mount onto the weather deck.

Empty Case Tray

Located beneath the loading tray is an empty case tray. When the loading tray swings up as the gun fires, the empty case tray swings up and aligns with the bore. When the breechblock drops to open during recoil, the extractors pull the empty case into this tray. When the loading tray swings down with a new round, the empty case tray swings down and aligns with an exit tube. At the same time the new round is being rammed into the bore, the empty case is struck by an ejector arm which ejects the empty case out through the exit tube and on to the ship's deck (figure 19–15).

Gun Operating Cycle

The list below is a brief description of the events in the 76 mm/62 operating cycle.

1. The gun mount is energized from a control panel below deck. Within four seconds the mount is placed in remote control on the azimuth for firing.

2. The revolving feed magazine rotates clockwise to index a round into the projectile hoist.

3. The projectile hoist lifts rounds vertically one above the other to the waiting rocker arm.

4. One rocker arm swings down as the other swings up.

5. The rocker arm ejects the round into the feeder drum which holds four rounds when filled and rotates in elevation with the gun.

6. A round is ejected into the loading tray which swings down and forward to the ramming position.

7. When the round is rammed and the breech block starts to rise, the out-of-battery securing locks release the housing. The nitrogen pressure built up in the counterrecoil recuperator forces the housing back into battery. By the time the housing has reached the in-battery position, the gun fires.

8. The housing recoils until it reaches its recoil travel limit, where it is caught by the out-of-battery securing locks.

9. The cycle is repeated.

The 20mm General Electric M61A1 Vulcan Gun

A gun which has been in service since 1964 is the General Electric, M61A1 Vulcan, 20mm, six-barreled gun (table 19–3). This gun (figure 19–16) is presently used in a number of U.S. and British aircraft, and

TABLE 19–3

Weapon Characteristics for the 20mm Vulcan-Phalanx, Gatling Close-in Weapon System

Caliber	20mm 76 caliber single gun
Mount weight (long tons)	1.3
Maximum rate of fire	1,000 to 3,000 per minute in shipboard mount
Ammunition feed system	Helical drum on mount
Cartridge weight	.22 lbs.
Muzzle velocity	3,650 ft/sec.
Ready to fire rounds	950
Range	1,625 yards
Number of barrels	6
Barrel life	20,000 rounds
Gun life	145,000 rounds
Deck space	54 square feet
Training velocity	@ 100°/sec.
Elevation velocity	@ 86°/sec.
Crew	0 (except for reloading)
Cooling	air, rotating barrels

Figure 19–16. The 20mm Vulcan six-barreled gun. It has been adapted for use in aircraft, ground vehicles, and ships.

in the newly developed shipboard Phalanx Close-in Weapon system (CIWS). The Phalanx CIWS will be used for defense against antiship cruise missiles. The Vulcan gun was selected for the Phalanx system because of its proven performance, high firing rate of 3,000 rounds per minute, light weight, and low cost. The Phalanx CIWS was described in Chapter 8.

The Vulcan gun employs the multibarreled principle first developed by Dr. Gatling in a gun used in the Civil War. The Vulcan gun has six rifled rotating barrels that fire 500 rounds per minute from each barrel. Since the barrels rotate as the gun fires, the rate of fire is multiplied by six, giving a total rate of fire of 3,000 rounds per minute for all six barrels. All barrels, rigidly clamped together, are attached to a rotating breech. As the breech rotates, cams operate the bolt for each barrel, which loads, fires, and extracts the rounds from its respective barrel. A 950-round capacity linkless feed ammunition drum is located immediately below the gun. Ammunition is served to the gun breech from the ammunition drum by a flexible conveyor belt loading system. Approximate range is three-quarters of a mile.

20

Magazines and Ordnance Safety

Introduction

The ever-present danger associated with munitions as well as the special problems of handling ammunition in ships have been the constant concern of the Navy since the Revolutionary War. Most problems with weaponry arise out of ignorance or carelessness.

Magazine History

About one hundred and fifty years ago a ship's magazine was primarily a place to store cartridges for gun propellants and small arms. Projectiles were kept in racks on the gun decks. Since wooden ships were even more vulnerable to fire than steel ships, magazines were even then located on the centerline, as far from enemy action as possible, and below the waterline, so that they could be quickly flooded. Magazine hatches and doorways were sheathed in copper and guarded by sentries, usually marines. A felt material called *dreadnought* covered the inside of the magazine to afford further protection from sparks.

Magazines have changed, but many essential design considerations have been retained. Projectiles have joined the propellants in the magazines, because they have become explosive too.

Magazine Types

The term *magazine* applies to any compartment, space, or locker which is used, or intended to be used, for the stowage of explosives or ammunition of any kind.

The term *magazine area* includes the compartments, spaces, or passages on board ship containing magazine entrances, which are intended to be used for handling and passing ammunition.

There are three types of magazines: primary magazines, ready service magazines, and ready service stowage magazines. Magazines are classified in this way by their location, ease of supply, and the security of their contents.

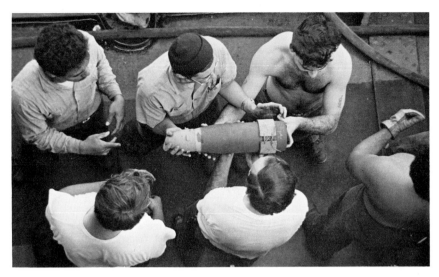

Figure 20–1. With fire hoses run out, the crew of the USS Richard B. Anderson (DD-786) pass five-inch projectiles while rearming from an ammunition ship under way in the Gulf of Tonkin.

Primary Magazines

The primary magazines are designed to store a ship's complete *peacetime* allowance of ammunition. These spaces are generally located below the main deck and, where possible, below the waterline. They are equipped with magazine sprinkling systems, insulation, and ventilation. They are kept locked.

Ready Service Magazines

These are stowage areas near the gun mounts. They provide a permanent stowage for part of the ammunition on board. The combined capacities of these and the primary magazines will hold the ship's *wartime* ammunition allowance (the allowance normally carried on board ships). Ready service magazines are equipped with insulation, ventilation, sprinkling systems, and locks.

Ready Service Stowage

These magazines are near the weapon to be served. They may be weather deck lockers, upper handling rooms, or bulwark (shield) racks. This stowage is normally filled only when the weapon is to be fired. There is little security for ammunition in these places, and least protection from the weather.

While magazines are designed to hold a single type of ammunition, and stowage in individual magazines is desirable, it is not possible in small ships because of space limitations and the requirements of the ammunition allowance list. The ammunition allowance list indicates the various types and amounts of ammunition to be carried in a ship as specified by the Naval Ordnance Systems Command. Magazine stowage requirements are contained in OP 4, Vol. 2, *Ammunition Afloat*. Mixed magazine stowage is allowed in small ships where space is severly limited. The type commander normally specifies the kinds of ammunition a multipurpose magazine may contain.

Magazine Security

In peacetime, all magazines and magazine hoists leading into magazine spaces are kept closed and locked, except when they are opened for inspection, ventilation, testing, or specially authorized work. These spaces are opened only when authorized by the weapons officer, who is responsible to the Commanding Officer for ensuring their security. Normally, the keys to all magazine spaces are kept by the Commanding Officer, but he may authorize the weapons officer to have custody.

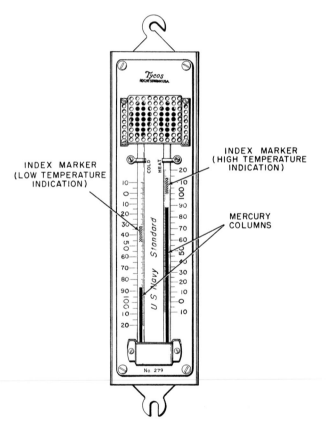

Figure 20–2. A maximum-minimum magazine thermometer.

Inspection of Magazines

All magazines are inspected every day to check for their safety and security, and to record daily magazine temperatures. This inspection is normally conducted by a gunner's mate petty officer. The most important item of the daily inspection is to check and record the temperature inside the magazine. The thermometers that are kept in each magazine are called maximum-minimum thermometers which indicate the maximum and minimum temperature that has occurred since the last inspection. The thermometer is a U-shaped, mercury-filled glass tube with two bulbs. The mercury columns in each tube should give the current temperature. The maximum temperature reading is taken by noting the bottom edge of the steel index marker against the right-hand scale. (For example, figure 20–2 shows it to be 100°F.) The minimum temperature reading is taken by noting the bottom edge of the steel index marker against the left-hand scale. (Figure 20–2 shows it to be 46°F.) After the temperatures are taken and recorded, the thermometers are zeroed by moving a small horseshoe magnet against the glass tube to draw the steel index markers down to the level of the mercury. The results are reported to the Captain and entered in the ship's deck log.

Magazine Sprinkling Systems

Flooding lines have been replaced with sprinkler systems installed on the compartment overheads and supplied with seawater from the ship's fire-main system. This change in basic design allows more flexibility in combating fires which might threaten the magazine from either inside or outside the space. The spray of water from above the fire has both a cooling and a smothering effect and is a quicker and more effective reaction to a fire. Furthermore, magazine sprinkler systems can completely flood a space within an hour. Compartments set aside as magazines are watertight to prevent the flooding of adjacent areas.

Sprinkling systems vary with individual ships and with types of ships. Detailed descriptions of the particular kind aboard a ship will be found in *Naval Ship Systems Command* (NavShipSysCom) publications and in the ship's *Damage Control Book.* In general, all sprinkling systems consist of a network of pipes arranged around the overhead of the magazine, connected by a series of valves to the ship's fire mains.

The major difference between systems is the method of opening the sprinkling control valve in the magazine. The systems vary in complexity. At one extreme is the simple piping arrangement in five-inch handling rooms, where opening a single manually controlled valve will cause the ready service racks to be drenched. At the other extreme is the automatically operated system with heat-sensing devices. The heat-sensing devices are connected to pilot valves released by air pressure (pneumatically) which will trigger other valves and release a flow of water to the spray nozzles.

Valves for sprinkling systems may be opened or closed either by local control at the valves or by remote control. There are three kinds of remote controls: (1) by hand, using shafting and gearing; (2) hydraulically, using control cocks and water from the fire main system, or control cocks and oil pressure supplied by hand pumps; and (3) automatically by means of temperature (thermopneumatic) control devices.

Magazine Sprinkler Control Valves, Sensors, and Alarms

Magazines have sprinkler systems which contain several kinds of valves. These valves serve different purposes but they are all actuated by hydraulic (oil or water) pressure. The controls that turn the sprinkler on or off are either hand-operated levers or heat-sensing devices. In either instance, they release fluid under pressure from the fire main causing further valve action to release seawater. A simplified diagram of a magazine sprinkler system is shown in figure 20–3.

The most significant valve is the *manual control* valve. It is installed in every sprinkler system, even the automatic systems. In the automatic system, it is used to close the sprinkler system. One manual control valve may be placed near a magazine group, and another at a location away from the magazine so the system can always be governed by

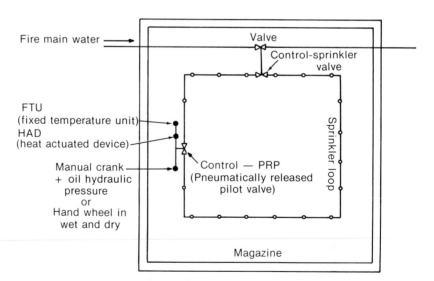

Figure 20–3. A simplified diagram of a magazine sprinkler system.

remote control—away from the fire. The valve has three positions: neutral, open, and closed. It is set in the neutral position when the situation is normal on board. In this position the valve blocks any flow of water from the fire main to the control piping of the system, which precedes the sprinkler piping. When the magazine is to be sprinkled, the valve is opened. This permits the pressure to pass through the *open loop* of the control piping to force open the magazine sprinkling valve, while the *closed loop* is blocked off. When the water is to be turned off, the manual control valve is closed, shutting water out of the open loop and the magazine sprinkling valve. The remaining water in the open loop is manually drained with a check valve.

The second important valve is the pneumatically released valve. If this valve receives a sudden charge of air from an expanding heat sensor globe in the automatic release system, it lets the water into the open loop of the sprinkling system. It is appropriately called a *pneumatically released pilot* (PRP) valve. Its function is the same as the *manual control valve* (figure 20–4).

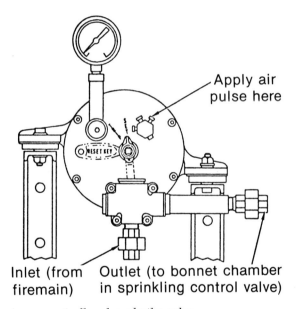

Figure 20–4. A pneumatically released pilot valve.

The third valve, called the *magazine sprinkler* valve, is dependent on fire main pressure from either the manual control valve or the PRP valve through the open loop. It can also be opened directly by hand. The sprinkler valve is simply held closed by a spring until pressure is applied through a small control line. This presses a diaphragm upward against the spring, lifting the valve seat. Once the pressure

Magazines and Ordnance Safety **271**

is released, the valve closes. The operating condition of the valve is checked every month in accordance with the planned maintenance system requirements.

Another kind of valve employed in magazine sprinklers is the *spring-loaded check* valve. It closes tightly against reverse flow to prevent water from backing through the system. Because spring-loaded check valves allow fluid to flow in only one direction, their presence makes it possible to install several control valves so the system can be operated from several stations on the ship.

Control Sensors

An alarm in the manually controlled sprinkler system alerts the crew when the temperature in the magazine rises past 105°F. It is a simple mercury thermostat which sets off a bell. A second kind of alarm warns the crew when there is either leakage in the sprinkler system or, in an automatic release system, when a fire is in progress and the sprinkler system is operating. This alarm is downstream from the magazine sprinkling valve, and when water passes it, it sets off a bell in Damage Control Central. The alarm consists of two electrodes in a section of pipe that is usually dry. After saltwater passes the sprinkling valve, it then passes the electrodes. This closes a circuit and activates the alarm bell.

Release Sensors

Release sensors are used in automatic systems. One of these sensors is designed to set off the sprinkler system when there is a rapid rise of temperature in the magazine, as would be the case in an explosion.

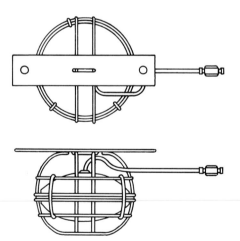

Figure 20–5. A heat-actuated device.

The device expands and opens the PRP valve, described above. It is called a *heat-actuated device* (HAD) (figure 20–5). Another device mounted adjacent to the HAD before the PRP, is used to set off the system when an unsafe temperature is reached (147°F) in the magazine. It is designed to combat smoldering fires. The device is a spring mechanism held in tension by silver solder. When the solder melts, the spring releases, setting off the PRP (figure 20–6). This invention is called a *fixed temperature unit* (FTU).

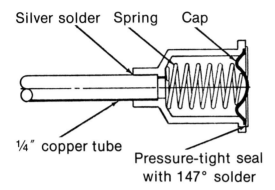

Figure 20–6. A fixed temperature unit.

Ordnance Safety Precautions

Although an officer who is assigned to a weapons billet should read and be familiar with *U.S. Navy Regulations* governing safety precautions in ordnance, it is useful to have a summary knowledge of the subjects covered by regulations in this category.

> The commanding officer must see that his officers and crew are instructed in ordnance safety. He is responsible for proper care, stowing, handling, and inspection of explosives, flammables, and fuels.

> The weapons officer must keep his spaces clean and well maintained and inspect them as necessary to ensure their good condition. It is his job to see that the crew are instructed in the safety orders.

> Great emphasis is placed on the need for every member of the naval service to be instructed in safe methods of handling the kind of ammunition used by his ship, aircraft, or station. Individual good sense is the key factor in the safety of shipmates.

The number of men assigned to a job involving the handling of ammunition will be restricted to an absolute minimum.

Reports of defective ammunition, containers, handling equipment, or violation of safety regulations should be reported to one's immediate superior.

Particular care should be taken to prevent safety signs and tags from being defaced or obliterated by paint.

Defective containers of ammunition should be tagged and set aside for return to the ammunition depot. The weapons officer should be called when defects are identified.

Rolling, dragging, throwing, or dropping containers of ammunition is forbidden. Naked lights, matches, steel tools, shoes with nails or cleats, or any other spark-producing substances are barred from the magazine.

Any fuzed case or projectile that has been dropped from more than four feet in the air should be set aside. The weapons officer should be called if this occurs.

Boiler tubes may not be blown during the handling of ammunition, and radio and radar transmitters must be secured.

Any person who sees a dangerous situation developing will immediately call out "Silence," thus freezing the situation until a safe solution can be implemented.

Ordnance References

The following publications are references with which every weapons officer on board a naval vessel should be thoroughly familiar.

1. *Ammunition Afloat* (OP 4, Vol 2) describes the general regulations for handling military explosives and hazardous munitions. It also describes stowage spaces for ammunition aboard ship and regulations for storing ammunition in a ship.

2. *U.S. Navy Ordnance Safety Precautions* (OP 3347) lists general safety precautions and establishes guide lines in the handling of all types of ordnance.

3. *Ordnance Safety Precautions, Their Origin and Necessity* (OP 1014) describes cases of ordnance casualties involving naval weapons since 1927.

4. *Rules and Regulations for Military Explosives and Hazardous Munitions* (Coast Guard 108) describes rules and regulations for handling ammunition in anchorages and at commercial piers set aside for the loading of explosives.

PART 4

Missiles

Shipboard guided missile systems are designed to destroy air and surface targets that threaten Fleet units. The area of coverage for any of the present combat missiles ranges from approximately 100 yards for point defense missiles, to more than 70 miles from the ship for area defense missiles. Of the many threats these missiles have to meet, the most difficult to detect, track, and destroy has been the enemy missile launched from submarines, ships, or aircraft.

Missiles now in service, or which are being introduced, are discussed in this Part, beginning with a general description of the components of a missile. Subsequent chapters will describe missile guidance, the complete missile system, and the Polaris/Poseidon fleet ballistic missile system.

21

Components of Guided Missiles

Figure 21–1. *The ship class of the Navy that specialize in area defense missiles is the cruisers.* Top, *the USS* Albany *(CG-10) fires two Talos missiles and an ASROC missile simultaneously;* below, *the USS* England *(CG-22) fires a Terrier.*

Subassemblies of the Guided Missile

The guided missile can be subdivided into the following principal components:

> Airframe
> Warhead
> Propulsion System
> Control and Guidance Systems

This chapter covers airframes, missile warheads, and propulsion systems.

Airframe

The guided missile airframe consists of the main body and airfoils which stabilize the missile in flight and control its flight path. In most missiles the main body is a slender, cylindrical structure which houses the internal components and determines the flight characteristics of the vehicle. Several types of nose sections are used as shown in figure 21–2. If the weapon's speed is supersonic, the forward section usually has a pointed-arch profile in which the sides taper. In missiles which fly at lesser speeds, the nose is frequently less sharp, or in some cases it is even blunt. Some missile forward ends are covered by a rounded radome which houses a radar antenna. The nose section can also contain an intake duct required for a jet power system.

Typical airframes usually terminate in a flat base. When the airframe contour is slightly streamlined at the rear, the missile is said to be "boat-tailed," like projectiles. Attached to the body are one or more sets of airfoils, which either provide lift or control the flight path and increase the missile's stability in flight. The basic types of airframe designs are distinguished principally by the location of the control surfaces with respect to the missile body. These types are the *canard*, the *wing-control*, and the *tail-control* designs.

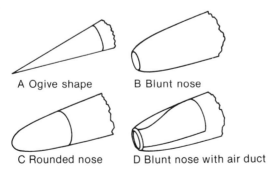

A Ogive shape   B Blunt nose

C Rounded nose   D Blunt nose with air duct

Figure 21–2. Missile noses.

In canard-control airframes (figure 21–3), small control surfaces are placed forward of the airframe's center of gravity. Fixed fins, usually larger than the control surfaces, are mounted on the tail section to increase flight stability.

In the wing-control design (figure 21–4), the wing-control surfaces are mounted at or near the center of gravity. The wing-control surfaces are larger than in the canard arrangement and provide considerable lift. Smaller fixed fins are mounted at the tail section of the missile body.

In the tail-control airframe (figure 21–5), the control surfaces are placed at the rear of the airframe. If wings are included, they are mounted amidships and contribute lifting force, but do not control the flight path. On some missile airframes with tail control, there are fins running along the side of the airframe instead of forward wings.

The fuselages of many guided missiles are made of one shell braced by inner bulkheads and longitudinal members. The body has several

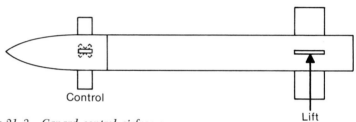

Figure 21–3. Canard control airframe.

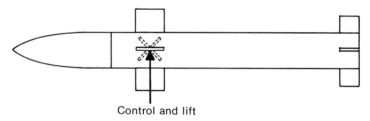

Figure 21–4. Wing control airframe.

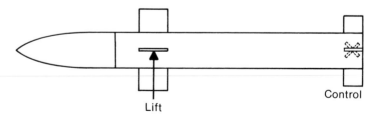

Figure 21–5. Tail control airframe.

cylindrical sections. Each section contains one of the essential units of the missile. These units are normally the propulsion system, the electronic control equipment, the warhead, and the fuze assembly. The separate unit construction makes possible the replacement and repair of the components. The sections are joined by various connections, which can be put together or dismantled easily. Access ports are provided in the shell through which adjustments to the components can be made.

Missile Warheads

The payload of a guided missile is its warhead, and the purpose for employment of the missile is to deliver its warhead to the target. Various warheads may be fitted on a missile, like gun projectiles, and detonated by one or more fuzes.

Some guided missile warheads are: *blast effect, fragmentation, continuous rod,* and *nuclear,* as well as *training* or *dummy* heads.

The Blast-Effect Warhead

The blast-effect warhead consists of a quantity of high-explosive material in a thin metallic case. The force of the explosion sets up a pressure wave which causes damage to the target. This type of warhead is most effective against underwater targets. Torpedo warheads are of this type. Blast-effect warheads have been used successfully against small ground targets, but are considerably less effective against aerial targets.

The Fragmentation Warhead

The fragmentation warhead uses the force of a burster charge to break the warhead casing into a number of fragments and to propel them with enough velocity to destroy or damage the target. Aerial targets are more susceptible to damage by fragments if the warhead explodes a short distance away, rather than in contact with the target. Against a partially protected surface target, a fragmentation warhead is most effective when exploded in the air above the target. Figure 21–6 shows this effect.

The Continuous-Rod Warhead

In the continuous-rod warhead, the burster charge is used to expand rods radially into a ring of metal which can lengthen and thus increase its diameter rather than produce an expanding shell of small fragments. The connected rods form two semicircles as they expand. The intent is to cause the connected rods, during their expansion, to strike the target and produce damage from cutting (figures 21–7 and 21–8).

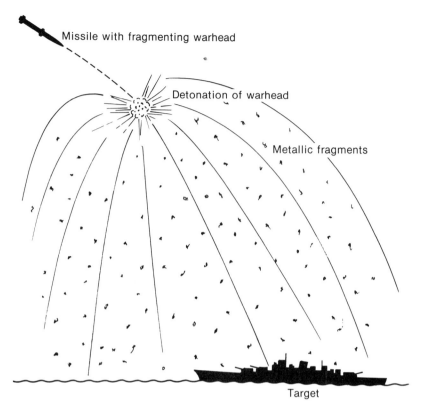

Figure 21–6. Effect of a fragmentation warhead on a surface target.

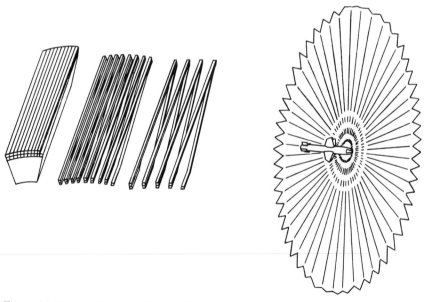

Figure 21–7. Continuous rod expansion.

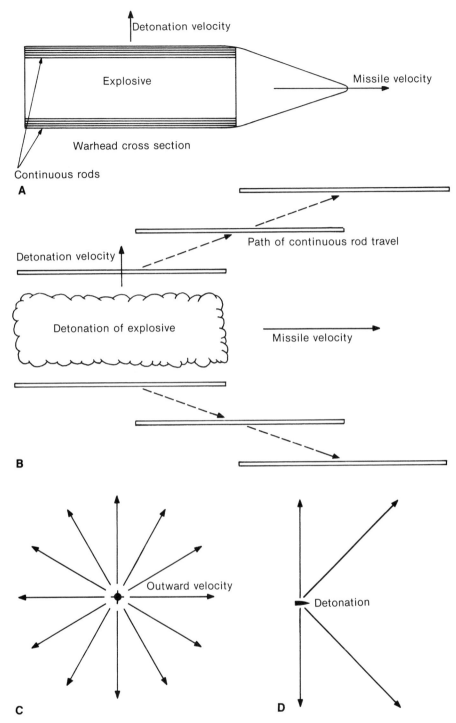

Figure 21-8. *The path of travel of the rods: (a) the warhead; (b) expansion after detonation; (c) front view of the pattern; (d) side view of the pattern.*

Nuclear and Thermonuclear Warheads

Missiles may be equipped with nuclear or thermonuclear warheads. The blast and radiation effects which result from the detonation of this warhead cause immediate physical damage to a large target area, and sickness and death to people who are a considerable distance from the explosion.

Special-Purpose Missile Heads

Two types of special-purpose missile heads are used in training and practice operations. These are (1) a dummy head which has only the outward appearance, the size, shape, and weight of a real warhead; and (2) an exercise head which does not contain any explosive material but otherwise contains the parts of a real warhead, so it can be assembled, disassembled, and tested for electrical continuity.

Propulsion Systems

A guided missile must move at a relatively high speed in order to intercept enemy missiles or aircraft and to decrease its chances of being intercepted when used offensively. Missiles are moved in a desired direction and at a desired speed in response to applied forces produced by the missile propulsion system. The missiles in the Navy surface-to-surface and surface-to-air missile categories have several different propulsion systems. The most common of these types is the two-stage, solid-propellant rocket. In two-stage rockets, the first stage is called the booster stage and the second stage is the sustainer stage. The second type of propulsion system combines a solid-propellant booster rocket with a ramjet sustainer engine. The final type of propulsion system is a solid-propellant rocket known as a *Dual Thrust Rocket Motor* (DTRM) which combines the booster and sustainer stages in one shell.

The two main classes of guided missiles are distinguished by the way they use oxygen. *Rockets* carry their own oxidizer and fuel. As a result, the rocket operates independently of its surroundings, and it can function either in a vacuum, under the water or at a very high altitude where oxygen is scarce. The *jet* carries its own fuel but has an air-breathing motor and so is limited to operating in the atmosphere.

Rockets

Rockets have three major parts: a propellant, a combustion chamber, and a nozzle. The propellant is a combination of the fuel and oxidizer, which cause a chemical reaction to generate the gases in the combustion chamber, which in turn pass through the exhaust nozzle at high velocity. Rockets may be further classified according to the state of the propellant used. The solid-propellant rocket is noted for its simplicity and relatively safe handling qualities; it is used in missiles launched from ships. Poseidon, Polaris, Talos, Tartar, Terrier, Standard, and Sea Sparrow are examples of naval missiles using solid propellants for propulsion. The liquid-propellant rocket is more complicated than the solid-propellant. As no liquid-propellant rockets are operational in shipboard missiles, they will not be discussed in this text.*

The major distinction in solid-propellant rockets is between *restricted-burning* and *unrestricted-burning* rockets. In the restricted-burning rocket, the propellant is allowed to burn on only one surface at a time (in the manner in which a cigarette burns). In the unrestricted-burning rocket, the propellant is allowed to burn on several surfaces at the same time, resulting in a relatively high thrust being produced for only a short period of time. Different amounts of thrust can be obtained by using different patterns of propellant grains.

In the case of both the restricted and unrestricted-burning solid propellants, it should be clearly understood that the propellant burns at a definite and controlled rate and that it does not explode. The propellant burning process is started by an electrically detonated squib which ignites a smokeless or black powder charge, which in turn ignites the propellant.

Atmospheric Jets

Atmospheric jets take air from the atmosphere, increase its pressure, and feed it into a combustion chamber where it is combined with the fuel and ignited. There are two methods of increasing the pressure of the incoming air. One way is with the use of a mechanical compressor. This principle is not currently used in Navy missiles. The other method employs the action of a diffuser. A diffuser is a duct of adjustable, hence varying, cross section designed to convert high-speed air flow into low-speed flow at increased pressure. This action is accomplished by changing the direction of the air flow through the diffuser stage.

The ramjet (sometimes called the flying stovepipe) is the latter type of jet, as shown in figure 21-9. The combustion process in the ramjet is continuous. It uses the action of the diffuser to create a "pressure barrier" which prevents the propellant gases from escaping in the forward direction. In order for the diffuser action to occur, the ramjet must be moving at a suitable speed prior to being ignited, as it cannot produce static thrust. Ramjets use liquid fuel as their burning agent.

---

* This excludes the liquid sustainer stage of the Talos missile, which is not a rocket but a ramjet engine.

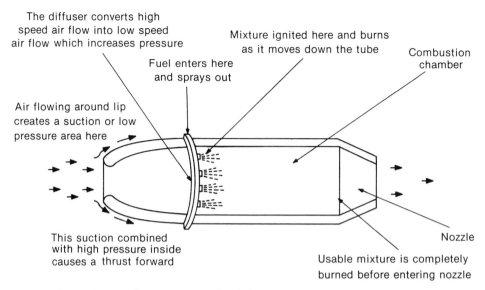

The diffuser converts high speed air flow into low speed air flow which increases pressure

Mixture ignited here and burns as it moves down the tube

Combustion chamber

Fuel enters here and sprays out

Air flowing around lip creates a suction or low pressure area here

This suction combined with high pressure inside causes a thrust forward

Usable mixture is completely burned before entering nozzle

Nozzle

Figure 21–9. The operating cycle of the ramjet.

Ramjets are classified according to whether they are operating at subsonic or supersonic speed, the basic difference being in the diffuser design. Both kinds operate in the manner shown in figure 21–9. Ramjets are limited in range only by the amount of fuel they carry. They can operate up to an altitude of about 90,000 feet.

Review of Propulsion Systems

Two-stage, solid-propellant rockets are the most commonly used rockets, because solid propellants have proven to be the most economical and the safest to handle among the fuels available. The booster rocket (first stage) provides a high thrust for about four seconds to propel the missile to a supersonic speed. As the booster motor burns out, it separates from the second stage (the sustainer rocket and payload). The second stage ignites immediately upon burnout of the first stage and provides a low-thrust push of long duration to sustain the missile's desired flight speed. It is not necessary for the sustainer stage to be burning when the missile reaches the target.

Dual Thrust Rocket Motor (DTRM)

The DTRM combines the booster propellant and sustainer propellant (figure 21–10) in the same casing, thereby eliminating the need for a long separate booster rocket and missile combination. The inner propellant of the DTRM propellant (figure 21–10) serves as the booster. It burns rapidly and provides the high initial booster thrust desired.

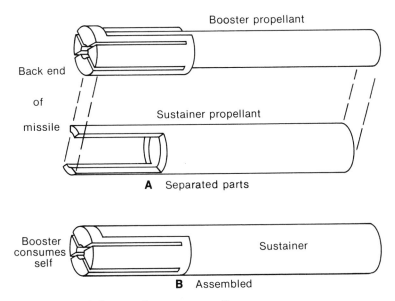

Figure 21–10. Dual thrust rocket motor propellant.

The outer portion of the propellant is the slow-burning sustainer which maintains the missile speed. The advantages gained in compactness from the two propellants in a single space is offset by the reduced amount of propellant used, which shortens the range of the missile.

Solid-Propellant Booster With Ramjet Sustainer

The booster again provides a short-duration, high thrust to push the missile to supersonic speed. It should be noted that the booster in this combination is an absolute necessity, because the ramjet sustainer engine is not capable of providing any thrust unless it is in motion. It is a very simple engine, since there are virtually no moving parts.

22

Ship-Launched Missiles

Introduction

The operational guided missiles in the Fleet today have their origin in a development program called "Project Bumblebee," which began at the end of World War II and culminated in 1957 with the first firing of the Talos missile. The advent of jet aircraft, especially high-flying aircraft, reduced a ship's reaction time for defensive measures, placed new requirements on her sensors, and made many antiaircraft guns useless, because they lacked the long-range firing capability. Currently, because of the successful development of long-range antiaircraft missiles, attacking aircraft are forced to attack at low altitudes. This has created a need for effective short-range missiles for close-in defense, and again places the airplane or missile within gun range.

Figure 22–1. A Talos missile launcher. The fins are not fitted for this training exercise on board.

The three missile systems that were developed in the last two decades for shipboard air defense are *Talos, Terrier,* and *Tartar.* The family of missiles used in the latter two systems is being replaced in the U.S. Navy with the *Standard* missile. The "three Ts" and Standard were developed to defend a large envelope of air space around Fleet units; as a result, they are called *area defense* weapons.

The low-flying air attack threat also caused the development of the concept of *point defense,* in which missiles are designed to protect the launching ship. One point-defense missile system adapts the *Sparrow* air-to-air missile to ship defense.

In the late 1960s, the surface-to-air missiles were given a limited surface-to-surface capability. However, the Navy has since undertaken the development of a ship- (or air-) launched missile specifically designed for striking at surface targets.

Talos

The oldest and longest-range U.S. Navy surface-to-air (SAM) missile is Talos (figure 22–1). Development began in 1944 at the Johns Hopkins Applied Physics Laboratory. The first firing at sea took place in 1959 from the USS *Galveston* (CLG-3) (figure 22–2). Talos is a two-stage missile weighing about 7,000 pounds. It is 30 feet long and has an effective range of over 70 miles. The missile airframe is basically a body for a ramjet sustainer engine, the warhead, and guidance system components. The propulsion system is a 4,000-pound booster and the ramjet sustainer. The antiaircraft warhead is a continuous-rod type with a proximity fuze for target detection and destruction. Talos can also carry a nuclear warhead or conventional high explosive for its

Figure 22–2. The USS Galveston *(CLG-3), shown in 1966, was the first ship to fire an operational Talos missile.*

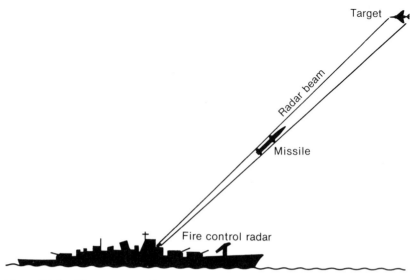

Target

Radar beam

Missile

Fire control radar

Figure 22–3. The concept of beam-riding missiles.

ancillary surface-to-surface mission. Modifications to the missile, including different kinds of warheads, run from A through H versions.

The missile is not guided during the boost phase. It switches to a beam-riding (BT)° guidance system (figure 22–3) and is stabilized in yaw, pitch, and roll after the booster engine burns out.

For maximum-range missions the Talos missile will continue to ride a beam. For shorter-range missions the missile switches in the terminal phase to *semiactive homing* (HT) (figure 22–4). This method is used because at long ranges it is less likely that the missile will be close to the target as there is more room for error in the fire control solutions and for target motion. As a result, echoes reflected by the target would be too weak for the missile to acquire for homing. At closer ranges, however, where the missile will be closer to the target, semiactive homing is preferable. It is more exact than beam guidance, and it follows the shorter path of intercept rather than flying a tail-chase pattern. For example, over a short course of 25 miles, semiactive homing allows the missile greater range than beam riding, because of its shorter flight path. Talos is by far the heaviest U.S. Navy SAM. The missile's reputation for high performance was sustained during the war in Vietnam when in 1968 the USS *Long Beach* (CGN-9) shot down two MIG fighter aircraft over Vietnam from her station in the Tonkin Gulf. The most common version of Talos is the HT version. Talos is scheduled to be replaced in the 1980s.

° B = beam (guidance system); T = tail (steering surface used).

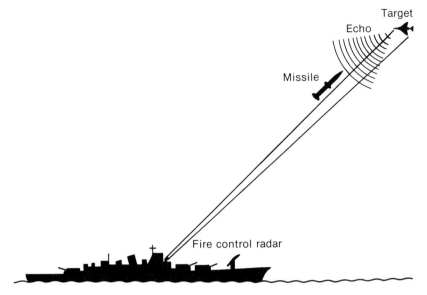

Figure 22–4. *The semiactive homing concept.*

Terrier

Terrier is an intermediate-range SAM (figure 22–5). The Terrier beam-riding (BT) version is a two-stage missile, about 27 feet long and weighing 3,000 pounds. The range of the Terrier BT is about 20 miles.

Figure 22–5. *A twin Terrier missile launcher.*

This kind of warhead is best suited to the tail-chase position the missile must take in the beam-riding version (figure 22–6). The BT missile can also carry a nuclear warhead. Like Talos, Terrier can be fired at surface targets that are outside a specified minimum range from the ship, which is the preliminary distance covered during the boost phase. The propulsion system consists of two stages of solid-propellant rockets. The booster rocket is 12 feet long and weighs about 1,800 pounds. It produces a high thrust for a short duration to boost the missile to supersonic speed. After booster burnout, the solid-propellant sustainer rocket ignites and produces a sustained thrust to get the missile to the target. The BT missile flies a ballistic path during the boost phase. It is stabilized and switched to beam-riding control from booster burnout to target intercept.

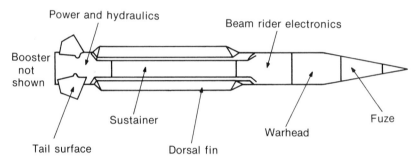

Figure 22–6. The components of the beam-riding Terrier (BT).

The Terrier Homing Missile (HT) is similar to the BT in size and weight; however, the internal component locations and functions are significantly different (see figure 22–7). The better efficiency of a semiactive homing flight path increases the missile range to more than 20 miles. The propulsion system is the same as that described for the BT version.

The HT warhead is a continuous-rod warhead with a proximity fuze. The HT missile does not have a nuclear capability; thus it is the most common version of Terrier. The guidance system employs ballistic flight during the boost phase, and after it is stabilized it is switched to semiactive homing for intercepting the target.

Tartar

The Tartar missile, which is the smallest and has the shortest range of the three surface-to-air missiles, was originally developed for use

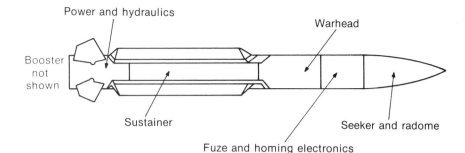

Power and hydraulics

Warhead

Booster not shown

Sustainer

Seeker and radome

Fuze and homing electronics

Figure 22–7. The semiactive homing Terrier (HT) top, drawing; *bottom,* after launching and booster separation.

on small ships (figure 22–8). However, the newest CGNs will be equipped with Tartar, a short-range SAM. The Tartar does not employ a separate booster rocket as do the other surface-to-air missiles; it uses a dual thrust rocket motor (DTRM). The Tartar, about 15 feet in length and weighing about 1,500 pounds, has an effective range of approxi-

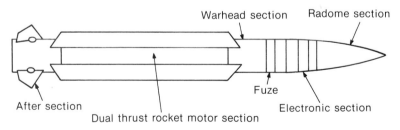

Warhead section   Radome section

Fuze

After section

Dual thrust rocket motor section

Electronic section

Figure 22–8. The Tartar missile.

mately 15 miles. The Tartar warhead and guidance system are the same as described for the Terrier HT missile.

Standard

As missile technology has advanced, developments have been made in the Fleet defense systems (figure 22–9). Two versions of the Standard missile are currently being produced.

One version, referred to as the "medium-range" Standard, basically replaces the Tartar missiles, while the other version, referred to as the "extended-range" Standard, replaces the Terrier missiles. Standard is a dual-purpose missile with a surface-to-air and a surface-to-surface capability.

The Standard missiles are equipped with conventional HE warheads with either point detonating or proximity fuzes. Whereas missiles of earlier design have hydraulically powered controls, Standard is the first completely electronic (solid state) system. Guidance is semiactive homing.* The medium-range version uses the excellent dual-thrust motor's solid propellant, while the extended range uses solid-propellant booster and sustainer rockets. Standard is intended to be the basic armament on board FFG, DDG, and CG classes of ships.

Sea Sparrow

Sea Sparrow is a missile intended for the local, short-range self-defense (point defense) of a ship. This category includes aircraft carri-

* A description is provided in the next chapter.

Figure 22–9. The Standard missile is fired from the USS Buchanan *(DDG-14).*

Figure 22–10. The Sea Sparrow missile is fired from a launcher on board an LST. Note the resemblance of the launcher to the ASROC launcher.

ers, and amphibious and service force ships (figure 22–10). The missile is designed to destroy cruise missiles, aircraft, and surface targets that attack the ship. The Sea Sparrow system is an adaptation of the Navy's air-to-air Sparrow missile. It consists of a single manual optical sight coupled with a CW doppler, radar director. The missile was developed in the late 1960s as the U.S. Base Point Defense System and has several variants that contain a number of improvements. A lighter and more automated NATO Sea Sparrow was produced which allows the engagement of two targets at one time. Work continues by the NATO group* to improve this version. Both the U.S. and NATO BPD Sea Sparrow systems require a ship's search radar for target detection. The second version has also been a cooperative NATO project called the Improved Point Defense System which substitutes U.S.-produced automatic medium-range target acquisition radar (TAS) for the optical system and adds a digital computer. When TAS is combined with the NATO Sea Sparrow, the overall U.S. system will be called the Improved Point Defense System. The present Sea Sparrow Mark III is 12 feet long, eight inches in diameter, and weighs about 450 pounds. The propulsion system is a single-stage, solid propellant. The warhead is a high-explosive fragmentation warhead, and the missile has a range of five to eight miles. It is fired from a modified ASROC eight-cell

---

* The NATO members participating in this venture are Italy, the Netherlands, Norway, and Denmark. Much work on shipborne surface-to-surface missiles has taken place in Italy. The Italians have developed three generations of these missiles.

Figure 22–11. A modified box launcher for Sea Sparrow on board the USS Harold E. Holt *(FF-1074).*

box launcher mounted on a 3-inch 50 caliber gun carriage (figure 22–11). The missile is guided by radar employing a director/illuminator which is optically trained on the target. The semiactive homing guidance system that controls the current version of Sea Sparrow is explained in Chapter 23.

Harpoon

The Harpoon surface-to-surface missile system for future shipboard installation is to be another adaptation of the air-to-surface Harpoon missile now under development and is expected to be in production in 1975 (figure 22–12). A submarine-launched version has been successfully tested. The ship version will add a rocket booster to the missile to bring the missile's initial speed up to the equivalent of the launching speed from a high-speed aircraft. It is an all-weather, antiship missile developed to counter the threat of enemy ships armed with antiship missiles. The degree of danger was made evident when the cruise missiles launched by an Egyptian missile boat sank an Israeli destroyer in the 1967 "Six-Day War." The characteristics so far made public by the Navy state that the missile's range will be more than 50 miles, with a radar terminal guidance (active-homing) system. Indications are that the missile will also be capable of mid-course corrections (command guidance) from the launching vessel to the missile. The ASROC box launcher will be used for Harpoon on ships that do not carry surface-to-air missiles. The ASROC launcher can fire salvos of Harpoon missiles to saturate an enemy's missile defenses. DDGs and CGs will have a slower rate of fire, because they have magazine launchers. Small ships and boats will be provided with newly developed individual canister launchers, each containing a single Harpoon. The canisters can be installed on board a ship in multiple groups, taking up less topside space than other launchers in use and requiring no below-deck space. They will be able to fire salvos. Because of the classification of this missile program, no further facts concerning the missile are known at this time. This missile is intended for ships that presently have no surface-to-surface missile capability.

Figure 22–12.   The Harpoon anti-ship missile is fired at a test range.

Missile Stowage, Loading, and Launchers

A missile and its associated fire control equipment must have stowage and launching facilities.

The two basic types of shipboard launching systems are the vertically and horizontally loaded launchers. The magazine assembly associated with each type of launching system is then determined by the method of loading the launcher. The choice as to which of these two systems is to be used is made in relation to the size of the missile and its associated booster. As illustrated in figure 22–13, the Tartar and its Standard successor missile, which have no external boosters, can very easily be loaded from a vertical position because of their short length. When an external booster to a missile is needed, such as shown for the Terrier missile in figure 22–14, the length of the

Figure 22–13. A Standard missile in the vertical loading position. Some vertically loaded launchers are designed to accept a mix of SAMs, SSMs, and ASROC.

Figure 22–14. A horizontal loading launcher for Terrier and Standard.

complete assembly almost precludes stowing the missiles in a vertical position. The launcher itself is basically the same as the Tartar design which is discussed later.

The Vertically Loaded System

As shown in figure 22–15, the Tartar missile is placed vertically in ready service rings directly below the launcher with its fins folded. When the missile launcher lines up its launcher arm rails at the transfer port in the deck, the stowage ring extends its rail up by a chain and pawl arrangement to match up with the launcher arm. When the missile is on the launcher arm rail, the fins extend to their flight position, the chain and pawl return to the stowage area, and the extended stowage ring retracts. The transfer port closes, and the launcher arms are free to train and elevate the missile to its firing position.

The Horizontally Loaded System

As stated earlier, it is impracticable to stow long missile (missile and booster) assemblies vertically; therefore, a horizontal loading system was produced in the mid-fifties. The missiles with boosters

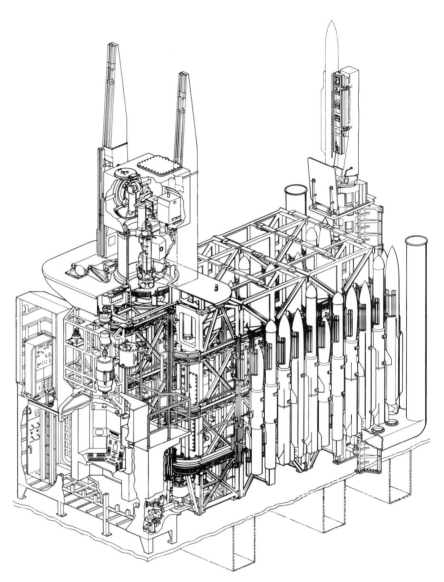

Figure 22–15. A vertical loading system for Tartar. This system can launch different kinds of missiles.

attached are stowed on horizontal ready service rings (figure 22–16). When a missile is to be fired, the ready service ring rotates to the designated missile by choice of warhead and guidance system and places it directly below the magazine doors. The magazine's doors open and the missile is hoisted by hydraulic rams up onto the loading rail in the assembly area. The rams retract and the magazine doors close. The missile fins are unfolded and the booster fins are manually

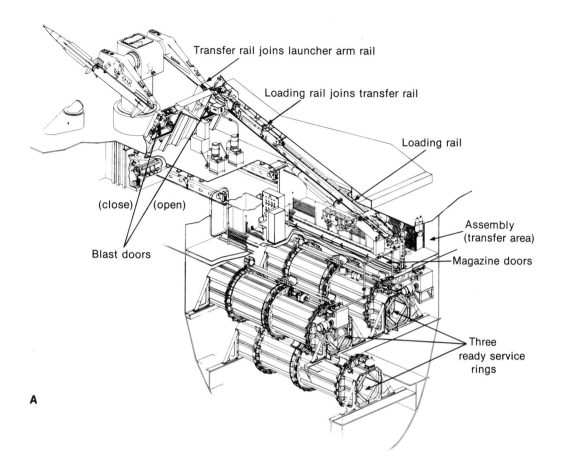

Transfer rail joins launcher arm rail

Loading rail joins transfer rail

Loading rail

(close) (open)

Blast doors

Assembly
(transfer area)

Magazine doors

Three
ready service
rings

A

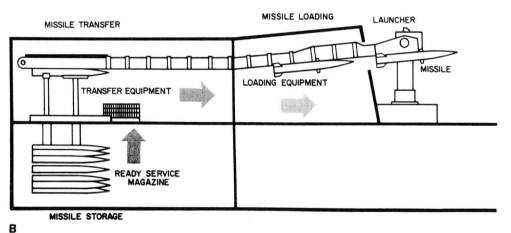

MISSILE TRANSFER

MISSILE LOADING

LAUNCHER

TRANSFER EQUIPMENT

LOADING EQUIPMENT

MISSILE

READY SERVICE
MAGAZINE

MISSILE STORAGE

B

Figure 22–16. Two horizontal loading systems for Terrier and Standard. (a) In the Mark 10 model there is an ASROC magazine, which is the lowest drum in the center. The illustration shows only one assembly area and loading system. (b) The second system can accommodate Terrier or Standard.

Ship-Launched Missiles **301**

put in place by crew members. The loading rail elevates to match up with the transfer rail. When the missile launcher is ready for the missile, the launcher lines up its launcher arm rails at the blast doors to the assembly area. The blast doors open and the transfer rail extends to match up with the launcher arm rail (figure 22–17). The missile is moved from the assembly area to the launcher rail by a chain and pawl arrangement. When the missile is on the launcher arm, the chain and pawl return to the assembly area and the extended transfer rail retracts. The blast doors close, and the launcher arms are free to train and elevate the missile to its firing position.

Figure 22–17. A Talos missile is loaded on the launcher by the transfer rail.

Figure 22–18. A modified Standard (MR) missile is fired from an ASROC launcher on board the destroyer escort USS Vreeland (DE-1068).

Figure 22–19. The "box" launcher offers the advantage of cellular construction allowing the ship to carry several weapons in one launcher. The other six cells shown have ASROCs in them.

Ship-Launched Missiles   **303**

Launching

A third and totally different launching system is the launcher discussed earlier in the ASROC description. This launcher has been adapted to launch either Harpoon or Standard missiles. Figure 22–18 shows an experimental installation of the box design to launch a Standard missile. The box launcher is adaptable to almost any kind of hull as it does not require internal stowage or launching space. Furthermore, some of its cells can carry ASROC while others on the same mount can carry Standard or Harpoon (figure 22–19). The box missile launcher is normally on board ships whose missions are not primarily related to surface and antiair warfare, such as aircraft carriers, ASW destroyers and destroyer escorts, amphibious, and auxiliary ships. The obvious disadvantage of the box design is the loading system. Reloading cannot proceed automatically and rapidly as in the total vertical and horizontal systems described above. Therefore, cruisers, frigates, and AAW destroyers will not normally carry a box missile launcher.

23

Missile Guidance

Introduction

The natural forces that affect a gun projectile also affect the missile in flight. All of these factors were introduced in Chapter 3. The most important variables in long-range trajectories are wind, gravity, centrifugal force, magnetic forces, and the Coriolis effect. They must be considered in computing the fire control solution.

Wind

Some missiles fly through the atmosphere for their entire flight, and others just at the beginning and the end of their flight. While it is traveling in the atmosphere, the force of the wind tends to push a missile off its intended course. Even though the magnitude and direction of the prevailing winds at various points on the earth are well known, they are changed by a number of factors—local topography, thermal updrafts due to local heating of the earth's surface, the distribution of high-pressure and low-pressure air masses, and storms and their associated turbulence. These changes to the desired trajectory must be considered in the guidance system.

Gravity and Centrifugal Force

The force of gravity tries to pull the missile back down to earth. The centrifugal force of the earth's rotation counteracts the effect of gravity to some extent. Centrifugal force is not a significant consideration in short missile flights.

Magnetic Forces

Some missile guidance systems use the strength and/or the direction of the earth's magnetic field as a reference for navigation. Both strength and direction of the magnetic field vary from point to point on the earth. Most of these variations are predictable, with reasonable accuracy, and can be compensated for in the missile guidance system.

Coriolis Effect

The Coriolis effect (a deflection because of the rotation of the earth) on a long-range missile depends greatly on the latitude at which the

Figure 23–1. The fire control antennae of the USS Conyngham *(DDG-17) are both tracking the same target for the Tartar/Standard (MR) semiactive homing, surface-to-air, single-arm missile launcher shown in the foreground. Only one radar director is actually illuminating the target, the other director is backing it up.*

missile is fired. The missile direction and length of flight are also deciding factors. Coriolis effect can be accurately predicted, and suitable corrections can be made by the missile guidance system.

Directing the Missile to the Target

After launching, the two aspects of missile fire control responsible for getting the missile to the target are missile *guidance* and missile *control.*

The *guidance* system includes the process of tracking, computing, and directing, while the *control* system involves the steering process. Without missile guidance and control, the accuracy of missiles at long ranges would be virtually impossible. Because of the interrelationship of the two systems, they are often referred to in this chapter as a single system.

A missile's guidance system is made up of components that are both internal and external to the missile. The guidance system orders the missile onto the desired flight path from the launcher to the target. This may be accomplished by using signals received from the ship, from the target, or from other sources. The missile control system maintains the missile in a proper flight attitude in relation to the desired flight path, compensating for ballistic variables and error.

Flight path guidance is broken down into these four distinct processes:

Tracking   The process by which the positions of the target and the missile are continuously established.

Computing   Positions, determined by tracking, are used to determine whether any corrective control directions are necessary to have the missile hit the target.

Directing   When the corrective directions have been determined, they are sent by signal to the missile.

Steering   When the signals reach the missile, they activate the power units which move the missile control surface.

The missile's flight attitude must be controlled and stable for the above four functions to work successfully. For example, if the tracking process showed the missile to be to the left of the flight path, the computing process would determine that a right turn was necessary. The directing process would transmit a right turn signal to the missile. If the missile were flying upside down, the right turn signal would make the missile actually turn to the left. To make sure that the missile is in the proper attitude, a device called an autopilot is made a part of the control system. The guidance and control systems work together, using the same control surfaces, to keep the missile on the desired flight path.

Control Systems

As stated above, the missile receives guidance signals after it has been launched. In order for the missile to respond to these signals, it must know its own movements and the position of its control surfaces.

In regard to its own movements, a missile in flight will have three rotational movements and three linear movements. As shown in figure 23–2, a missile has a rotational movement about the center of gravity of the missile in pitch (on the lateral axis), yaw (on the vertical axis), and roll (on the longitudinal axis).

The three linear movements are a lateral movement, a vertical movement, and a movement in the direction of thrust (figure 23–3).

A missile has a control-surface/position-detecting device to tell where each control surface is.

After the missile computer network receives the guidance signals, movement information, and control surface position information, it produces error signals. These error signals actuate servo mechanisms that reposition the control surfaces to bring the missile back on the desired flight path (figure 23–4).

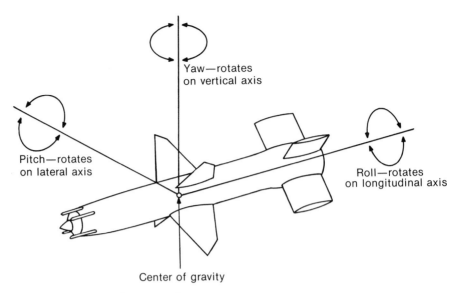

Figure 23–2. *Missile rotational movements.*

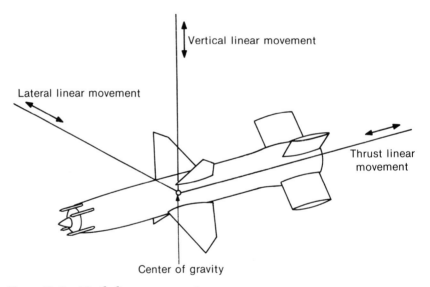

Figure 23–3. *Missile linear movements.*

Missile Flight Phases

A missile flight path can be broken down into three general phases. These three phases are shown in figure 23–5 for the Tartar, Terrier and Talos missiles. The initial phase is called the *boost* phase. During the boost phase, the booster rocket provides the missile with an accel-

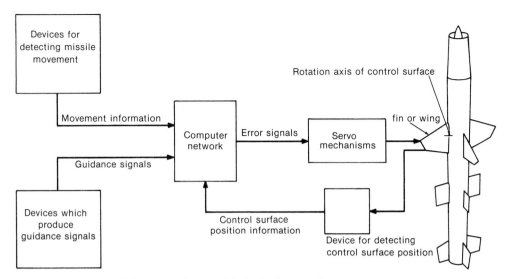

Figure 23–4. A block diagram of a simplified missile control system.

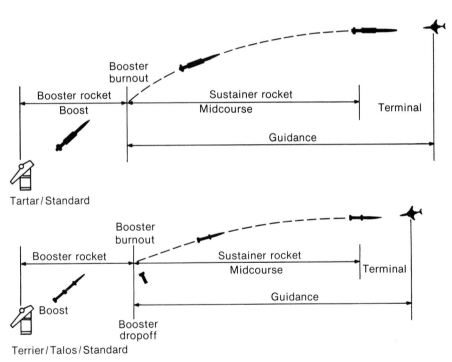

Figure 23–5. Phases of missile flight.

eration of speed from zero at the launcher to a desired speed at the end of the phase. The second phase is called the *midcourse* phase. During the midcourse phase, the missile has its longest flight in both time and distance. Also, during this phase, a sustainer rocket in the missile keeps the missile at the speed that it attained during the boost phase. The final phase is the *terminal* phase where the missile is very close to the target. Guidance of the missile is maintained in both the midcourse and terminal phases. It should be noted that guidance becomes more and more critical as the missile gets nearer to the target. Therefore, the terminal phase responses to any corrections to the missile flight path must be made very quickly or the missile might miss the target. Some missiles will have a combination of two of these phases, depending on the design. When this happens, the characteristics and requirements discussed above will still be required for the total flight path.

General Missile Guidance Systems

The general categories of missile guidance systems that are used in missiles are *preset, command, beam-riding, homing,* and *composite.* The selection of the guidance system or combination of systems to be used in a particular missile is determined by the tactical use of the missile.

In preset missile guidance systems, the characteristics of what the missile is to do while in flight are set into the missile prior to launch. Once the missile has been launched, these orders cannot be changed. The V-1 and V-2 rockets used by the Germans during World War II had a preset guidance system. After they were launched they climbed to a set altitude. They then flew at that altitude for several minutes. At the end of the preset time, the rocket motor was turned off and the missile dove in a ballistic trajectory to its target.

Polaris and Poseidon fleet ballistic missiles are successors of the preset type, having inertial navigation systems which adjust the ballistic flight path programmed at launch. New ship-launched combat missiles are being designed in this category—the Italian surface-to-surface missile, Otomat, reportedly uses inertial guidance and an altimeter to guide the missile in its midcourse flight.*

In the command guidance systems, the flight path of the missile is directly controlled at all times by a radio or radar command link from the launching station. This system was successfully employed in the Regulus missile. It is used in such surface-to-surface missiles as the U.S. Navy Harpoon ship-launched missile (under development),

---

* *Weyer's Warships of the World,* 1973.

the Italian Sea Killer missile family, and in the guidance of target drones. Many foreign naval missiles are guided by command.°

Beam riding guidance systems are a modification of the command guidance system. The missile carries the equipment necessary to generate self-correcting flight orders, which bring the missile onto the center of the guidance beam transmitted by the ship. Since the center of the beam is focused on the target, the missile should hit the target. Operational beam riding missiles, such as one version of the Terrier missile, were described in Chapter 22.

There are three kinds of homing guidance systems—*active, semiactive,* and *passive.* All three of these systems have a mechanism that permits them to "see" the target. When it is said that a missile sees a target, the missile is actually receiving energy reflected or originating from the target. These target reflections are used by the missile to determine its flight path computations. The way that the target is illuminated determines whether the system is active or semiactive. In the active homing system, the missile transmits a beam at the target to produce the reflections. In the semiactive system, the missile relies on some friendly external source to produce the reflections of the target; for example, the launching ship's radar. Passive systems may use heat, radar emissions, or sound from the target to which they are attracted.

Composite systems are in widespread use in modern naval missiles. They combine the best features of several guidance systems in the flight of the missile. Most missiles today combine some of the guidance methods defined above.

Command Guidance

Command guidance systems are characterized by the fact that the flight of the missile is controlled at all times by the launching station. This is accomplished by transmitting steering orders through the fire control radar beam or by a radio signal.

Beam-Riding Guidance

The main difference between beam-riding guidance and command guidance is that the command system transmits orders directly to the missile. The beam-riding missile has been designed so that the missile is able to compute its own steering orders based on its position relative to the center of the guidance beam (figure 23–6). As the missile moves off the radar beam axis (the carrier frequency), the missile receives

---

° Examples are the Australian ASW missile Ikara, the U.S. Bullpup air-to-surface missile, the Israeli Gabriel, and the Soviet Styx and Strela missiles.

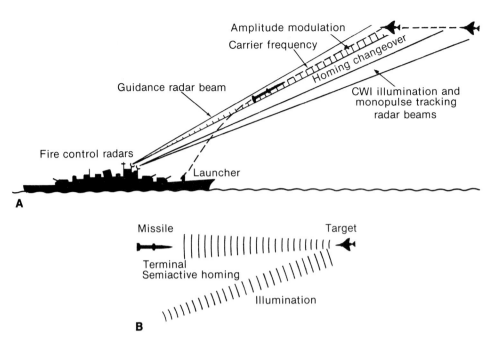

Figure 23-6. Concept of a beam-riding guidance system. (a) Two separate fire control radar directors are used in this example; (b) semiactive homing is employed in the terminal phase when this system is in use.

the radar signal in amplitude modulated form. The amount of AM expresses the distance from the center. A phase comparison technique will give the general orientation or direction toward which the missile must go to correct. The following radar beams are used in beam-riding guidance systems. Together they make up the external guidance system required to direct the missile to its target.

Tracking beam   A tracking beam as in gun fire control radars is a very narrow beam that provides present target position data to the ship's missile fire control system for problem solving.

Capture Beam   This is a wide angle radar beam whose axis is parallel to the guidance beam. Its function is to initially capture the beam-riding missile after the boost phase. It is needed because of separation from the fire control. When the missile is at the center of the capture beam, practically speaking, it is also at the center of the guidance beam (figure 23-7). After a predetermined interval the missile will shift from the capture beam to the guidance beam for a reference (figure 23-8).

Guidance Beam   This is a narrow beam that provides the missile a reference line to the target. The guidance beam is superimposed on the tracking beam; that is, the two beams are trained and elevated

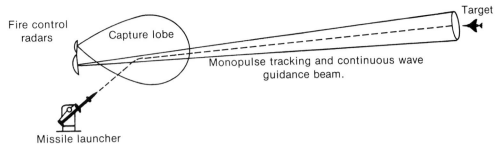

Figure 23–7. When the missile is launched, it enters the capture lobe. The capture lobe aligns the missile with the guidance beam.

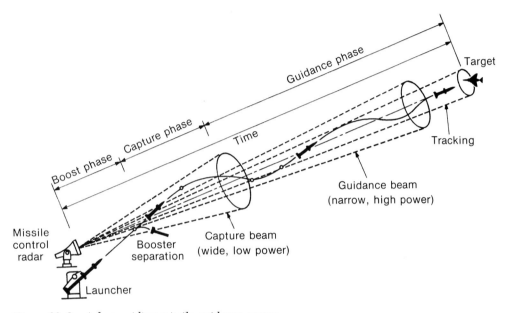

Figure 23–8. A beam-riding missile guidance system.

together and occupy the same space. The guidance beam is therefore on target whenever the tracking beam is on target. In some beam-riding fire control systems, the guidance beam can be offset from the tracking beam (figures 23–6 and 23–9). The guidance beam is placed on the future target position by the ship's missile fire control computer, thus eliminating a tail chase by the missile. The Talos missile system employs this type of guidance, but in the terminal stage of the flight, the Talos missile changes over to semiactive homing. Thus in an antiaircraft firing the offset feature permits the missile to reach a high altitude, where its ramjet sustainer propulsion system operates more efficiently. The missile is therefore able to achieve greater speeds and

Figure 23–9. Offsetting the guidance beam from the tracking beam is shown by the different positions of the fire control directors above the missile launcher.

ranges. In an antisurface role, the guidance beam keeps the missile away from the false radar targets of the water surface by being offset, until the very last portion of the flight. This characteristic permits the missile and guidance beam to be directed so that the flight path is not distorted or affected by the water surface.

Another type of beam-riding guidance is a version of the Terrier system. In this system, the guidance beam is pointed at the target. These missiles ride the guidance beam all the way to the target. Since the radar beam always points at the target, a tail chase by the missile will develop (figure 23–10).

Some basic drawbacks to the beam-riding systems are the size of

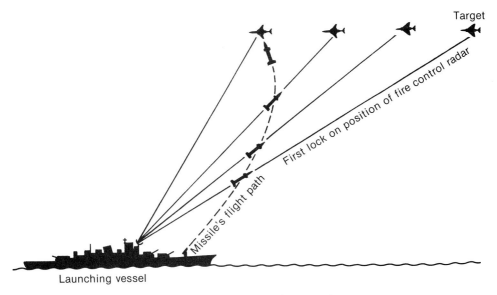

Figure 23–10. *The flight pattern of a single beam-riding missile.*

the required launching installation, the narrowness of the radar guidance beam, and the limitations in the effective range of the guidance beam for missile control.

With a narrow guidance beam, there is more of a chance that the target can evade the missile by maneuvering. The tail chase situation of a beam-riding version of Terrier (BT) results in an inefficient flight path.

Homing Systems

In an *active homing system* the missile itself generates the target illumination signal. This could be a radio, radar, or laser signal. Once the signal has been reflected by the target, the missile guidance equipment picks up the echo. Then the missile homes on the echo. There are currently no active homing missiles in service on U.S. Navy ships, because of several electronic warfare susceptibilities. Two new missiles, Harpoon and Sea Phoenix, may employ active homing radar in the terminal flight phase in the ship-launched version. Disadvantages of active homing in missilery include the need for a source of high power energy in the missile for transmitting the homing signal. This in turn imposes weight and power limitations on the missile, affecting range and warhead. Furthermore, once the missile has been launched the ship has no further control over the missile in flight. The danger is that the missile may not find the desired target, because it will home on the best echo return in the area. An example of this problem might

Missile Guidance **315**

be when a friendly ship was close to an enemy vessel being taken under fire by another U.S. ship.

Finally, active homing betrays the approach of an enemy missile, giving the enemy ship's electronic support measures equipment a bearing to guide sensors and weapons. Advantages of active homing missile guidance include: relieving the launching platform of missile guidance throughout the missile's flight path, which allows the firing ship to engage many more targets at once; or it allows small vessels to carry sophisticated missiles, such as the PGH, PG, and PHM type boats. Moreover, a surface ship firing an active homing missile at another surface target is free of the range limit imposed by the line-of-sight characteristic of radar. As a result, if the launching ship does not need to illuminate the target with its fire control radar, its missiles can seek surface targets at greater distances, over the horizon from the firing ship. This is particularly significant for small vessels which sit low in the water and have a very small radar horizon (figure 23–11).

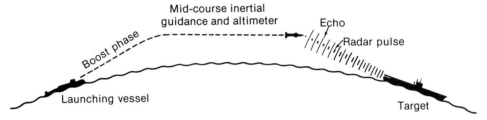

Figure 23–11. The active homing principle used in a long-range flight.

Semiactive Homing Guidance Systems In a semiactive homing system, the missile receives returning target illumination signals from the target upon completion of the boost phase of its flight. These illumination signals do not originate from the missile or the target, but are normally produced by the ship's radar which has directed a radar beam at the target. Once the radar beam has been reflected by the target, the guidance sensing equipment in the missile picks up the echo (figure 23–12) and steers a collision course to the target. The advantages of this guidance system are: (1) permits the use of shipboard longer-range, higher-powered transmitters; (2) more space internally within the missile for additional explosive material; (3) more space for the sustainer propellant to increase missile range; and (4) more space for guidance equipment to increase missile accuracy. One of the disadvantages of this system is that the transmitting ship cannot break off the attack and direct its radar illumination beam at another target while the missiles are in flight. A second disadvantage is the relatively large size of the missile-launching installation.

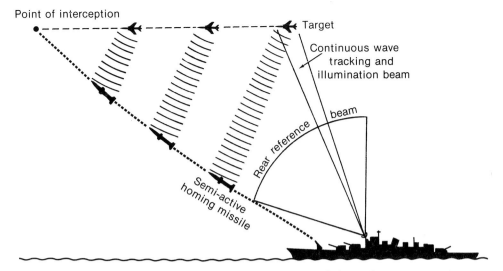

Figure 23–12. The flight concept of a semiactive homing guided missile.

These also apply to beam-riding missiles. New developments are in progress to overcome the guidance problem.*

In addition to the echoes from the target, the semiactive homing system uses the radar radiation from the launching station to maintain positive control over the missile, as in the Terrier homing version. This beam serves to prevent a semiactive homing missile from seeking the launching ship rather than the target, and it gives the missile the distance it has traveled from the launcher. This radiation is called a *rear reference signal.* An additional device installed in all current, semiactive homing guidance systems is an antenna mounted in the nose of the missile which employs the Doppler principle: the missile receives a lower frequency signal as it flies from the launching ship, and a higher frequency signal as it approaches the target. The missile steers toward the higher frequency signal. The same antenna is used to locate the target by receiving the echo of the illuminating signal. This highly directional nose antenna is called the *seeker head.*

The launching station computers determine where the seeker head should look to see the target after the missile has been launched. These position orders are then sent to the missile before launching. After the boost phase and after the seeker head has found the target, a computer in the missile guidance uses the tracking seeker head information to produce missile steering orders. These steering orders take the missile out of the line of sight from the launching station to the target and steer the missile along a collision course with the target.

* The AEGIS project is a U.S. Navy program directed at correcting this limitation.

Even though there are variations in speed, changes in path, and maneuvers by the target, the missile computer will change the missile path to maintain the correct collision path.

Passive Homing Systems   In the passive homing system the missile receives its guidance from such sources emanating from the target as heat, electromagnetic emissions, or sound. In this kind of system, the missile must first be placed near the target. Except for losing the ability to control which target the missile will attack after it has been fired (strongest emission), the passive system has many advantages. They include more available space for explosive material, sustainer propellant for increased range, and control equipment. This system is used in aircraft-launched missiles, such as the Sidewinder heat-seeking missile. Passive systems are relatively vulnerable to decoys that emit more energy than the target. Like active homing guidance in the terminal phase, passive homing permits a launching ship to fire at a target over its horizons. Therefore, missiles equipped with passive homing guidance are well adapted for the surface-to-surface role.

Composite Guidance Systems

Any of the above described methods of guidance could be used in combination with each other in order to maximize the reliability and flexibility of a missile performing its mission. An example of a missile which uses the composite system is Talos, which employs a beam-riding method in the mid-course phase of its flight, and then switches to semiactive guidance in its terminal phase. The newest French and Italian surface-to-surface missiles Exocet and Otomat have preset inertial guidance and altimeter correction in their midcourse flight and active homing in the terminal phase. The Soviet Strela missile family appears to be command guided with passive homing in the terminal phase.

24

The Complete Guided Missile System

The Weapon Control System

The need for rapid handling and evaluation of target data, from detection to destruction, has brought into being a system concept beyond the traditional fire control system. A system used for the control of a particular battery has been known as a fire control system, but the introduction of new data-processing equipment integrated with the equipment for control of all the ship's batteries, and the ability to operate the ship's batteries, and the ability to operate the ship's armament in coordination with other ships in company, have given rise to the new term *weapon control system* (WCS). Such a system is not restricted to a weapon type, but is a group of interrelated pieces of equipment which controls the delivery of effective fire on selected targets. It includes equipment that is only indirectly involved in weapon control.

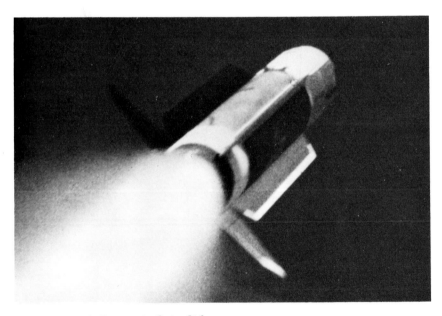

Figure 24–1. A Tartar missile in flight.

The weapon control system is composed of a *weapon direction system* (combined with a Naval Tactical Data system if installed), as well as one or more fire control systems.

Weapon Direction System

Fundamentally, the WDS acts as a clearinghouse for target information to provide the earliest designation and acquisition of a target.

This area has been the subject of rapid and continuous development.

Originally the system for the transfer of target information inside the ship from one part of a weapon control installation to another was called target designation equipment. Its primary function was sending target information to the fire control system from the ship's sensors. But, as the field of weapon control developed, target designation no longer completely described the equipment's functions, and the name was changed to weapons direction system. The WDS still forms a link between the ship's own search sensors and the ship's fire control systems.

Naval Tactical Data System

The *Navy Tactical Data System* (NTDS) is closely related to the ship's weapons direction system, but it works with other ships and aircraft. It is made up of data-processing, display, and transmitting and receiving communication equipment (figure 24–2). NTDS is employed to integrate the individual ship's weapons into a total force of ships with central tactical direction whenever the ship is steaming in company with other ships.

The NTDS makes it possible to exchange target information with the ships in the force, and through NTDS equipment, a ship's weapons become part of all the weapons at the disposal of the task force commander.

The NTDS accepts data into its computer by electronic transmission from other ships or transmits different kinds of information generated by the ship to other units in company. The ability of a ship to integrate herself with other ships and aircraft in facing the entire threat environment mounted by the enemy, offers better protection to the force as a whole and provides flexibility in the employment of weapons. In this way the individual assets of each ship are brought to bear, while their weakest areas are covered. For example, if an incoming cruise missile were detected by one ship, she would automatically pass all target information provided by her sensors to the other ships. Every ship's weapons direction system would then be able to designate the

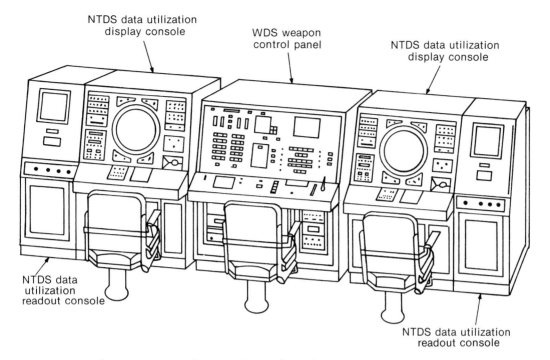

NTDS data utilization display console

WDS weapon control panel

NTDS data utilization display console

NTDS data utilization readout console

NTDS data utilization readout console

Figure 24–2. The weapons control area in the combat information center.

target data to its own fire control system for each missile and gun battery. The batteries then have the necessary preliminary information to acquire and track the incoming missile. Orders to fire can be given by the task force commander, or by individual ships' commanding officers as the tactical situation requires. Usually the screening ship best equipped and positioned for the task would be assigned to fire.

The weapon control area in the combat information center (figure 24–3) contains manned NTDS consoles that are used for the evaluation of contacts. A weapon control panel is located in the weapon control area and provides a means to assign a target to a fire control system, load the missile launcher, fire the missile, and monitor data flow between the NTDS computer and the fire control and launching system (figure 24–4). When a target is received from NTDS and the ship's search radars, it is tracked and evaluated in CIC. After the weapon type is selected, it is assigned to a particular fire control system to ensure the highest probability of a kill consistent with director availability and safety. If missiles are to be employed, the target is acquired by the fire control system, and the WDS assigns the appropriate missile launcher to it.

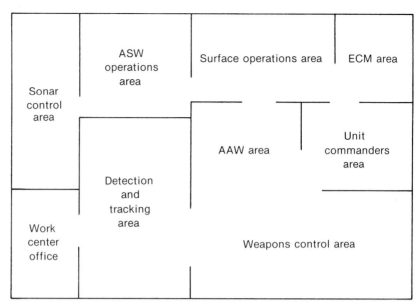

Figure 24–3. A plan view of a CIC on board a guided missile destroyer.

Internal Missile Firing Sequence in the WCS

The missile fire control problem and its solution is basically the same as other fire control problems. There is a processing of the target information from detection to target destruction in the following order:

> Target detection
> Target identification
> Target evaluation
> Target designation/fire control system
>   acquisition
> Fire control solution
> Weapon assignment
> Missile launching

Target Detection/Identification

A long-range air search radar from a ship must be able to intercept an air target before it can attack the ship. To afford maximum warning, the air search radar sends out high-powered wide pulse as the antenna rotates 360 degrees. *Identification Friend or Foe* (IFF) determines whether an echo is an enemy or a friendly unit.

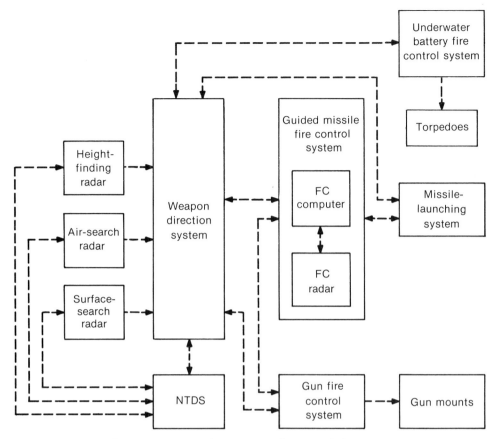

Figure 24–4. The data flow in a missile system employing NTDS.

Target Evaluation

Once an echo has been identified as being an enemy aircraft, it must be evaluated in the overall defense picture in CIC. These are some of the questions asked during target evaluation:

Is the enemy target going to pass close enough to the ship to be within range of the ship's missiles?

Does the enemy target intend to attack the ship? What would the enemy target launch against the ship?

What is the last possible time that the ship can launch a counterattack on the target?

Should there be more than one enemy target, the ship's weapons must be designated to attack the most threatening target. This target evaluation is accomplished by the weapon control system.

Target Designation/Fire Control System Acquisition

Once a target has been evaluated as being a threat to the ship or to the ship's mission, the target must be turned over (designated) to a fire control system—guns or missiles—and acquired by that system.

Fire Control Solution/Radar Functions

The missile director radar has the two-fold function of acquiring and tracking the target and, in many missile systems, also of providing radar beams for guiding the missile to the target. A missile radar consists of two basic groups of equipment—an antenna group above deck and a power/control group below deck. The antenna group consists of an antenna with a pedestal to support it, the electrical and mechanical components to move and stabilize the antenna, and the transmitting, receiving, and associated microwave circuits. Some antenna groups also contain gyroscopes which stabilize the radar antenna. The power/control group consists of the various power supplies and the radar consoles which operate, monitor, and control the antenna group and radar set. The antenna group is not manned; it is completely monitored and controlled by operators located in the radar room near the antenna. During normal operation, the radar room operators only monitor the equipment to insure that it is functioning properly. Target location is fed to the missile radar set via the fire control computer from the weapon direction equipment. If the antenna has not acquired the target from the designation information, the fire control computer automatically starts a search program which moves the radar antenna until it finds the target, similar to the action of gun fire control radars. The WDS is not restricted to receiving its information from the search radar. A designation to the missile radar can come from ESM equipment, which may have obtained an accurate bearing to a target emitting electro-magnetic waves and will position the radar on the target. Similarly, an optical line of sight can be used to position the radar. When the target is found, the system automatically locks on the target and starts to track it. If the ship has more than one fire control system, it is possible to pass designation from one radar set to another called *interdirector designation* (IDD). Because the information from one radar set to the other radar set is accurate, a computer search program is not necessary; therefore, IDD goes through a fire control switchboard instead of repeating the data input from another computer.

When the radar set has acquired the target, radar tracking circuits automatically keep the radar beam on target. The computer receives the target position information from the radar and sends it continuously to the computer where the target's rates of movement are calculated.

The second function of many shipboard missile fire control radar sets is to transmit radar beams that will provide control signals to the missile and guide it to the target. For a beam-rider missile, the radar set simultaneously transmits *tracking*, *capture*, and *guidance* beams. When a semiactive homing missile is being guided, the radar set transmits *rear reference*, *illuminating*, and *tracking* beams.

Fire Control Solution/Computer Functions

As in any fire control problem, the fire control computer calculates the necessary information for the missile to hit the target. With the advances in radar tracking units and highly sophisticated computers developed for missile systems, no operating personnel are necessary at the computer. Most missile fire control computers operate automatically in one of three modes—*air-ready*, *designation*, or *track*.

Air-ready Mode This is the standby situation for the computer. Electrical power is on but the computer is not receiving any information; therefore, it is not generating any guidance or missile launcher orders. The computer does send positioning signals to the radar antenna and launcher to place them in a predetermined position, known as the "air-ready position."

Designation Mode When the computer receives a designation command from the director assignment console, it positions the radar antenna on the indicated bearing and elevation and changes the range gate of the radar to the indicated range. Once this has been accomplished, the target should be acquired by the radar. If the target is not acquired by the radar, the computer automatically moves the radar antenna in a preset search pattern until the radar acquires the target. Once the radar has acquired the target and started to track, the computer automatically goes into the track mode of operation.

Track Mode In the track mode of operation, the computer solves the fire control problem by aiding the radar in tracking the target and receiving error signals from the automatic radar tracking circuits. It also provides the Weapon Direction System with such tactical data as present target position, future target position, and time of flight (missile time to target intercept).

Weapon Assignment

The weapon assignment is accomplished at the Weapon Control Panel. With the tactical data of the target's present and predicted intercept positions being received from the computer, the combat systems officer in CIC can determine from the WCS which missile launcher to use. Once the launcher has been assigned and the missile is ready to fire, the command to fire is made by the combat systems officer by closing the firing key located on the weapon control panel.

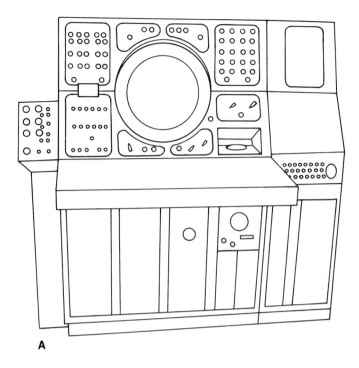

A

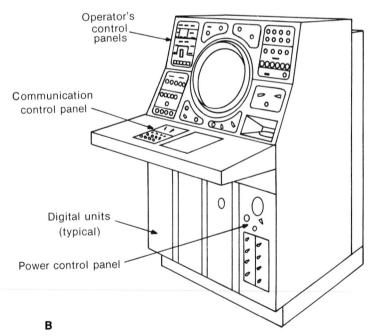

Operator's
control
panels

Communication
control panel

Digital units
(typical)

Power control panel

B

Figure 24–5. (a) *NTDS data use console;* (b) *NTDS data input console.*

Missile Launching

The primary functions of any missile launching system are to (1) stow the missile until needed, (2) assemble additional items (fins, etc.) on the missile prior to firing, and (3) load the missile on the launcher ready for firing. However, to understand the need for these particular functions, it is first necessary to understand the sequence of events of the missile launch. Take, for example, the sequence of events in the horizontally loaded missile launching system. It begins when a *missile select* command is transmitted from the weapon control panel to the launcher station. The missile select command in this example may be for a beam-riding Terrier or a semiactive homing Terrier. The missile select command may also be for an ASROC if the launcher has a dual purpose, as in the *Belknap* class of CGs. All of these types of missiles may be loaded on the same ready-service ring in the missile magazine.

Once the missile to be fired has been selected, the missile launching station receives a *load order* from the weapons control panel. The load order tells the launching station what action to take with the selected missile in one of four loading orders—"hold," "continuous," "single," and "unload." The "hold" order puts the system in a standby position with the selected missile being readied for flight. The "continuous"

Figure 24–6. The missile is fired.

order tells the system to keep supplying missiles to the launcher. The "single" order tells the system to load one missile on each launcher arm, and not to bring any more missiles into the assembly area. The "unload" order tells the system to remove any missiles on the launcher arm.

Summary

The weapons problem develops as soon as an enemy target is detected in CIC. The target position information is passed to the NTDS by own ship's sensors or NTDS data. It is tracked and evaluated by the NTDS consoles (figure 24–5). Once it has been evaluated as the most threatening target, the target information (range, bearing, elevation, course, and speed) is passed to the Weapons Direction System for reevaluation with respect to the availability of a missile system and the capability of that system. When this has been completed, the target is designated to a fire control system for acquisition and tracking. While the fire control system tracks the target and solves the fire control problem, a launcher is assigned and the missiles are loaded. When the target is within range of the weapon, the missile is launched (figure 24–6). With everything functioning properly, the target will be destroyed.

25

The Fleet Ballistic Missile System

Figure 25–1. The Fleet ballistic missile submarine USS Andrew Jackson *(SSBN-619) as seen from the starboard bow, with the missile hatches in view aft.*

Introduction

The Fleet Ballistic Missile Weapon System consists of a nuclear-powered submarine (figure 25–1), 16 Polaris or Poseidon missiles, and all the equipment necessary to supply intelligence to, and to launch the missiles when the submarine is either submerged or on the surface. The submarine serves as a mobile launching platform, having a cruising range limited only by provisions and crew. It can remain submerged for extended periods, and when deployed in its operating area, is not easily detected by enemy forces. As a defense against hostile action by an enemy, the submarine is provided with the most modern torpedo fire control system and its associated detection devices.

The nuclear submarine provides an all-weather, mobile launching base for the missiles and offers maximum readiness conditions and minimum vulnerability to detection and countermeasures. The submarine houses the missiles and all equipment required for ship operation, navigation, missile preparation, and missile launching (figure 25–2).

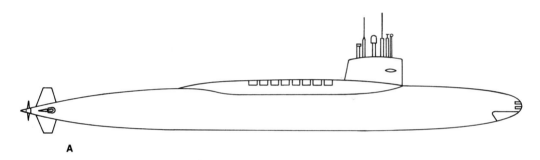

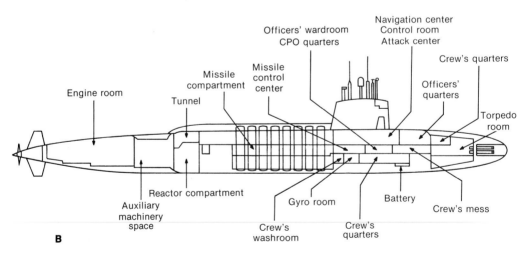

Figure 25–2. (a) *Profile view of the SSBN;* (b) *a cutaway view of the interior of the SSBN.*

The submarine weapon system is composed of the ship subsystem, FBM fire control subsystem, navigational subsystem, the missile subsystem, and the launching system.

Ship System

The SSBN submarine (ship subsystem) supplies electrical, hydraulic, and pneumatic power to all weapon system components; and temperature control, monitoring, and compensation devices to the missile and launching systems. Interior communication equipment provides liaison between the various weapon system stations.

As an integral part of its watertight hull, the submarine's structure forms 16 outer (mount) tubes to accommodate the 16 inner (launcher) tubes, which support and protect the missiles before they are launched. Also, the ship subsystem supplies ship data (rudder angle, stern plane angle, and reference ship heading) to the navigational system.

Fire Control System

The purpose of the FBM fire control system (figure 25–3) is to prepare and to fire the 16 missiles in a minimum amount of time. The fire control system is composed of all the equipment needed to erect the missile guidance system inertial platform to the local vertical, to determine the true launching bearing, to store and compute target data, and to send the data to the guidance computer.

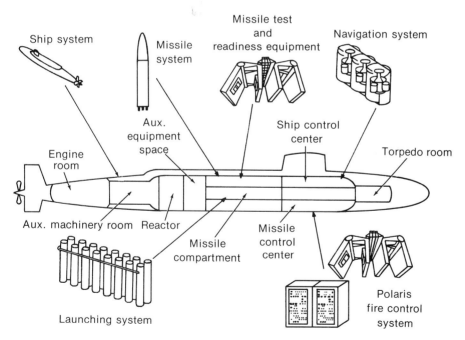

Figure 25–3. The weapon system.

Navigation System

The function of the navigation system is to determine position, velocity, and attitude of the boat (heading, roll, pitch, yaw, heave, and sway); and to transmit this data continuously to the fire control system. This information is provided by inertial navigation equipment, celestial and radio navigational aids, computer groups, and auxiliary equipment.

The navigation system ensures that the FBM weapon system is always provided with precise navigational information. This accuracy must be maintained while the submarine is operating anywhere in the navigable waters of the world. The Ship's Inertial Navigation System (SINS) is the primary instrument used for navigating.

SINS is based on the principles of inertia. Every movement of the submarine is recorded with reference to the stable element in SINS. Included in the equipment are numerous gyros and accelerometers whose function it is to detect, record, and designate to the fire control system the submarine's position and speed, and to establish true north and a vertical reference. SINS, then, acts like a dead reckoning tracer-/analyzer. It also has the ability to weigh, analyze, and make corrections to its dead reckoning solution based on optical and Loran observations.

Inertial Guidance

Inertial guidance is defined as a guidance system designed to project a missile over a predetermined path, wherein the path of the missile is adjusted after launching by devices wholly within the missile and independent of outside information. These devices make use of Newton's second law of motion. This law, which relates acceleration, force, and mass, states that the acceleration of a body is directly proportional to the force applied, and inversely proportional to the mass of the body. Accelerometers will detect any change in vehicular motion. To understand the use of accelerometers in inertial guidance, let us first examine the principle of accelerometers in general terms.

An accelerometer, as its name implies, is a device for measuring the force of an acceleration. In their basic principles, such devices are simple. For example, a pendulum, free to swing on a transverse axis, could be used to measure acceleration along the fore-and-aft axis of the missile. When the missile accelerates, the pendulum will tend to lag aft; it tends to remain where it was when the movement started. The actual displacement of the pendulum from its original position will be a function of the magnitude of the accelerating force. Another simple device might consist of a weight supported between two springs (figure 25–4). When an accelerating force is applied, the weight will

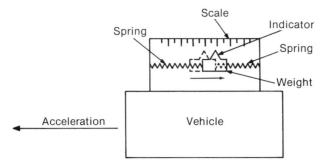

Figure 25–4. An elementary spring-mounted accelerometer.

move from its original position in a direction opposite to that of the applied force. The movement of the mass (weight) is in accordance with Newton's second law of motion.

A simple illustration of the principle involved in the accelerometer is the action of the human body in an automobile. If an automobile accelerates forward, the occupant is forced backward in the seat. If the auto comes to a sudden stop, he is thrown forward. When the auto goes into a turn, the occupant tends to be forced away from the direction of the turn. The amount of movement is proportional to the force causing the acceleration. The direction of movement in relation to the auto is opposite to the direction of acceleration.

With an inertial guidance system, a missile is able to navigate, from launching point to target, by means of a highly refined form of dead reckoning. Dead reckoning is simply a process of estimating your position from information on (a) previously known position, (b) course, (c) speed, and (d) time traveled. For example, assume that a ship's navigator determines his ship's position by astronomical observations with a sextant. The ship's position, and the time, are marked on the chart. Assume that the ship then travels for three hours on course 024, at a rate of 20 knots. From the known position on the chart, the navigator can draw a line representing the ship's course. By measuring off on this line a distance representing 60 nautical miles (20 knots times 3 hours), the navigator can estimate the ship's new position by dead reckoning. If the ship changes course, the navigator will mark on the chart the point at which the change occurred, and draw a line from that point representing the new course.

A missile with inertial guidance navigates in a similar way, but with certain differences. It determines the distance it has traveled by multiplying speed by time. But it cannot measure its speed directly if it is traveling at supersonic velocity outside the earth's atmosphere. However, it can use an accelerometer to measure its acceleration, and determine its speed by multiplying acceleration by time. To summarize:

$$\text{Velocity} = \text{Acceleration} \times \text{Time}$$

$$\text{Distance} = \text{Velocity} \times \text{Time}$$

The acceleration, of course, is not constant. It may vary because of uneven burning of the propellant. It will tend to increase as the missile rises into thinner air. Positive (forward) acceleration will become zero at burnout. If the missile is still rising at that time, it will have a negative acceleration because of gravity; if it is still in the atmosphere, it will have a negative acceleration because of air resistance. Acceleration will cause a constantly changing speed, and changing acceleration will change the rate at which the speed changes. If the missile is to determine accurately the distance it has traveled under these conditions, its computer circuits must perform a double integration. Integration is the process of adding up, or getting the algebraic sum, of all the instantaneous values of a changing quantity. Thus the integrators act as computer elements.

The Missile

The Polaris A3 and Poseidon missiles use a solid propellant. They have three stages, designed to deliver nuclear warheads to enemy targets within a range of 500 to 2,500 nautical miles from its launch point. They can be sent to sea aboard SSBN submarines operating at extended ranges from home and advanced bases. Solid propellant grains cast in the rocket motor cases are stable for long storage periods, eliminating the need for fueling operations on board. They provide a high thrust-to-weight ratio, and produce maximum thrust almost instantaneously after ignition. A two-stage propulsion system is used to attain the desired range. The final stage (reentry body) of this three-stage missile is a true ballistic device, traveling through the low-drag environment of space on the momentum supplied by the two propulsion stages. This third stage, still subject to the gravitational pull of the earth, follows a ballistic trajectory to the target (figure 25–5).

Launching System

The function of the missile launching system is to stow, protect, and eject the 16 missiles. The missile is launched using a controlled release of high-pressure steam. The steam is produced by a gas generator beneath the base of the missile. Some systems use high pressure air for ejection, but most systems now use steam pressure in the ejector. This results in a flameless launch, with rocket ignition occurring at

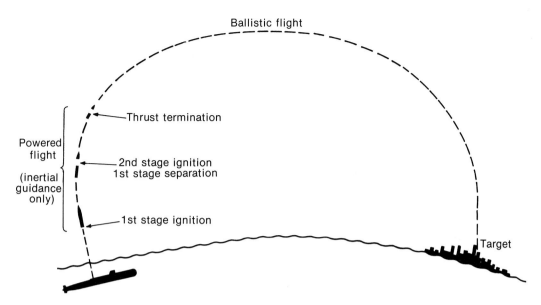

Figure 25-5. A Poseidon missile trajectory.

a safe height above the submarine. Incorporated in the launching system are features providing resilient mounting of the missile to prevent shock and vibration damage during storage aboard the submarine. The functions of the pre-launch, launch, and post-launch operations are continuously controlled and monitored within the launching system.

Flight Sequence

In a submerged launch, ignition of the first stage rocket takes place shortly after the missile breaks the surface of the sea. This is the beginning of powered flight and the inertial guidance portion of the trajectory. The first stage propels the missile far into the atmosphere. The first stage then separates, and the second stage rocket motor propels the missile to a point above the earth's atmosphere. When the missile has reached the proper velocity and point in the trajectory, the reentry subsystem separates and the warhead, or warheads, follow a ballistic trajectory to the target. The time of separation determines the range which the missile warhead will span. The range can be varied in this way, as previously indicated, from 500 to 2,500 nautical miles.

Since there are no external control surfaces on the missile, changes in the trajectory are made by deflecting the jet stream from its motors. A precomputed ideal trajectory is preset into the missile. The preset

Figure 25–6. The USS Henry L. Stimson *(SSBN-665) during a high-speed surface run.*

information takes into account the movements of the target, the launching point, and the missile with respect to space during the time of flight. The velocity which the missile must attain along its trajectory for the release of its warhead is also preset on the time of flight. The launching submarine determines its launching position and the position of the target on the earth's surface is determined from charts. While in the power stage of flight, the missile continuously measures its linear accelerations on the basis of its inertial system and alters its trajectory to offset the outside forces causing unwanted accelerations. When the missile is on a proper trajectory and a correct velocity has been attained, the warhead is released and proceeds toward the target with no further correction possible.

The warhead dives toward its target at a steep angle and at several times the speed of sound. The materials for the outer surface of the warhead have been developed to resist the temperatures generated by friction with the atmosphere at reentry speeds, and suitable insulation is provided between the outer skin and the internal components to prevent damage to the warhead.

PART 5

Antisubmarine Weapons

Long before the submarine was successfully developed as the best vehicle from which to fire weapons that could pierce a ship's hull underwater, men managed to perfect the principal underwater weapons later employed in submarine warfare. By 1805, Robert Fulton was able to demonstrate a practical way to sink ships by exploding a charge of gunpowder against a ship's hull. He called his weapon a *torpedo*. The next step was getting the weapon to the point of impact. This led to a search for a delivery system which was more selective and reliable than floating mines down upon the enemy with the tide or current.

The first effort was to equip the steam launch with a spar torpedo. A charge with a contact fuze was suspended at the end of a long spar. The boat then approached the target ship and, just before contact, the spar was lowered to strike below the waterline. The next effort was focused on finding a self-propelled torpedo which could be fired from a safe distance.

The first so-called "locomotive" torpedoes were American inventions steered by wires trailed behind the torpedo. These efforts are reflected in the current Mark 48 torpedo. However, the most successful self-propelled torpedo was perfected by a Scotsman named Robert Whitehead, who began working with an Austrian naval officer, Captain Giovanni Luppis, in 1862. The torpedo ran independently on a preset course. Inaccuracies in maintaining course and depth were eliminated in the 1890s by an Austrian engineer, Ludwig Obry, who invented a satisfactory gyroscope for steering control.

The modern torpedo was adopted by all major navies for use by both submarines and destroyers against surface ships by the turn of the century, despite the fact that the combination of submarine and torpedo was described by one British naval officer as "underhand, unfair, and damned un-English." [*]

This Part explains the sensors, weapons, and fire control concepts as they are combined and applied in U.S. Navy antisubmarine systems.

[*] Attributed to Admiral A. K. Wilson in 1902. Quoted in *From the Dreadnought to Scapa Flow*, vol. 1. (London: Arthur J. Marder, 1961).

26

Principles and Operation
of Shipboard Sonar Systems

Figure 26–1. One of the latest hull-mounted sonar domes is the AN/SQS-26 bow sonar transducer.

340

Introduction

On surface ships, echo-ranging equipment, called *sonar* (*sound navigation and ranging*), is installed to determine ranges and bearings of submarines by means of sound waves. In some cases, it is used for such navigational purposes as locating reefs, submerged objects, and buoys. There are two general modes in a ship sonar—passive and active.

Both of these sonar modes receive echoes or sound noises by means of a transducer. The transducer is located on the centerline just aft of the bow, or on the bow of the ship (figure 26–2). It is located there to keep it as far away as possible from the noise of the ship's machinery spaces and propellers. The sonar receiving and indicating equipment (called the *stack* or *sonar control indicator*) is located in a compartment called *sonar control*. The signal transmitting equipment (active sonar only) is usually located as near as possible to the transducer.

The Principles of Passive and Active Sonar

A passive sonar can only listen for sounds in the water to detect an enemy submarine. When the hydrophones in the sonar dome pick up the sound of a target, the only information that can be derived is a bearing to the target. However, should two hydrophones or more be separated by a known distance (baseline), then range to the target can be determined. The separated hydrophones can measure the curvature of the sound wavefront, thus the radius (range) to the source as shown in figure 26–3. Tactical applications of passive sonar go well beyond the scope of this introduction, and will not be discussed here. Instead, the reader should refer to the NWIP 24-2 series, ATP 1 (A), Volume 1, and the NWP 24 series. Passive sonar is extensively em-

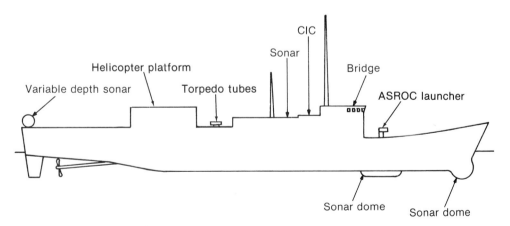

Figure 26–2. General shipboard locations of sonar equipment.

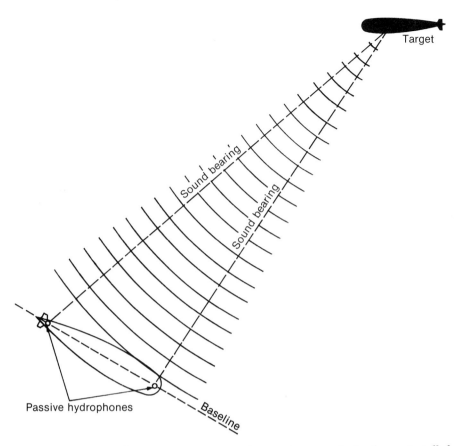

Figure 26–3. Finding range to a target, using passive sonar hydrophones, installed a known distance apart. A computer provides range solution.

ployed by the U.S. Navy in ASW, in sonobuoys dropped from aircraft (figure 26–4), in sonar dipping helicopters (figure 26–5), in submarines, and in fixed and towed cable arrays. All destroyer-type ships have a passive and active hull-mounted sonar capability, while ASW helicopters and aircraft also have both passive and active capabilities through the use of sonobuoys. Some destroyer-type ships have a variable depth sonar that is towed below the layer at variable depths which can detect submarines by passive or active means.

An active sonar basically consists of (1) a transducer (dual-purpose equipment for both transmitting and receiving sound), (2) electronic transmitting equipment (to generate the sound pulse), (3) receiver equipment (to amplify the echoes received), (4) display equipment cathode ray tube to provide a video picture of the received sound), and (5) loudspeakers or headphones (to reproduce the received signals audibly). Bearing and range to the sonar contact is read from the

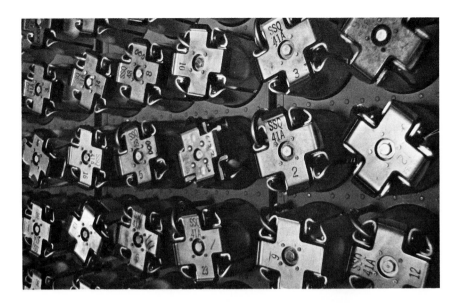

Figure 26–4. Top, *sonar buoys, also called sonobuoys, arranged in their racks aboard a navy patrol aircraft. Below, the sonar buoys shown with one of the four fins extended horizontally. The fins slow the fall of the sonobuoys. After they have hit the water, the buoys drop hydrophones, which provide passive or active sonar coverage of the area to the aircraft overhead.*

Figure 26–5. A carrier-borne ASW helicopter (SH-3 Sea King) lowering its sonar transducer.

display equipment. Bearing of the target is determined by observing the bearing dial which is mounted on the scope. Range is obtained by the electronic equipment measuring one half the time that it takes for the pulse to go out and the echo to return. The equipment then indicates the actual range to sonar contact directly on the scope display.

All active sonars are a combination of two echo-ranging systems that function simultaneously. One system provides a continuous video (sight) display of acoustic reception from all directions on the *cathode ray tube* (CRT). The other system provides an audio response of acoustic reception on a desired bearing. Both the video and audio systems are used when tracking a sonar contact. The video image is used for more exact tracking of the sonar contact in bearing and range. The audio system provides for more accurate identification (classification) of the target by determining echo quality and strength.

The video system scans electronically on each bearing for any echoes of the transmitted pulse. Any echoes received will appear as bright spots on the face of a cathode ray tube (CRT) in the same way as a radar presentation is made on the face of a cathode ray tube. Each spot then appears at the correct bearing on the CRT, at a distance from the center which is proportional to the range of the returning echo. The target is then tracked in bearing and range by the sonar operator. The active sonar can transmit at different frequencies.

Basic Active Sonar System—The Transducer

A transducer is a device that converts energy from one form into another. An example is the changing of electrical energy into mechanical energy or vice versa. This is the principle by which sonar transducers operate.

Electrostrictive Process of Energy Transformation

The electrostrictive process in transducers relies on the ability of certain manmade ceramics to produce a mechanical force when a voltage is applied; or conversely, produce a voltage when a mechanical force is applied.

When ferroelectric material such as lead zirconate titanate compound is placed in an electric field, it changes in dimensions. This effect is very similar to the piezoelectric effect found in some natural crystals whose oscillations change in step with changing electrical or mechanical forces. For the ceramic material to acquire the piezoelectric characteristic, an extremely high voltage is initially applied to the material for several minutes to polarize it permanently. Then, as alternating current is applied, the material will shorten or lengthen with each half-cycle to set up mechanical vibrations at the desired frequency.

Ceramic transducer elements are used in modern sonars and have high sensitivity, high stability with changing temperatures and pressure, and relatively low cost. Their greatest advantage lies in the mechanical properties of the material, which allow construction of almost any reasonable shape or size. A certain number of ceramic elements, usually eight or nine depending on type sonar, are stacked vertically and are called a *stave*. Staves are arranged into a cylinder shape to form the transducer.

In order to transmit a pulse, electrical energy is supplied to the transducer elements where it is converted to acoustical energy (pulse). In order to receive an echo, the transducer elements reconvert the acoustical energy (returning echo) into electrical energy. The sonar dome protects the transducer elements and reduces the noise caused by water turbulence around the elements.

Operation of the Active (Echo-Ranging) Mode

The operation of any active sonar system in its active mode occurs in four major sequential phases: *transmission, reception, video presentation,* and *audio presentation.*

Transmission

The sonar equipment sends an electrical pulse through amplifying equipment to the transducer. The transducer converts the high electrical energy to high acoustical energy, which is sent into the water around the transducer. The receiver equipment is automatically turned on after the pulse has been transmitted (figure 26–6).

Reception

When the returning sonic energy is received by the transducer, it is converted into electrical energy. Since the transducer is physically

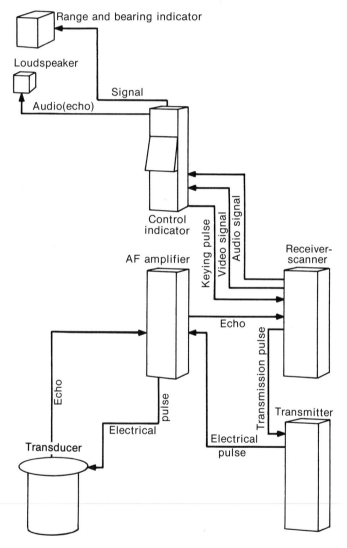

Figure 26–6. A sonar system in a simplified schematic diagram.

Figure 26–7. Hydrophones being installed on a sonar stack. The stack is attached to the hull and protected by a pressurized sphere made of a heavy fabric compound.

separated into individual staves (vertical rows of hydrophones), the returning echoes will only hit a certain number of staves (26–7). The electrical signal representing the target echo is sent to the preamplifier to be amplified. After amplification the echo is sent to the receiver. Because the echo only hit some of the staves of the nearly circular transducer, the bearing of the target can be determined after processing in the receiver. Range is also determined in the receiver by measuring one half the time required by the pulse to go out to the target and return. In the receiver, the echo is processed by the audio and video scanners for the projection of usable signals by the control indicator and the speaker.

Video Presentation

A video display is used to classify and track target echoes received by the sonar. The type of display will depend on the type sonar found on board ship. The SQS-23 and SQS-29 series sonars will have a PPI display, while the newer SQS-26 sonar will have a PPI and B-scan display. These displays will be found at the control equipment for the sonar (figure 26–8). An approximately 7-inch cathode ray tube (CRT) is employed for the PPI presentation which receives electrical signals from the video receiver-scanner and provides the sonar operator with a picture (pip) of the true bearing and range (figure 26–9) to the contact. The B-scan display found only in the SQS-26 is a 17-inch rectangular CRT that is used to present sonar range vertically and bearing horizontally.

Figure 26–8. A sonarman on board the USS Berkeley *(DDG-15) mans sonar search equipment during fleet training exercises.*

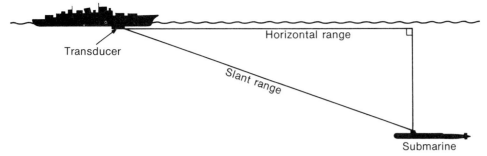

Figure 26–9. The difference between horizontal range and slant range.

PPI Cathode Ray Tube Presentations

In the active mode of operation, the CRT may be in either of two presentations—*ship center display* (SCD) or *target center display* (TCD). The SCD mode is used for searching for sonar contacts. The TCD mode is used for actual tracking of the contact once it has been established.

Ship Center Display (SCD)

In the ship center display, the sonar transmitting ship is located at the center of the CRT scope display. For discussion, one complete cycle of the display on the CRT from one transmission pulse to the next will be used. The sequencing of this display is automatically controlled within the operator console. Figure 26–10 shows all the information on the CRT scope at one time. In actual operation, each component is printed separately.

The sonar operator turns the bearing knob to the true bearing in which he desires to search and receive echoes. He then turns the range knob to an established range for that type of search. The sonar equipment then prints a line, called a *cursor*, on the face of the CRT at the indicated bearing and range.

After the sonar equipment prints the cursor, the sonar equipment automatically keys the transmitter, and a pulse is sent out by the transducer. A spiral electronic sweep appears at the center of the CRT scope and increases in diameter at a rate proportional to the time it takes the transmitted pulse to pass through the water. With this sweep being in synchronization with the rotating video receiver scanner, the presence of a returning echo will produce a bright spot on the face of the CRT. The bright spot (echo) will correspond to the slant range and true bearing of the object reflecting the pulse.

At the same time that the sweep is increasing in diameter, a broken line, bearing 180 degrees relative from own ship's course, is displayed

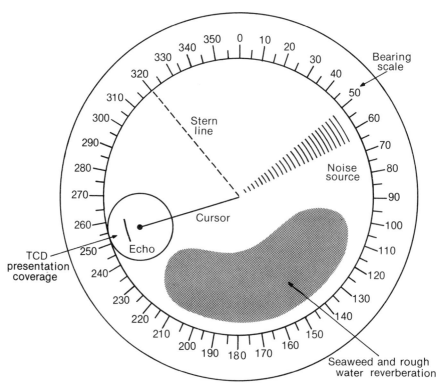

Figure 26–10. The cathode ray tube showing a ship-centered display.

on the scope. This line indicates where the ship's stern is in true bearing and is called the *stern line*. The stern line is used to assist the sonar operator to visualize the ship's heading without cluttering the visual presentation in the area of search ahead of the ship. It is also used to establish a reference point from which to search in set patterns.

Since the equipment receives a video picture from every direction except a few degrees of the stern (baffle area), all noise sources are shown on the CRT. The noise produced by the ship's screws prevents the reception of target echoes astern. A noise source such as a cavitating propeller will show up as a bright spoke or wedge (figure 26–10). Reflected echoes from such things as seaweed and rough water will show up on the CRT as a large brightened area.

Most sonar sets can change the actual size of the echo printed on the CRT. This capability is called *sum* or *difference*. In the *sum* of operation, the left, right, and center video signals from the transducer are shown on the CRT, which provides a broad, easily seen pip for an echo. When a good echo has been detected during search, the

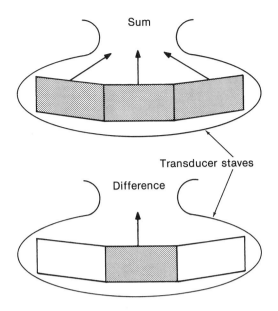

Figure 26–11. Top, *the sum mode;* bottom, *the difference mode.*

equipment is switched to *difference.* Here the left and right video signals are not displayed on the CRT and the target echo becomes small and sharp (figure 26–11). This makes it possible for the sonar operator to track the target more accurately both in range and bearing. *Sum* is used during search, and *difference* is used during attack. When the transmitted pulse has traveled a preset distance, controlled by the operator, one cycle of operation has ended. A new pulse is transmitted and the cycle is repeated.

Target Center Display (TCD)

Once a target shows up as a result of the ship center display, actual tracking may begin using target center display. The end of the cursor, instead of the ship, (figure 26–12) now becomes the reference point for the center of the CRT scope. The TCD greatly expands the picture on the CRT scope of the area in the immediate vicinity of the end of the cursor. When the cursor is near or on the target, the target contact will also show up on the CRT. In most cases, the transmitting ship will be off the CRT scope presentation as it is shown in figure 26–12. The enlarged picture in TCD operation greatly aids the sonar operator in the tracking of a sonar target. The TCD presentation continues at the option of the sonar operator during the rest of the time the contact is held.

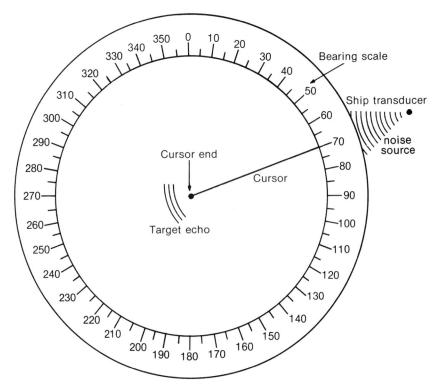

Figure 26–12. The cathode ray tube showing a target-centered display. The cursor end always remains in the center of the CRT.

Audio presentation

The amplified electrical signal received from the receiver-scanner is changed into an audible frequency sound and sent to a headset or loudspeaker located at the control indicator. Here it is used in target identification and Doppler determination.

Passive Mode

When the sonar operator turns the sonar control knob to the passive or listen mode position, the transmitter section of the sonar equipment is placed in standby and does not send electrical energy to the transducer. As in the active mode, the same cursor is printed on the CRT scope, but the transducer does not send out a pulse. Also, the same spiral electronic sweep starts at the center of the CRT and expands outward. Should any noise sources be received at the transducer, they are printed as the sweep expands.

The AN/SQS-23 Sonar Sets

The AN/SQS-23 sonar (figure 26–13) combined good features of the preceding sonar sets and also lowered the transmission frequency for greater range. One advance made prior to the introduction of the SQS/23 series was the *rotating directional transmission* (RDT) mode. When a transmission pulse assembly switch was added to previous sonar sets, the transmitted pulse could be concentrated into a narrow sector of the transducer. This provided for greater transmission power

Figure 26–13. The AN/SQS-23 sonar of the USS Barry *(DD-933) is seen in drydock in Boston.*

with resultant improved sensitivity and range. It also provided for a narrow selected bearing and a directional beam of power, and added a new type of transducer that would operate at a greatly increased power-output level. As a result, accurate ranges and bearings at ranges greater than those obtained on previous equipment were obtained. The AN/SQS-23 sonar is found on many destroyers today.

AN/SQS-26 Sonar

The AN/SQS-26 surface sonar systems (figure 26–14) perform the ASW functions of submarine detection, classification, localization, and tracking at target ranges that, under most conditions, greatly exceed those of previous shipboard sonar systems. Then sonar systems achieve increased range capability by operating in a low transmission frequency band with greater transmitter output power. They also use a variety of operating modes to exploit both direct and indirect acoustic paths.

Figure 26–14. A view of the AN/SQS-26.

A brief description of the various active operating modes follows.

Bottom Bounce (BB)   This mode is accomplished by using automatically selected transducer angles to reflect the sound beam up from the ocean floor normally 500 fathoms or deeper. Preselected transmission angles cause sound to be reflected from the bottom into regions not normally possible.

Convergence Zone (CZ)   This was previously explained in an earlier chapter.

Omnidirectional Transmission (ODT)   This mode uses a direct path in the conventional manner above and below the layer.

Passive   This may be used concurrently with or independently of any active mode of operation. Reception is dependent upon noises produced by the target.

The type of mode used depends upon water conditions, depth of the water, and the tactical situation.

Variable Depth Sonar (VDS)

One of the major problems of detection and tracking is that a target can run below the previously described thermocline or take advantage of water conditions that block good sonar coverage. A solution to this problem has been to place the transducer below the thermocline depth. *Variable depth sonar* (VDS) provides a means to lower a transducer into shadow zones which could not be penetrated by sonar emissions from the hull-mounted transducer (figure 26–15). The VDS (figure 26–16) is lowered from the ship's stern and towed at the desired

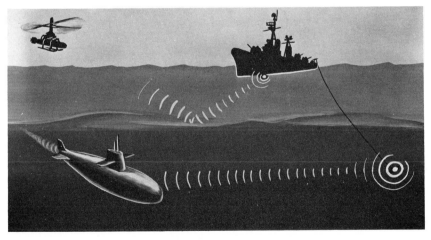

Figure 26–15. The special value of variable depth sonar is shown in this conception of layer interference with sonar search by a hull-mounted transducer.

Principles and Operation of Shipboard Sonar Systems   **355**

Figure 26–16. Top, *a variable depth sonar installed on board the* USS Francis Hammond *(DE-1067); bottom, another kind of installation on the stern of the USS* Morton *(DD-948), which was part of the ASW conversion of the* Hull *class destroyers.*

depth. It is connected electrically to the sonar electronic equipment in the same manner as the hull-mounted transducer. The transducer is installed inside a hydrodynamically shaped body to ensure a minimum of turbulence around the transducer. Transmission and reception principles of the towed transducer are the same as for the hull-mounted transducer.

27

Antisubmarine Weapon and Delivery Systems

Introduction

The current weapon employed by U.S. Navy surface ships against submarines is the torpedo. Older systems such as the depth charge and its descendant, the depth bomb pattern thrown ahead of the ship (hedgehog), are not in common use. There is a depth bomb for the ASROC missile which can replace the torpedo. Parenthetically, most surface ships do not carry mines either, although a number of ship types such as destroyers and amphibious ships can be employed to supplement the minelayer.

The main differences in systems are the means of delivering the torpedo from the ship to the vicinity of the submarine. The Navy also has several different marks of homing torpedoes available for use.

Figure 27–1. The torpedo is an interesting case of a weapon being fully developed for Fleet use before its ultimate target, the submarine. The ship's ASW torpedoes are located in three launching stations: overhead in the helicopter; in the triple tubes on the port side of the ship beneath the forward stack; and forward of the superstructure in the ASROC launcher.

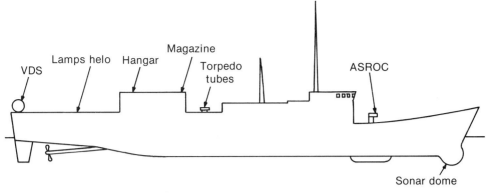

Figure 27–2. *General locations of ASW weapons and weapon control stations on board ships of the U.S. Navy. Actual positions vary by class of ship; other topside equipment was omitted for the sake of simplicity.*

Figure 27–2 is a composite drawing showing the general shipboard location of torpedo delivery systems, weapon control stations, and sensors.

Background of the Homing Torpedo

From the time the torpedo became operational in the U.S. Navy in the last quarter of the nineteenth century (figure 27–3), until World War II, torpedoes were designed to sink surface ships by following the course set into their gyro mechanisms. They would run in a straight line until they either ran out of power or struck a target. Examples

Figure 27–3. *A Whitehead torpedo being loaded into the stern tube of a torpedo boat in the 1890s.*

of this type of torpedo are the Mark 14 and 16, 21-inch, air-steam torpedoes.

During World War II, two new features were introduced into torpedoes. Electric propulsion was the first feature, which resulted in a wakeless torpedo that could not be visually detected from the vessel or target under attack. The second feature completely changed the principles used to guide the torpedo and resulted in a homing type torpedo that would seek out the target and attack it.

The homing feature became indispensable in the torpedo when the submarine replaced the surface vessel as the main target of this weapon. As the mission of the torpedo changed, new torpedoes became smaller because less explosive was required under high pressure to damage a submarine hull. The surface ship discarded depth charges in favor of ASW torpedoes.

Description of the Homing Torpedo

A surface-launched homing torpedo is initially gyro controlled in order to get the torpedo reasonably close to the target. This gyro-controlled run is called an *enabling run* (figure 27–4). At the end of this run (enabling point), the torpedo exploder is armed, the homing mechanism (passive/active sonar) is activated to search for the target, and the influence device or contact firing mechanism is set to function. The maneuvers that are made by the torpedo after the enabling run has been completed are called the search pattern. These patterns may be helical, zigzag, circular, or snake runs, and they may include a

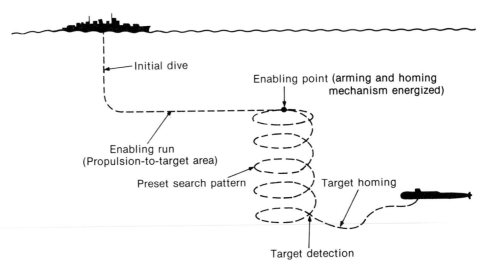

Figure 27–4. *A characteristic run of a homing torpedo.*

zone of fixed water depth. They may also include the torpedo searching from search floor to surface and back to search floor again. When the torpedo homing mechanism detects a target, the torpedo attacks the target.

In general, there are two types of homing torpedoes—*active* and *passive*. The active acoustic torpedo does not depend upon the sound emitted from the target. The torpedo generates and transmits its own acoustic energy (sonar), which is used for its self-directing homing information. This energy has a fixed, controlled frequency and beam width and is reflected by the target. The torpedo is designed to steer to this particular reflected echo. The reflected echo is converted into electrical signals which control the operation of the torpedo rudder and elevator control surfaces, causing the torpedo to home on the target.

The passive acoustic torpedo homes on the acoustic energy radiated by the target. This received acoustic energy is converted into electrical signals, which control the operation of the torpedo rudder and elevator control surfaces to steer the torpedo toward the noise source.

Torpedo Fuzes

Torpedoes are normally armed both mechanically and electrically. The exploder is armed mechanically after it leaves the launching station. The exploder mechanism is also armed electrically by a timing device after the torpedo has traveled either a preset distance, (after the enabling run of the tube-launched torpedo) or when it reaches its search depth (for helicopter or ASROC launched torpedoes). The fuze detonates either by contact or by sensing the proximity of the target. The contact fuze is similar to the point detonating fuze described in Chapter 17. The influence fuze employs one of several principles to become active—sensing the strength of target echo, magnetic disturbance, or Doppler effect.*

Propulsion of Torpedoes

Except for the two latest torpedoes, the Mark 46 and the Mark 48, most U.S. torpedoes are powered by batteries and electric motors. Some of the battery systems become active when the torpedo enters the water. Seawater is used as the electrolyte of the battery. The Mark 46 engine employs a solid fuel propellant in the Mod 0, and a liquid fuel in the Mod 1. The Mark 48 is propelled by the same liquid fuel used in the Mark 46 Mod 1.

* Using the Doppler principle, a sonar detects movement by the difference in frequency between random echoes from impurities and foreign matter in the water and the frequency of the target echo.

Torpedoes in Service

The Mark 44, 46, and 48 are representative of U.S. Navy torpedoes currently in service. Below is a brief description of their characteristics.

Mark 44 Mod 0

The Mark 44 Mod 0 torpedo is electrically controlled and propelled. It uses an active acoustic homing system and can be launched from surface craft or aircraft.

The torpedo is designed to attack submerged submarines cruising at moderate speeds. After the enabling run, the torpedo searches for a target by active acoustic means while maneuvering in a vertical helical path. Echoes from the target cause the torpedo to steer toward the target until point contact with the target is made. If the torpedo loses the target echo, it will search for a short time in the same general direction in which it is traveling. If it is unsuccessful in relocating the target, it will resume a helical search.

The acoustic homing system of this torpedo has a passive feature that allows the torpedo to home in on an acoustic noise source whose frequency level is within the correct sensitivity range of its receiver. The passive element increases the attack capabilities of this weapon. When the torpedo rises above a preset depth, the passive homing feature is eliminated by a ceiling device which prevents the torpedo from attacking the launching ship.

Passive torpedoes are not effective against targets which do not create or emit measurable noises. They can often be evaded by stopping engines or by using a simple noisemaker which misleads or misdirects the torpedo away from the actual target. Surface vessels use a noisemaker towed astern. Submarines use a noisemaker which can be placed in the water away from the submarine and left there to attract the torpedo.

Mark 46

The Mark 46 torpedo has a diameter of 12.75 inches, but is longer and heavier than the Mark 44. It is a replacement for the Mark 44 and can be launched from aircraft or ships. It homes on its target with an active-passive acoustic homing head, either following the target's radiated noise, or if the target is silent, searching for the target with active sonar (figure 27–5).

Mark 48

The newest torpedo entering service in the Navy is the Mark 48 (figure 27–6). It is an extremely elaborate and sophisticated weapon

Figure 27–5. *The Mark 46 torpedo being launched from a triple tube launcher.*

Figure 27–6. *A nuclear-powered attack submarine arms with Mark 48 torpedoes.*

and is presently serving only in submarines. It is guided with an active-passive terminal homing head, and it is provided with command guidance by wire in the first part of its run. The torpedo is reported to be able to dive deeper and to have a higher speed than its predecessors. The Mark 48 is approximately 19 inches in diameter.

Delivery Systems

At present, torpedoes may be launched by tube, by helicopter, and by rocket. Each method covers a different zone around the ship.

Homing torpedoes may be launched from surface vessels using torpedo tubes. Many homing torpedoes can have the search depth set in electrically, just before launching. Torpedoes dropped by helicopter are preset so that when they are dropped near the target, they seek the desired depth and go into the preset search pattern without going through the enabling run stage, previously described in arming the fuze.

Torpedo Tubes

Torpedo tubes serve the following purposes:

They house and protect the torpedo (including such things as heating in cold weather) until the instant of firing.

They provide a means for setting such things as torpedo gyro angle and running depth, up to the instant of launching.

As expulsion of the torpedo begins, they trigger the torpedo to start its own engine and gyroscope.

They expel the torpedo with compressed air with sufficient force to clear the firing ship and to provide the necessary speed and direction to keep the torpedo on its firing course until its engine develops enough power for self-propulsion.

Above-Water Torpedo Tubes and Locations

Shipboard torpedo tubes are either trainable or fixed. Fixed tubes are usually mounted so that their muzzles protrude through some part of the ship's hull. Trainable tubes require a large clear deck area—a location such as the weather deck. From this location, torpedoes can be fired through limited arcs of train to one or the other side of the ship.

Some of the advantages and disadvantages of using either a fixed or trainable torpedo tube follow:

Greater torpedo initial gyro angles must be set into torpedoes fired from a fixed tube. This is a disadvantage because torpedoes tend to depart more widely from their predicted courses when fired with large rather than with small initial gyro launch angles.

Fixed tubes have a weight advantage because they do not need the training mount, training gear, etc.

Fixed tubes must be carried on both sides of the ship, whereas a trainable tube can be located on the centerline to launch to either side of the ship.

Fixed tubes may be located in a protected location and kept away from the elements; an example would be the USS *Truxtun* (CGN-35) or the *Garcia* and *Knox* classes.

Fixed Tubes

Figure 27–7 shows a Mark 25 single barrel, fixed-type, nontrainable torpedo tube normally mounted singly on each side of the ship. The interior tubes are mounted athwartships within the superstructure with their muzzles extending through the sides of the deckhouse. This torpedo tube can also be mounted on a weather deck. When mounted externally, it will normally be located aft of the number one stack to afford it some protection against waves that might come over the bow. The tube components are constructed of a lightweight aluminum alloy. The torpedo is launched from the tube by a blast of compressed air. This tube was designed to launch a 21-inch torpedo. Adapter rings may be inserted into the tube to permit launching a 19-inch diameter torpedo.

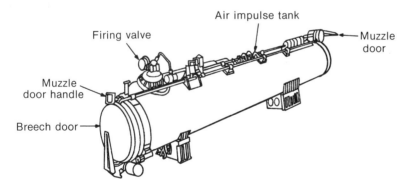

Figure 27–7. the Mark 25 shipboard, non-trainable torpedo tube.

Trainable Tubes

The Mark 32 torpedo tube is currently the most common tube in the Fleet. It launches 12.75 inch torpedoes, such as the Mark 44 and

Mark 46. There are two ways of mounting the Mark 32, one of which is the typical triple tube trainable mount shown in figure 27–8, and one is a nontrainable bracket version. They may be supplied with compressed air from ship generators with which to expel the torpedo or from bottles carried on board vessels not equipped with compressed air generators. Except for the way in which they derive their air supply, the two versions of the Mark 32 are similar.

The complete trainable torpedo tube assembly consists of three separate and independently fired tubes that are mounted on a common training gear. The tubes and training gear are equipped with thermostatically controlled internal electric heating units for cold weather. Each barrel is fired independently by an electric firing circuit. The electrical firing key is usually located in close proximity to the tube. Manual firing is possible for emergencies. The mount has no train power drive and must be trained manually with the train hand wheel.

The tubes are arranged in a triangular group. Each barrel is fabricated of plastic reinforced with fiberglass to make it as light as possible. The breech mechanism covers the back end of the tube, and the muzzle cover is at the launching end. Along the top surface of the tube are two openings, one located toward the muzzle and the other toward the breech. The opening near the muzzle is for attaching lanyards from the torpedo to the tube to start the torpedo and to enable the exploder to arm. An electrical plug is located under the cover at the breech to set electrical commands into the torpedo before launching.

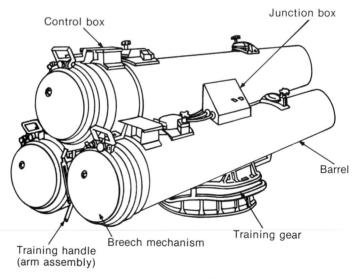

Figure 27–8. The Mark 32 trainable torpedo tube.

The muzzle cover is a fiberglass-reinforced plastic assembly that has a rubber ring which seals the cover over the mouth of the tube. After the torpedo is loaded into the tube through the breech end, the breech mechanism, consisting of a rubber-lined fiberglass-reinforced plastic air flask with controls, valves, and fittings on it, is bolted in place. On command from the control box, the firing valve in the breech mechanism releases a blast of compressed air into the after end of the tube to eject the torpedo. The control box is an aluminum water-proof box located on the breech end of the tube with buttons on the after side providing either electrical or manual triggering of the firing valve. A junction box located over the training gear houses the connections between the ship's electrical supply and the electrical heating system of the barrels and training gear.

A nontrainable version of this torpedo tube is installed in some ships' helicopter superstructures with the muzzles extending through the forward bulkhead. Instead of being arranged in a triangular group, the nontrainable version only uses two barrels which are mounted one over the other or next to each other.

Helicopters

Helicopters have long since become invaluable members of the Navy's ASW forces. The ASW helicopter mission has been the domain of the large helicopter and in particular the Sikorsky SH-3 helicopter. The use of a large helicopter is dictated by mission requirements which entail a large payload of sophisticated equipment and by an operational concept under which the helicopter is based together with complementary fixed-wing aircraft on an aircraft carrier. On the other hand, the destroyer has also long played a major ASW role with its basic ASW mission being the escort of convoys or task units. In ASW, as in other naval missions, time and developments conspire to make ASW weapons and weapon systems obsolete at an alarming rate. The nature of today's submarine threat, with increasing numbers of fast, deep-diving nuclear boats, poses a serious challenge to current ASW systems. This challenge is being met by combining the versatility and capability of the helicopter with the destroyer in the *light airborne multipurpose system* concept (LAMPS) (figure 27–9).

LAMPS has a two-fold primary mission: antiship missile defense and ASW (figure 27–10). The antiship missile defense mission of LAMPS provides the destroyer with the ability to detect enemy missile launching ships over the ship's radar horizon with the helicopter's radar and equipment for detecting enemy electronic missions. Armed with a Harpoon missile now under development, LAMPS helicopters will be able to attack hostile ships.

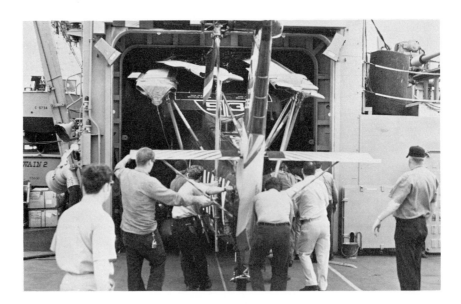

Figure 27–9. The Light Airborne Multi-purpose system (LAMPS) is a small manned helicopter, shipborne, that carries various weapons and sensors. Top, *a Kaman SH2F Seasprite helicopter is moved into its hanger on board the* USS Wainwright *(CG-28).* Bottom, *landing on deck of the* USS Harold E. Holt *(FE-1074).*

On an ASW mission, the LAMPS helicopter proceeds to the place of most recent contact by the ship or other detecting ASW forces. The helicopter would then pinpoint, classify, and attack the submarine with torpedoes. Its detecting equipment will include active and passive sonobuoys, magnetic anomaly gear, and radar.

The Seasprite (SH-2F) is the LAMPS helicopter currently in service. Secondary functions of the Seasprite include all-weather search and rescue, plane guard duties, gunfire, observation, personnel transfer, and vertical replenishment. The Seasprite can float should it have to land in the water because of an engine failure.

Figure 27-10. *The Seasprite LAMPS helicopter carrying a torpedo under the port strut and several kinds of sensors, including the radar mounted below the nose, the EW gear on the starboard strut, and a MAD probe aft.*

The LAMPS system includes equipment aboard ship to aid the navigation of the helicopter during night and foul weather operations. There are also navigation aids in the helicopter. The integration of the helicopter with the ship requires close coordination in the tactical employment of the ship's sensors with those of the helicopter. For example, the ship may launch the helicopter to assist in detection efforts, or alternatively it may launch the helicopter after initial detection and direct the helicopter to the area of last known position of the submarine (datum).

Antisubmarine Rocket (ASROC)

Another system for launching torpedoes or depth bombs at submarines is ASROC. ASROC is an assembly of a missile booster behind a torpedo or depth charge. The ASROC missile (figure 27-11) is a supersonic, ship-launched, solid fuel, ballistic rocket.

ASROC is a stand-off weapon designed for the destruction of sub-

Figure 27–11. An ASROC being fired from the USS Aylwin *(FF-1081). The eight-cell launcher is clearly visible through the smoke.*

marines at intermediate ranges. This is achieved by the delivery of the weapon through the air to a point in the water from which it can either attack the submarine with a torpedo, or if it has the submarine within its lethal radius, with a depth charge. The unguided missile is made up of the payload which is propelled by a rocket motor and stabilized by an airframe throughout the powered flight. The airframe and rocket motor separate in accordance with firing orders from the underwater battery fire control system. From separation to

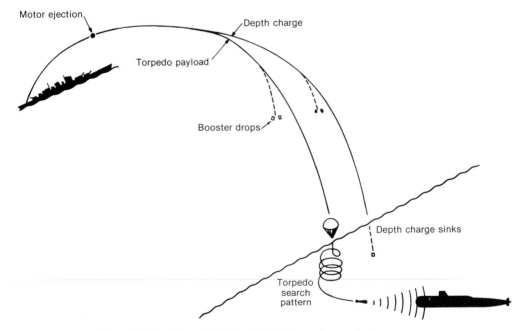

Figure 27–12. The ASROC missile flight and torpedo drop.

370 Introduction to Shipboard Weapons

entry of the water, different methods of stabilization are employed in the weapon. The descent of the depth charge through the air is stabilized by fins. A torpedo parachute decelerates the torpedo to a safe speed to avoid damaging its highly sensitive transducer nose cap and electrical components when it enters the water (figure 27–12).

Before the missile is launched, the submarine must be located by sonar. The sonar range and bearing and other pertinent data are then transmitted to the ASROC fire control system located in the underwater battery plotting room. The fire control system automatically computes the future target position as explained in a following chapter. It then sets a time-to-separate order into the timers on the airframe and keeps the launcher trained on the desired water entry point. When the fire control system has a solution, the missile can be fired at will by simply closing the firing circuit.

ASROC Launchers

There are two kinds of ASROC launchers. The most common kind is the so-called "box" design shown in figure 27–13. This launcher contains eight cells for eight ASROCs. There are four over-and-under

Figure 27–13. The ASROC "box" type launcher. This launcher is the most common in the Fleet. It cannot be automatically reloaded, but on board some of the newest frigates it can be conveniently reloaded from the magazine in the superstructure.

units called *guides* which may be elevated separately. The cells are mounted on a modified three-inch gun carriage. The box may be forward, midships, or aft, depending on the class of ship. When the missile is to be fired, the box is trained to the desired angle (45°). The rocket ignites in the cell, blowing out the weather shield in the back of the cell. Meanwhile, the forward port for the cell opens and the rocket blasts off. The box launches cannot be automatically reloaded in most of the ships in which it is installed.

Some destroyer escort classes have semiautomatic reloading systems in the bridge structure aft of the ASROC launcher.

Combination Launcher

The *Belknap* class of CG is equipped with a combination launcher that can handle ASROC or other missiles (figure 27–14). In this process, moving the ASROC from the magazine to the launcher rail can proceed automatically, firing one missile at a time. In this system there are three drums horizontally arranged below decks in an inverted triangle with the two drums on the top containing ASROC and other missiles. The bottom drum contains Terrier or Standard missiles. When an ASROC is to be fired, the left or right loader drum, depending on whether a depth charge or torpedo is selected, rotates, indexing a round onto a loading rail. The rail carries the ASROC through the open door of the magazine and pushes it onto the launcher arm. The rail retracts inside the magazine and the doors close. The launcher then trains and elevates the required number of degrees, and the ASROC is fired. If another ASROC is to be fired, the cycle is repeated. The system for loading missiles is described in Chapter 22.

Magazine and Loading Systems

From the description of the tube and ASROC launching systems, it is evident that the magazine and loading equipment have individual variations peculiar to the ship type considered. The ASROC launcher installed on the older *Gearing* class destroyers can be reloaded by hand from a magazine on the main deck behind the launchers. Subsequent classes of destroyers and missile destroyers must rearm manually from another ship or ashore after they have fired their ASROCs from the launchers, since they do not carry ASROC magazines. Some cruisers and frigates carry box launchers. Of all the large destroyer types in the Navy, only the *Belknap* class provides an automatic loading system for ASROC.* The box launcher is the only version found among the

* The ships of the *Spruance* class will incorporate an automated loading machine below deck for reloading ASROC. The system loads vertically into the elevated box launcher.

Figure 27–14. Top, *the combination launcher installed on the bow of the USS* Belknap *(CG-26) handles ASROC and/or other missiles. Bottom,* an ASROC loaded on the Belknap's *launcher rail trained outboard.*

Antisubmarine Weapon and Delivery Systems **373**

destroyer escort classes. Therefore, reloading is manual in the older DEs, while in the newer classes, such as the *Knox* class, loading is semiautomatic from the bridge structure.

Depth Charges

Until this point, the scope of the discussion of surface-launched underwater weapons has been restricted to the torpedo. It should be recognized nevertheless that the depth charge, which had such widespread use in both World War I and World War II, still has a practical application in modern antisubmarine warfare for surface ships on escort duty. The depth charge may have tactical value when an attacking submarine has closed the main body of a formation or entered inside it to use her torpedoes to best effect. At this point the depth charge can be used to place the attack submarine on the defensive (as in an *urgent* torpedo attack by the escort). Nevertheless, the detonation of the charge must be close to the submarine. Therefore, given the need for proximity, the sinking rate, and the need for the escort to leave the charge well behind her, attacks by escorts on modern submarines are not likely to succeed with depth charges. If the submarine is attacking the escort with steam torpedoes, dropping a depth charge while evading the torpedo may be the best chance the escort will have. Certainly there are some environmental water conditions (e.g., hard bottom) which favor the use of depth charges over homing torpedoes. Coast Guard vessels and certain classes of naval ships and auxiliaries would carry depth charges in wartime.

28

Antisubmarine Warfare Fire Control

Figure 28-1. Sonarmen plot an attack against a submarine on the underwater battery fire control equipment of the USS Berkeley (DDG-15).

Introduction

Antisubmarine warfare is in a state of constant evolution, and new weapons are added from time to time to the U.S. Navy inventory. In this chapter, we present a view of fire control as it relates to torpedoes launched from a ship's torpedo tubes, helicopter (LAMPS), or ASROC launcher, because ASW fire control is the link between the ASW weapons and sensors described in earlier chapters that together form the entire weapon system.

The fundamental problem of fire control is to direct a weapon launcher in such a way that the weapon will be directed to the target.

In the surface fire control problem, the fire control director/radar tracks the target and measures range and bearing. Elevation of the target would be zero in this case. This data is sent to the gun fire control computer where rates of target motion are calculated, and used

375

to predict the future target position. Ballistic variables—initial velocity, superelevation, drift, and wind—are added to achieve an aiming point for the gun mount. If the computations are correct and problem conditions remain unchanged after firing, the projectile will hit the target.

In antisubmarine warfare, the fire control problem is similar to the surface problem. Submarine slant range and bearing information is obtained from the sonar equipment. This information is transmitted to the underwater battery fire control computer, and the future target position is solved in the same way as in the gun fire control surface problem. Since the submarine is below the horizontal plane, an estimate of submarine depth must be entered into the underwater battery fire control computer. In the case of ASROC, various ballistic corrections are added to the future target position to get launcher train and elevation orders. No ballistic corrections are required for a torpedo launched from a surface tube or helicopter.

Mark 32 Surface Vehicle Torpedo Tubes (SVTT) Fire Control

The Mark 32, Mark 44, and Mark 46 torpedoes are currently in use with the launching systems described.

The fire control problem for the Mark 32 tube-launched torpedo is not solved entirely by a computer. The *underwater battery fire control system* (UBFCS) helps by providing such target information as bearing, range, target course, and target speed to the ASW attack team. Torpedo search instructions are determined by environmental and attack parameters that exist during the attack. These instructions, including search depth, are set into the torpedo through the UBFCS equipment.

The ship is maneuvered into the proper launch position by the ASW attack team in CIC, whose function is to recommend courses to steer to the OOD. The final phase of the attack can be accomplished by CIC, the sonar control indicator (stack) operator, or the ASW officer at the UBFCS attack console. Normally, the ASW officer will be given control in the last stage of the attack to guide the ship into proper firing position before the torpedo is launched. After weapon release, control of maneuvering the ship is returned to CIC to guide the ship clear of the target area.

Light Airborne Multipurpose System (LAMPS) Fire Control

A general description of LAMPS was provided in Chapter 27. The LAMPS helicopter, in the ASW mode, gives the destroyer force a long-range ASW attack and task force screening capability. A fire control problem does not exist in the strict sense of the phrase, as in the case of torpedo tubes and ASROC. If a submarine is detected by the surface ship's sonar system, LAMPS will be launched to aid in classification through the use of passive or active sonobuoys and Magnetic Anomaly Detection (MAD) equipment. If the sonar contact is classified as a "probable" submarine, the helicopter can drop a homing torpedo on top of the submarine. This eliminates the elements in a fire control problem and the requirements for problem solving. An NTDS* data link, or other suitable links, provide for an exchange of information between the helicopter and surface ship.

Asroc Fire Control

ASROC uses one of two weapons to combat a submarine: a homing torpedo or a depth charge. Either payload provides a weapon standoff capability unmatched by torpedo tubes. The solution of the problem is indicated in the following steps, beginning with the decision to fire a selected missile (either torpedo or depth charge) at a target.

1. The system is stabilized. The roll and pitch of the ship is compensated for, therefore the fire control problem is solved in respect to the horizontal plane.

2. The rates of target and own ship's motion are measured and generated continuously in the computer to enable the ship to shoot at the future target position rather than at the present position.

3. The basic solution is corrected continuously by computing the effect of weathercocking wind (true wind combined with the apparent wind caused by own ship's motion). This error is eliminated by a correction to launcher train and elevation order. Launcher elevation is always 45 degrees above the horizontal plane plus or minus a correction for weathercocking wind. This angle of elevation will give the maximum range of the missile.

4. Other ballistic corrections that refine the solution are entered manually into the fire control equipment.

The basic attack problem is to determine a future target position and to launch the missile so that the payload enters the water at the optimum position (figure 28–2).

After locating a target, the sonar transmits target bearing and range information to the fire control system, and the solution of the problem begins. Future target position is computed from target motion quantities. The water entry point for the payload is generated by the com-

---

* The purpose of the computerized naval tactical data system (NTDS) is explained in Chapter 24.

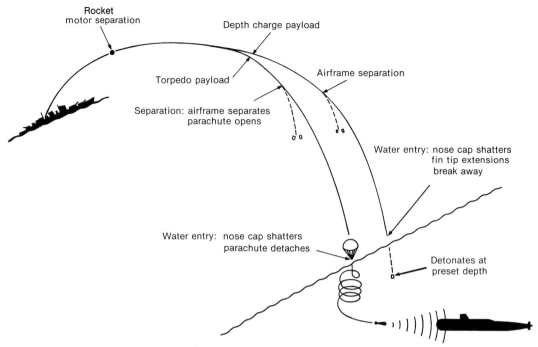

Figure 28–2. Flight sequence of the ASROC payloads.

puter. Taking into account the water entry point, wind direction and speed, air density, own ship motion, and internal missile ballistic quantities, an aiming point is computed for the ASROC launcher. The fire control system generates firing orders and transmits them to the ASROC missile and launcher.

Underwater Battery Fire Control System (Mark 114) Components

The UBFCS (Mark 114) solves the ASROC and torpedo tube attack problem, generates missile launching orders, prepares the missile for firing, provides a means for the Commanding Officer to control missile firing, and sends missile designation data to the gun fire control director for missile tracking during flight (figure 28–3). As previously explained, the same system provides target and ship data to CIC for a torpedo tube launching by way of the attack console.

Attack Console (Mark 53)

The *attack console,* a transistorized analogue computer, is the data processing center of the fire control system. The computer processes own ship data, target data, and ballistic quantities. It provides data to sonar to aid tracking and position-keeping. During tracking, the attack console receives the target position data from the sonar equip-

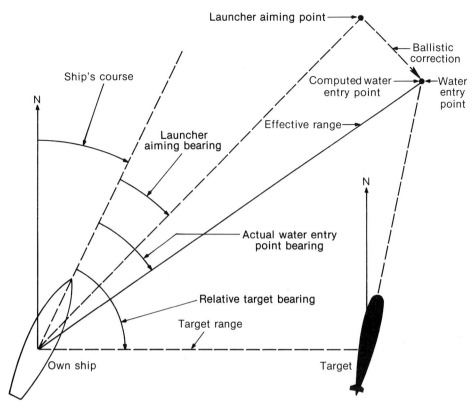

Figure 28–3. A simplified diagram of the ASROC fire control problem.

ment, it develops rates of target motion, and it uses these rates to keep the cursor on the sonar control indicator (stack) automatically positioned on the target. When the target has been lost by sonar, the console will maintain the control indicator cursor on the assumed position of the target, using the last target rates developed. The computer also supplies launcher train and elevation orders for ASROC, rocket motor and airframe jettison orders, and torpedo settings for the ASROC payload and torpedo tubes. The console designates to the gun fire control director the ASROC water entry position for the missile while it is tracking the missile in flight. This helps to confirm the accuracy of the fire control solution by checking the actual water entry point against the desired water entry point contained in the solution. As in gunfire spotting, any discrepancy between the two results in an updating of the solution to increase accuracy in subsequent firings.

Relay Transmitter (Mark 43)

The *relay transmitter* (Mark 43) tests, programs, and monitors the selected ASROC missile.

Relay Transmitter (Mark 44)

The *relay transmitter* (Mark 44) makes the attack console compatible with the gun fire control system, missile fire control system, and weapons direction system aboard ship. This unit sends designation data (bearing and range) to the gun fire control director for ASROC missile tracking. As the ASROC payload enters the water, the fire control director will send the bearing and range to the water entry point to the attack console.

Position Indicator (Mark 78)

The *position indicator* (Mark 78), located on the bridge, is a data repeater unit that provides the Commanding Officer a display of his own ship, the target, and tactical information about the weapon. This information is displayed automatically and continuously to give a complete picture of the attack as it develops. The position indicator also has a control switch that grants approval to fire an ASROC missile.

Summary

With the development of modern ASW homing torpedoes, the fire control problem does not have to be solved as precisely as in the gun fire control problem. Once the submarine has been detected and classified, the biggest problem in ASW today, modern underwater battery fire control systems can solve the fire control problem for ASROC, provide tactical information to CIC for tube-launched torpedoes, and provide target position information to LAMPS through an NTDS data link. The Mark 114 UBFCS has proven to be reliable, and it will not be replaced until newer systems are developed as the state of the art changes.

Equipment Nomenclature System

Electronic equipment aboard U.S. Navy ships is designated by a standard nomenclature system. Nomenclature designations are used mainly as the short title of a piece of equipment. These designations are unclassified, whereas the actual name of the equipment may sometimes be classified. The nomenclature system is called the *Joint Electronics Type Designation System* ("AN" system) for communication and electronic equipment.

The AN nomenclature is assigned to complete sets of equipment and major components of such equipments. The AN nomenclature is not assigned to minor components of electronic systems or to small parts, such as capacitors and resistors. Articles having other adequate identification in American war standard or joint Army-Navy specifications will normally not have an AN designator.

Complete systems of equipment are designated by three indicator letters that follow AN and signify kind of installation, type of equipment, and purpose. For example, this appendix enables determination of what the AN/SPS-10 is and where it may be used. A check of the table shows it to be surface radar, search, model 10. The component indicator letters in use can be found in *Electronics Installation and Maintenance Book*, NavShips 900,000.

First Letter

Installation

A — Airborne (installed and operated in aircraft).
B — Underwater mobile, submarine.
C — Air Transportable (inactivated, do not use).
D — Pilotless carrier
F — Fixed
G — Ground, general ground use (include two or more ground type installations).
K — Amphibious

M — Ground, mobile (installed as operating unit in a vehicle which has no function other than transporting the equipment).

P — Pack or portable (animal or man).

S — Water surface craft.

T — Ground, transportable.

U — General utility (includes two or more general installation classes, airborne, shipboard and ground).

V — Ground, vehicular (installed in vehicle designed for functions other than carrying electronic equipment, etc., such as tanks).

W — Water surface and underwater.

Second Letter

Type of Equipment

A — Invisible light, heat radiating.

B — Pigeon

C — Carrier

D — Radiac

E — Nupac

F — Photographic

G — Telegraphic or teletype.

I — Interphone and public address.

J — Electro-mechanical (not otherwise covered).

K — Telemetering

L — Countermeasures

M — Meteorological

N — Sound in air

P — Radar

Q — Sonar and underwater sound

R — Radio

S — Special types, magnetic, etc., or combinations of types.

T — Telephone (wire)

V — Visual and visible light

W — Armament (peculiar to armament, not otherwise covered)

X — Facsimile or television

Third Letter

Purpose

A — Auxiliary assemblies (not complete operating sets used with or part of two or more sets or sets series).

B — Bombing

C — Communications (receiving and transmitting)

D — Direction finder and/or reconnaissance
E — Ejection and/or release.
G — Fire control or searchlight directing
H — Recording and/or reproducing (graphic meteorological and sound)
L — Searchlight control (inactivated, use "G")
M — Maintenance and test assemblies (including tools)
N — Navigational aids (including altimeters, beacons, compasses, racons, depth soundings, approach and landing)
P — Reproducing (inactivated, do not use)
Q — Special, or combination of purposes)
R — Receiving, passive detecting
S — Detecting and/or range of bearing
T — Transmitting
W — Control
X — Identification and recognition.

Numerals

Model Numbers

1   2   3   4   etc

Fourth Letter

Modification Letter

A   B   C   D   etc

Glossary

Automatic guns   Automatic guns use case ammunition in which some of the energy of the propellant explosion is used to open the breech, eject the empty case, and operate a device which loads another round of ammunition. An automatic gun will continue to fire as long as the trigger is closed.

Ampul   A small glass vessel which is completely sealed. It contains electrolyte in a proximity fuze.

Battery   The weapons installed on a ship are called that unit's battery. On a ship armed exclusively with guns, the main battery would be the largest caliber guns on board. On ships with missiles, the main battery has been extended to mean the weapons on board with the greatest potential. On an attack submarine the main battery is her torpedoes.

Bourrelet   The bulge at the forward part of a projectile before it begins to taper.

Brisance   The rapidity with which an explosive develops its maximum force.

Caliber   An expression of the measurements of a gun. A gun is designated first by the diameter of the bore of the gun measured across the muzzle from land to land, then by the length of the gun. The diameter is divided into the length of the gun barrel. The result is the length of the gun expressed in *calibers*. A 6-inch caliber gun, 25 feet in length, is called a 6-inch, 50 caliber gun, or 300 inches ÷ 6 inches = 50 calibers.

Chase   The elongated part of the gun barrel between the forward part of the powder chamber and the muzzle.

Cold gun   When one can place a hand on the barrel without discomfort.

Cook-off   The explosion of a projectile or a propellant charge in a gun bore due to the heat of the barrel alone.

Detents   A safety mechanism in a fuze that must be unlocked or

384

withdrawn from position before the fuze can set off the warhead or projectile.

Elevation The elevation angle of a gun is the angle that the gun bore axis makes with the deck, measured in a plane horizontal to the deck.

Gun The term *gun*, when properly defined, designates the tube or barrel through which the projectile passes. In current usage, the term also refers to the whole mount assembly of which the barrel is but a part.

Hangfire A delay in the detonation of the propelling charge in a gun (the possibility of a hangfire after 20 seconds have elapsed since the last firing attempt is slight).

Hot gun When one cannot place a hand on the outside of a barrel because of the heat.

Housing The housing of a gun is a box-shaped structure joined to the gun barrel with a bayonet joint. On most intermediate caliber guns, it also houses the breech mechanism. Since it is attached to the gun barrel, it becomes a recoiling part.

In Battery A gun in its firing position. A gun moves out of battery during recoil and returns to battery during counterrecoil.

Initial Velocity (IV) The speed at which a round leaves the muzzle of a gun barrel (muzzle velocity).

Lapping Head A cylindrical metal file used to remove such corrosive and foreign material from a gun barrel as unburned powder grains, copper residue and the like.

Linear Rate Fire Control System A linear rate fire control system uses the linear values of target position measured between a point of original sighting and a second position in the director's line of sight. A computer receives the values of the two target positions and compares them for time difference. It then predicts future target position from the linear movement (velocity) of the target, with relation to the time of flight required by the projectile to reach a collision point. Linear rate systems are well suited to long-range engagements and shore bombardment.

Mark Term used with a number to identify a specific design of gun or piece of equipment, which in turn is frequently followed by a Mod (modification) number to identify the variety of equipment within the type; an example would be Mark 42 Mod 10.

Misfire The complete failure of a gun to discharge.

Mount The mount is the entire structure built into the ship's hull that contains the gun. It supports the gun, secures it to the hull, and provides for its train, elevation, recoil and counterrecoil.

Ogive The curved portion of an arch: the tapered section of a projectile.

Pointing(er) The term pointing has the same meaning as elevating and depressing combined. The *pointer* is the member of the gun crew who elevates and depresses the gun.

Rapid-Fire Guns These are guns which load, fire, eject empty cases, and operate the breech using a source of energy other than the energy of the propelling charge, as in the 3″/50 caliber gun.

Recoil Recoil is the gun's reaction (in the opposite direction of the projectile's travel) to firing as it is contained by the slide and retarded by the recoil mechanism. The recoil mechanism or brake absorbs the force of the moving gun as it moves in the direction opposite to the path of the projectile.

Relative Rate Fire Control Systems These systems use angular rates of target motion determined by the movement of the director using gyroscopic lead-computing sights or other computing systems. Relative rate systems are best suited to engaging close-in aircraft.

Rotating Band A soft metal or plastic band fixed near the base of a gun projectile which, when rammed into the gun barrel during loading, is engraved by the lands. This creates a tight fit for the projectile in its travel through the bore, preventing the propelling gases from escaping from behind the round and imparting the required spin.

Sabot A lightweight bushing which carries a sub-caliber projectile during its travel through the gun barrel.

Sea Return A term applied to the radar image of the sea's surface. The radar signals reflected by the surface of the ocean can confuse the operator of the radar scope because the cathode ray tube will show these signals, thus masking the pips of the contacts the operator is tracking, or by concealing new contacts.

Semiautomatic guns Semiautomatic guns use case ammunition in which some of the energy of the propellant explosion is used to open the breech, eject the empty case, and open a device that will automatically close the breech when another round is loaded. Semiautomatic guns must be loaded by hand as in the 5″/38 caliber gun, or by power-driven loading equipment.

Slide On all guns larger than 20mm, the slide is the structural part which supports the gun, housing, and other recoiling parts, and permits them to move in recoil.

Train(er) To *train* a gun is to alter the position of the gun bore axis in relation to a plane perpendicular to the deck as measured from the ship's centerline. The *trainer* is the member of the gun crew who controls the horizontal movement of the gun.

Bibliography

Books

Almanacco Navale 1970–71. Giorgio Giorgerini and Augusto Nani. Rome: Rivista Marittima, 1970.

Digital Computer and Control Engineering, R. S. Ledley. New York, N.Y.: McGraw-Hill, 1960.

Digital Computers Basics (NavPers 10088). Washington, D.C.: U.S. Navy, 1968.

Electronic Analog and Hybrid Computers, G. A. Korn and T. M. Korn. New York, N.Y.: McGraw-Hill, 1964.

Fire Control Technician 3 (NavPers 10173-series). Washington, D.C.: Bureau of Naval Personnel, U.S. Navy.

Fire Control Technician 2 (NavPers 10174-series). Washington, D.C.: Bureau of Naval Personnel, U.S. Navy.

Fire Control Technician 1 & C (NavPers 10175). Washington, D.C.: Bureau of Naval Personnel, U.S. Navy.

Fundamentals of Acoustics, Laurence E. Kinsler and Austin R. Frey. 2nd ed. New York, N.Y.: John Wiley and Sons, 1964.

Fundamentals of Sonar, J. W. Horton. Annapolis, Maryland: Naval Institute Press, 1959.

Gunner's Mate G3 & 2 (NavPers 10185). Washington, D.C.: Bureau of Naval Personnel, U.S. Navy.

Gunner's Mate G1 & C (NavPers 10186-series). Washington, D.C.: Bureau of Naval Personnel, U.S. Navy.

Jane's Weapon Systems 1972–73. 4th ed. Edited by R. T. Pretty and D. H. R. Archer. London: B.P.C. Publishing, Ltd., 1972.

Jane's Weapon Systems 1970–71. 2nd ed. Edited by R. T. Pretty and D. H. R. Archer. London: B.P.C. Publishing, Ltd., 1970.

Les Flottes de Combat 1972. Henri Le Masson. Paris: Editions Maritimes et D'Outre-Mer, 1971.

Naval Airborne Ordnance (NavPers 10826-series). Washington, D.C.: Bureau of Naval Personnel, U.S. Navy.

Naval Ordnance, Officers of the Department of Ordnance and Gunnery, U.S. Naval Academy. Annapolis, Md.: U.S. Naval Institute, 1915, 1921, 1936.

Naval Ordnance and Gunnery, Volume 1—Naval Ordnance (NavPers 10797). Washington, D.C.: Bureau of Naval Personnel, U.S. Navy.

Naval Ordnance and Gunnery, Volume 2—Fire Control (NavPers 10798-series). Washington, D.C.: Bureau of Naval Personnel, U.S. Navy.

Naval Orientation (NavPers 16138-series). Washington, D.C.: Bureau of Naval Personnel, U.S. Navy.

Ordnance Publication 0, Index of Naval Ordnance Systems Command Ordnance Publications. Washington, D.C.: U.S. Navy.

Ordnance Publication 4, Ammunition Afloat. Washington, D.C.: U.S. Navy.

Ordnance Publication 1014, Ordnance Safety Precautions: Their Origin and Necessity. Washington, D.C.: U.S. Navy.

Ordnance Publication 1233A, Mk 63 GFCS, Schematics. Washington, D.C.: U.S. Navy.

Ordnance Publication 1549, Service Life of U.S. Naval Gun Barrels. Washington, D.C.: U.S. Navy.

Ordnance Publication 1600, Mk 56 GFCS. Washington, D.C.: U.S. Navy.

Ordnance Publication 1631, Ammo Hazard Classification. Washington, D.C.: U.S. Navy.

Ordnance Publication 1664, U.S. Explosive Ordnance. Washington, D.C.: U.S. Navy.

Ordnance Publication 1692, 3″/50 Gun Range Tables AA Projectile. Washington, D.C.: U.S. Navy.

Ordnance Publication 1695, Mk 63 GFCS. Washington, D.C.: U.S. Navy.

Ordnance Publication 1753, 3″/50, Gun Mount, Description and Operation. Washington, D.C.: U.S. Navy.

Ordnance Publication 1764, 5″/54 Gun Mount, Description and Operation. Washington, D.C.: U.S. Navy.

Ordnance Publication 1795, 3″/50 Gun Range Tables Surface Firing. Washington, D.C.: Bureau of Naval Personnel, U.S. Navy.

Ordnance Publication 2173, Handling Equipment for Weapons and Explosives. Washington, D.C.: U.S. Navy.

Ordnance Publication 2215, Navy Gun Type Ammunition. Washington, D.C.: U.S. Navy.

Ordnance Publication 2238, Identification of Ammunition. Washington, D.C.: U.S. Navy.

Ordnance Publication 2329, Terrier. Washington, D.C.: U.S. Navy.

Ordnance Publication 2448, Talos and Terrier CGN-9 Class. Washington, D.C.: U.S. Navy.

Ordnance Publication 2512, Guided Missile Complete Round, Descrip-

tion and Operation. Washington, D.C.: U.S. Navy.

Ordnance Publication 2665, Mk 13 GM Launching System. Washington, D.C.: U.S. Navy.

Ordnance Publication 2680, Terrier DLG-6 Class. Washington, D.C.: U.S. Navy.

Ordnance Publication 3000 (1st rev.), Weapon System Fundamentals. Vol. 1. *Basic Weapons,* Vol. 2. *Analysis of Weapons,* Vol. 3. *Synthesis of Systems.* Washington, D.C.: U.S. Navy.

Ordnance Publication 3063, Safety Precautions Terrier and Standard. Washington, D.C.: U.S. Navy.

Ordnance Publication 3115, Mk 22 GM Launching System. Washington, D.C.: U.S. Navy.

Ordnance Publication 3138, Tartar, DEG-1 Class. Washington, D.C.: U.S. Navy.

Ordnance Publication 3322, Safety Precautions, Talos. Washington, D.C.: U.S. Navy.

Ordnance Publication 3347, USN Ordnance Safety Precautions. Washington, D.C.: U.S. Navy.

Ordnance Publication 3392, 5"/54 Gun Mk 45. Washington, D.C.: U.S. Navy.

Ordnance Publication 3408, Tartar DDG-31 Class. Washington, D.C.: U.S. Navy.

Ordnance Publication 3590, Mk 12 GM Launching System. Washington, D.C.: U.S. Navy.

Ordnance Publication 3625, Mk 63 GFCS. Washington, D.C.: U.S. Navy.

Ordnance Publication 3713, 5"/54 Gun Mk 42 Single Mount. Washington, D.C.: U.S. Navy.

Ordnance Publication 3834, Mk 25 GM Launching System. Washington, D.C.: U.S. Navy.

Oto Melara SPA, "76/62 Compact Gun Mount," mimeographed, Oto Melara, La Spezia, 1972.

Navy Missile Systems (NavPers 10785 series). Washington, D.C.: U.S. Navy.

Principles of Naval Ordnance and Gunnery (NavPers 10783-series). Washington, D.C.: U.S. Navy.

Principles of Optics, Max Born and Emil Wolf, 3rd ed., Oxford, England, Pergamon Press, 1965.

Shipboard Electronic Equipments (NavPers 10794-C). Washington, D.C.: U.S. Navy.

Shipboard Electrical Systems (NavPers 10864-B). Washington, D.C.: U.S. Navy.

Ships and Aircraft of the U.S. Fleet, compiled by John S. Rowe and

Samuel L. Morison. Annapolis, Maryland: Naval Institute Press, 1972.

A Study of Maritime Mobile Satellite Services. Vol. 1.: *Merchant Vessel Population and Distribution: Present and Forecast.* Robert P. Thompson. Washington, D.C.: U.S. Coast Guard, U.S. Maritime Administration, Department of Transportation, 1970.

The 3″/50 Gun (NavPers 10110). Washington, D.C.: U.S. Navy.

The 5″/38 Gun (NavPers 10111). Washington, D.C.: U.S. Navy.

Weyer's Warships of the World 1973, compiled by Gerhard Albrecht. Annapolis, Maryland: Naval Institute Press, 1973.

Periodicals

O'Neil, William D., Lieutenant Commander, U.S. Naval Reserve (Ret.). "Gun Systems for Air Defense," *U.S. Naval Institute Proceedings,* March 1971, p. 45.

Philip, John S. "A New Breed of European Missiles," *Aerospace International.* May-June 1972, pp. 25–30.

Index